Ritual and Religion in the *Xunzi*

SUNY series in Chinese Philosophy and Culture

Roger T. Ames, editor

Ritual and Religion in the *Xunzi*

Edited by
T. C. Kline III and Justin Tiwald

SUNY PRESS

Cover art: *Offering a Yellow Goat in Sacrifice to the Kitchen God*, Huang Yue, Qing dynasty. Ink on paper. Used with the permission of the National Palace Museum Collection, Taipei, Taiwan (Republic of China)

Published by
STATE UNIVERSITY OF NEW YORK PRESS
Albany

Printed in the United States of America

For information, contact
State University of New York Press
www.sunypress.edu

Production, Laurie Searl
Marketing, Kate R. Seburyamo

Library of Congress Cataloging-in-Publication Data

Ritual and religion in the *Xunzi* / edited by T. C. Kline III and Justin Tiwald.
pages cm. — (SUNY series in Chinese philosophy and culture)
Includes bibliographical references and index.
ISBN 978-1-4384-5195-4 (hc : alk. paper) 978-1-4384-5194-7 (pb : alk. paper)
1. Xunzi, 340 B.C.–245 B.C. Xunzi. 2. Philosophy, Confucian. I. Kline, T. C., [date], editor of compilation. II. Tiwald, Justin, editor of compilation.
B128.H7R58 2014
181'.112—dc23 2013027107

10 9 8 7 6 5 4 3 2 1

Contents

Acknowledgments

This volume was conceived as a companion to the earlier anthology on Xunzi's philosophy—T. C. Kline III and Philip J. Ivanhoe, eds., *Virtue, Nature, and Moral Agency in the "Xunzi"* (Indianapolis, IN: Hackett, 2000). Although that volume collected together an excellent set of essays, both old and new, it was not sufficient to reveal the depth and scope of Xunzi's Confucian vision. To deepen our understanding of Xunzi's conception of Confucianism, it is necessary to approach his work as both a religious vision and a philosophical system. Philosophers and Sinologists writing in Europe and America have often overlooked this necessity. In the hope of remedying past omissions and pointing forward in a new direction, Justin Tiwald and I offer this collection of essays as a beginning to a more rich, nuanced, and compelling understanding of Xunzi's vision, and Confucianism in general, that takes account of religious as well as philosophical dimensions.

I thank the following for permission to reprint chapters that appear herein: Roger T. Ames for permission to republish Edward J. Machle's "Xunzi as a Religious Philosopher," originally published in *Philosophy East and West* 26.4 (1976), pp. 443–461; Oxford University Press for permission to republish Philip J. Ivanhoe's "A Happy Symmetry: Xunzi's Ecological Ethic," which appeared with the subtitle "Xunzi's Ecological Thought" in the *Journal of the American Academy of Religion* 59.2 (1991), pp. 309–322; and State University of New York Press for permission to republish Robert C. Neville's "Ritual and Religion: A Lesson from Xunzi for Today," which appeared in his collection of essays, *Ritual and Deference: Extending Chinese Philosophy in a Comparative Context* (Albany: State University of New York Press, 2008), chapter 3.

As with any large project, this collection did not spring fully formed from the head (or hand) of any one person. I have been aided along the way by a community of generous and wise individuals, generous in their gift of time and effort, and wise in their balanced guidance. Philip J. Ivanhoe and Eric L. Hutton have been invaluable and staunch friends since this project's inception. It would not exist without their support. Lastly, I owe an unpayable debt to De-nin Lee for her unbending support, when by rights it should have bent long ago.

—T. C. Kline III
Lisbon Falls, Maine

Notes on Conventions

There are three notes with regard to textual conventions. First, all romanizations of Chinese are in Pinyin except for proper names, of either people or published works, that are traditionally romanized in some other system. To keep the text consistent, romanizations in quoted sources have also been changed to Pinyin. In addition, in order to better distinguish proper names, the romanizations of proper names or titles precede the Chinese characters rather than follow them.

Second, translations found in the text are from readily available editions of the Chinese texts or from the contributors themselves. In places where contributors disagree with a translation and have altered it, these altered translations are identified as "adapted" in the citation. References to other translations of the passage can also often be found in the endnotes. References to translations are by page number, except in the case of John Knoblock's translation. For Knoblock's translation, references use his own system of chapter and section notation—chapter number followed by section number.

Third, whenever possible, citations of Chinese sources refer to the recent series of concordances edited by D. C. Lau and Chen Fong Ching and published by the Chinese University of Hong Kong's Institute of Chinese Studies 香港中文大學中國文化研究所 and the Commercial Press 商務印書館 in Hong Kong. We have chosen to use these texts as standard rather than the Harvard-Yenching series. The advantages are that the new series is in print and can be purchased. Furthermore, the printing itself is more readable than the earlier typeset of the Harvard-Yenching series. All references to the *Xunzi* are to the concordance in this series: 荀子逐字索引 *A Concordance to the Xunzi*.

Introduction

This collection of essays has been gathered together in order to support and develop the claim made by Edward Machle that Xunzi 荀子, a third-century-b.c.e. Confucian philosopher, is a religious philosopher. Or to put it differently, if we wish to fully understand Xunzi's work, we must recognize that his various philosophical positions are embedded within a developed religious vision. Unfortunately, in most modern scholarship on Xunzi, it has been the exception and not the rule to recognize the importance of Xunzi's religious vision in the overall shape of his work. Instead, scholars have regularly accused Xunzi of being antagonistic toward religious practice.[1] This accusation often emphasizes Xunzi's critical evaluation of his contemporaries' religious interpretation of ritual practice. Xunzi strikes many scholars as an early Confucian exemplar of secular and proto-scientific philosophical inquiry. Like Freud or Marx, he is believed to be presenting a conception of ritual practice that explains away or reinterprets in a secular psychological framework what was previously conceived of in religious terms. Much of this overemphasis on Xunzi's critique of religious practice arises from mistaken conclusions drawn from an examination of Xunzi's ritual theory.

To understand how these interpretations of Xunzi might come about, consider the image on the cover of this book. The painting depicts a family offering a goat for sacrifice at the end of the lunar year. Mother, father, and kneeling son offer the sacrifice at an altar, while the remaining two sons light firecrackers. The image shows us a common scene of Chinese ritual activity. In addition, the colophon tells us that this image depicts Yin Zifang and his family. Yin Zifang's story is first recorded as a biography in the *Houhanshu* 後漢書 *History of the Later Han*. It reads as follows:

> During the time of Emperor Xuan 宣帝 (73–49 b.c.e.) lived Yin Zifang 陰子方, who had achieved the utmost of filial piety and possessed benevolence and compassion. Once when Yin Zifang was seeing to the morning cooking on the day of sacrifice at the end of the lunar year, the kitchen god appeared to him. Zifang twice showed obeisance and received blessings. His household had a yellow goat, and he sacrificed it to the kitchen god. From this point onward, Yin Zifang rapidly rose to fame and fortune. His fields measured over ten thousand acres. His chariots, horses, servants, and slaves compared with those of the ruler of a state. Zifang often said, "My children and grandchildren are bound to be strong and mighty." Three generations have followed and are still flourishing and prosperous. For this reason the descendants often offer a yellow goat to the kitchen god at the sacrifice for the end of the lunar year.[2]

The story of Yin Zifang combines three significant elements. First, it mentions the level of moral cultivation and achievement of Yin Zifang. He is declared to have reached the height of filial piety, an important Confucian virtue achieved only through a long process of moral cultivation. Second, in recognition of this achievement he is visited and blessed by the kitchen god. It is implied that this blessing and the riches and prosperity that follow from it are a reward for his achievement in moral cultivation. Third, Yin Zifang and his descendants, having been blessed, continue to perform the ritual sacrifice of a yellow goat. One could argue that Yin Zifang, through his own human efforts, cultivates a virtuous disposition, which is then recognized by a god, who rewards him for the accomplishment. Ever after, Yin Zifang and his descendants sacrifice a yellow goat to acknowledge the kitchen god and maintain their prosperity.

This interpretation of Yin Zifang's story is paradigmatic of a type of early Chinese religious interpretation, and although this kind of interpretation of ritual practice was quite common in the third century b.c.e.—as well as in the later Han from when the story derives—it is precisely this type of interpretation that Xunzi wholeheartedly rejects. Within this understanding of ritual practice, the prosperity of Yin Zifang and his descendants is directly due to the blessing of the kitchen god, maintained through the sacrifice of the goat, and only indirectly due to his own efforts in moral cultivation.

Xunzi rejects the interpretation of ritual practice offered in the story of Yin Zifang. He repudiates the supernatural and literal interpretations of ritual symbols and actions and instead explains them in terms of their ability to shape and re-form human behavior, bringing individuals into harmony with themselves, their society, and the greater cosmos. He further refutes any interpretation of ritual performance that either involves the interaction between humans and supernatural beings, such as the kitchen god, or ties prosperity and success only indirectly to human efforts at moral cultivation through ritual participation.

The fact that Xunzi repudiates this sort of account has led scholars to conclude that he is antagonistic toward religious practice. However, what we find in Xunzi is *not* a critique of religious practice as such but rather a critique of certain forms of religious practice and interpretations of religious practice—the forms that treat rituals and supernatural beings as mere instruments of personal advantage and interpretations that fail to appreciate the proper function of ritual in moral cultivation. What underlies Xunzi's critique, we believe, is not an unqualified rejection of religious practice but a careful and penetrating interpretation of religious practice. As we will see shortly, all of the contributors to this volume argue in one way or another that Xunzi's understanding and explanation, and in some cases reinterpretation, of ritual practice constitute a compelling and sophisticated ritual theory embedded in a broader religious vision. In what follows, we briefly recount Xunzi's views about ritual, describe the context in which he advances them, and explain how each of the essays explicates and develops his broader vision of ritual and religion.

To start, Xunzi considers himself a follower of the Confucian tradition and is committed to the project of moral cultivation laid out by Kongzi 孔子 (Confucius). He believes that the teachings of Kongzi reveal the proper and only way to successfully cultivate virtuous human dispositions. By acquiring these virtues through participation in the Confucian ritual order, a person can become a 君子 *junzi*[3] or, in rare instances, a sage 聖人 *shengren*. Individuals who have achieved the level of *junzi* or sage are in turn capable of teaching others to follow the Confucian Dao 道 and bringing harmony and order to Chinese society. Moreover, it is only through the efforts of the *junzi* and sages that the Dao is brought into existence and maintained from one generation to the next. Central to this project of moral cultivation and teaching is participation in the Confucian ritual order.[4] By the third century b.c.e., when Xunzi was writing, Confucianism, and especially participation in the Confucian ritual order, had come under attack from other schools of thought.[5] Many of these figures presented sophisticated and compelling critiques of the Confucian vision. Fully engaged in the intellectual culture of his time and well aware of these critics, Xunzi developed his understanding of ritual practice in order to justify the Confucian tradition in light of what he took to be both internal misinterpretations and external critiques.[6]

Of the critiques external to the Confucian tradition, Xunzi primarily recognizes two schools of thought as significant threats—Mohism and Daoism. Although the grounds for their critiques differed, both Mohists and Daoists disputed the claim that ritual practices were important and salutary components of the good life. Mozi 墨子 argued that Confucian ritual practice wasted limited human and natural resources. As he saw it, the Confucian ritual order did not succeed in producing order and prosperity for the people but instead led to excessive expenditures and conflict. Mozi and his supporters rejected the ritual order because it did not provide the necessary institutions or guidance for strengthening and developing the state. Alongside Mozi, the Daoist critique, primarily found in the *Zhuangzi* 莊子, rejected any form of ritual practice that rested on participants committing themselves to normative ethical standards such as right and wrong, or good and bad.[7] Commitments to such standards cloud the mind and prevent the individual from being able to perceive the patterns of the Dao in the world and respond to them in an open and spontaneous manner. As will be apparent from the essays in this volume, Xunzi responds to these challenges in various ways, often adopting and adapting much of the position of his adversary in order to strengthen his own argument.

Still other threats to proper interpretation and practice of ritual were internal to the Confucian tradition. Xunzi believed his Confucian predecessor Mengzi 孟子(Mencius) held a conception of human nature and understanding of moral psychology that was a dangerous deviation from the original vision of Kongzi.[8] Rather than emphasizing the external guidance of the rites and the teachings of the sages, Mengzi's conception of moral cultivation focused wrongly, according to Xunzi, on the internal cultivation of an innate moral sense. In other words, Mengzi failed to properly appreciate the importance of ritual practice and the manner in which participation shaped human dispositions to act in accordance with the Dao. It was this misinterpretation of Kongzi's teachings that Xunzi believed was central to Mengzi's philosophy and must be corrected. Xunzi's theory of ritual practice as central to moral cultivation is meant to rectify Mengzi's misrepresentation of Kongzi's teachings.[9]

In sum, recognizing himself as a follower of the Confucian tradition, a tradition under assault from various external and internal sources, Xunzi developed a conception of ritual practice and moral cultivation in order to defend the Confucian ritual order from its detractors by providing a sophisticated and comprehensive explanation of ritual participation that would prevent future generations from misinterpreting the original Confucian teachings. To this end, Xunzi's ritual theory remains embedded in the framework of the Confucian religious vision.

While this volume aims to support and defend Machle's claim that Xunzi be read as a religious philosopher, it should be noted that Machle was not the first Western scholar to take Xunzi seriously as having a significant religious vision. In 1945, A. R. Radcliffe-Brown delivered the Henry Myers lecture at the Royal Anthropological Institute, entitled "Religion and Society," in which he argues that Xunzi has a ritual theory and a conception of religious practice. Later published as a chapter in his book *Structure and Function in Primitive Society*, the essay as a whole focuses on the broader question of the relationship between religion and society and the role played by ritual practice in this relationship.[10]

Radcliffe-Brown begins his essay by reiterating an earlier approach he developed to the study of religion. Rather than focus on the beliefs of a given religion, a form of scholarship that he finds prevalent in Western religious studies of the early twentieth century, he advocates that we instead examine the social function of religion within a given society. His approach to the study of religion can best be summed up in his own words:

> [A]n orderly social life amongst human beings depends upon the presence in the minds of the members of a society of certain sentiments, which control the behavior of the individual in his relation to others. Rites can be seen to be the regulated symbolic expressions of certain sentiments. Rites can therefore be shown to have a specific social function when, and to the extent that, they have for their effect to regulate, maintain and transmit from one generation to another sentiments on which the constitution of the society depends. I ventured to suggest as a general formula that religion is everywhere an expression in one form or another of a sense of dependence on a power outside ourselves, a power which we may speak of as a spiritual or moral power.[11]

Radcliffe-Brown further claims that this approach to religion and ritual is by no means new but can be found in the work of Xunzi. The rest of the essay then examines several religions in practice. In each case Radcliffe-Brown applies his approach to ritual in order to reveal the social function of religion, the way in which it provides the bonds that tie society together into a community.[12] These bonds, in their various forms in different cultures, express a sense of dependence that Radcliffe-Brown, and we believe Xunzi, takes to be central to the social function of religious practice. In considering this sense of dependence, we can distinguish two aspects. On the one hand, we can depend on others to help us in the face of the difficulties and vicissitudes of life in the natural and social world; yet, on the other hand, "we must submit to the control of our conduct by rules which are imposed."[13] The Confucian ritual order provides the means by which to get things done in the world and enables the proper expression of human values and emotions. Yet, at the same time it restrains and shapes the forms of behavior that are permissible in human interaction. Although Radcliffe-Brown's analysis of religion and ritual may be somewhat outdated, it is surprising to see that as early as the 1940s a prominent American scholar of religion had recognized Xunzi as a religious philosopher and ritual theorist. Radcliffe-Brown locates ritual practice as central to his conception of religion, a role that helps us understand how Xunzi conceived of the connections between ritual, religion, and social relationships. Furthermore, as will become apparent as you read the essays in this volume, later scholars of Xunzi owe much to Radcliffe-Brown and functionalist approaches to religion.

Each of the essays in this volume aims to reveal some aspect of Xunzi's religious vision and the ritual theory that underlies that vision. The essays have been organized into three groups—those that focus on Xunzi's overall religious vision, those that more specifically discuss his ritual theory, and those that examine Xunzi in a comparative religious perspective. Let us turn now to the first of these groups, Xunzi's religious vision.

Essays in this section of the volume address Xunzi's religious vision, his general understanding of religious practice and its relation to society and to the greater cosmos within which society exists. Together, these two essays reveal key elements of Xunzi's religious vision, such as the social function of religious practice, the proper religious interpretation of ritual practice, and the source and justification of religious reverence for the ritual order.

The first of these two essays, Edward Machle's "Xunzi as a Religious Philosopher," offers a compelling explication of Xunzi's philosophical orientation toward religious belief and practice. Xunzi, he argues, is not a mere critic of religion, nor is he wholly an apologist but rather what Machle calls a religious philosopher. The distinctive aim of the religious philosopher is "to make sense of the received religious tradition as a way of continuing to be part of it."[14] He may be thought of as engaging in what Thomas Kasulis has more recently described as metapraxis, the explanation and justification of ritual practice from within a given religious tradition.[15] In order to show why we should treat Xunzi as a religious philosopher, Machle begins by considering the more prevalent argument that Xunzi is antagonistic to religion and religious practice. His examination of these claims leads Machle to focus on two central components of the prevailing argument that he believes result from a misunderstanding of Xunzi's work.

The first of these components is Xunzi's rejection of the type of religious interpretation revealed in the story of Yin Zifang discussed earlier. Xunzi explicitly rejects certain ritual practices as well as specific interpretations of ritual practice. Machle argues that Xunzi's rejection of certain ritual practices and interpretations of ritual practice should not be construed as a rejection of religious practice as a whole, nor is it a rejection of all religious interpretations of ritual practice. Xunzi does indeed reject practices and interpretations founded on the physical efficacy of the rite, such as physiognomy and sacrifices for healing sickness. However, he still accepts and advocates participation in religious rites, such as the rain sacrifice and funerals, when accompanied by the proper interpretation, an interpretation that focuses on the psychological and social function of the rite in creating and maintaining harmony and community. According to Machle, funerals, then, become an important rite for explaining Xunzi's conception of religious practice. Funerals are a kind of performance and practice that addresses itself to both humans and spirits 神 *shen*. Yet they are not ultimately concerned with putting corporeal beings in communication with noncorporeal ones. Ritual participants should sacrifice to the spirits "as if" they were present. As Machle describes it, for Xunzi, ritual practice becomes a matter of humane culture (his translation for 文 *wen*) and not magical manipulation. Ritual situates the individual harmoniously in society and the natural world.

Discussion of the relationship of humans and spirits in the funeral rites leads to a discussion of the second component on which Machle focuses, namely, Xunzi's naturalistic, nonanthropomorphic conception of Heaven 天 *tian*.[16] Xunzi's conception of Heaven deserves attention because he appears to reject the earlier Confucian portrayal of Heaven as having anthropomorphic characteristics such as will and consciousness. Both Kongzi and Mengzi speak of Heaven as having a will and being aware of and concerned about the activities of human beings. Xunzi does not share this view of Heaven. Yet, according to Machle, the human relationship with Heaven is still religious. "Xunzi includes all proper responses to Heaven's action under his rubric of *li*. . . . A ritual response to natural initiative is surely in some proper sense religious."[17] Xunzi demythologizes the conception of Heaven, while still maintaining a religious interpretation of the human relationship to Heaven. Through examining the misunderstanding of Xunzi's rejection of forms of ritual practice and his conception of Heaven, Machle defends his claim that Xunzi is indeed a religious philosopher and in doing so highlights Xunzi's interpretation of ritual practice and the relationship between human beings and Heaven.

Philip J. Ivanhoe, in the second essay in this section, describes the complexity and nuance of Xunzi's understanding of the relationship between humans and the greater cosmos as embodied in the Confucian ritual order, or Dao 道. Ivanhoe separates Xunzi's position from that of other theorists and explains why religious reverence constitutes a central element of Xunzi's relationship to the Dao. According to Xunzi, the Dao, embodied in the ritual order, accomplishes at least two tasks. First, it leads humans out of the state of nature that Xunzi describes in the beginning of chapter 19 of his work, and second, it provides us with avenues for the satisfaction of basic human desires, as well as "opening up new and profound sources of satisfaction, sources which are available only to those who are inside and committed to the project of the Confucian Way."[18] The Dao takes into account the character of human nature as well as the capacities and limitations of the nonhuman realm. It weaves the human and natural worlds into a seamless and harmonious whole that allows all things to flourish. According to Ivanhoe, the capacity of the Dao to bring about this harmonious cosmos deservedly elicits religious reverence, a reverence that can be found throughout Xunzi's writing. "The Way inspired profound respect, awe, and nothing less than reverence in those who understood it. They alone realized that through the Way the sages joined human intelligence with the vast, complex, and staggering power of Nature to produce a harmonious and magnificent result."[19] Through this essay, Ivanhoe expresses the scope and depth of Xunzi's understanding of the Dao and explains why it would be worthy of the religious reverence that Xunzi affords it. In the process of this explanation, Ivanhoe also distinguishes Xunzi's religious vision from nonreligious visions, such as that of Hobbes, as well as alternative Chinese visions, such as those of Mengzi and Zhuangzi.

In the three essays of the second section of this volume, the focus shifts to Xunzi's ritual theory. In recent years ritual studies has become a field unto itself. It is recognized that ritual practice is an important element of religious experience and an equally important subject for the study of religion. Xunzi, like many present-day scholars, was interested in the forms, function, and role of ritual in the complete human life. For him, Confucian ritual was an integral part of the good life. To explain and justify the role of ritual participation in the good human life, Xunzi developed a rich and sophisticated ritual theory. The three authors of these essays approach Xunzi's theory from slightly different standpoints, bringing various theoretical interlocutors into the conversation. They begin from a position shared with Xunzi, namely, that human beings are born unfinished and must undergo a process of cultivation before they become fully human and humane. One of the difficult tasks in understanding Xunzi's work involves explaining the complex process of moral cultivation, the means by which ritual participation shapes each individual life from an originally inchoate and petty existence into the humane and harmonious existence of the *junzi* or sage. In each case, these authors bring to light the process by which Xunzi believes ritual shapes human life and in doing so bring Xunzi into the present conversation in ritual studies.

Perhaps more explicitly than either of the other two authors in this section, Robert Neville finds in Xunzi's ritual theory a valuable resource for contemporary discussion of ritual. Neville addresses three main points: the connection between Xunzi's ritual theory and Charles Peirce's semiotics, ritual's role in the proper formation of desire, and the function of ritual within religion as integrating desire at different levels of individual and social organization. Throughout the essay Neville works from a definition of ritual, influenced by his interest in semiotics, that is as broad as Xunzi's own. Ritual includes "all conventions, all learned signs and sign-shaped behaviors."[20] Ritual constitutes the very fabric of human interaction. Neville goes so far as to say that "civilization itself depends on ritual mastery in the sense that humaneness cannot arise unless there are ritual social habits that allow of its expression."[21] Statements such as this one also make clear Neville's debt to Peirce and semiotics, a connection that he draws in the first substantial section of the essay. In some sense, ritual becomes another way of discussing the semiotics of human interaction. Human beings engage in a symbol-laden ritual dance with one another. Through the signs and symbols of this dance we engage with the realities of human existence. Especially in the case of religious symbols, we would have no way to engage certain realities without these symbols. By bringing Peirce's semiotics to bear on Xunzi's theory, Neville offers a set of tools for understanding the significance of ritual activity.

Neville develops this significance further by considering how ritual shapes even our inner life, our desires. Human beings are biological creatures, born with innate reactions to our environment. Desires are a powerful component of these innate reactions. As such they also pose a special problem for Xunzi and early Chinese philosophers in general. According to Xunzi, our desires do not originally lead to harmonious interaction with others or the natural environment. Our desires are often too powerful or weak and lack a full and proper specification of their objects and means of satisfaction. This problem is resolved by ritual participation and ritual mastery. Through culturally learned signs, behavior can become organized and given significance in ways impossible to achieve without ritual. The shaping and organization of impulses through ritual mastery takes place on several levels. As Neville explains, the most basic of these levels is the integration and organization of the individual personality. We become moral agents. As human beings we must next integrate ourselves into our family and eventually our larger community. "Each level achieves a ritual integration and intensity by weaving a pattern on the lower level. But that is a kind of force, a constriction. The lower levels pay a price by being integrated into the dance of the higher levels."[22] We willingly undergo this process of higher and higher levels of integration, despite the price paid by lower levels, because the higher levels of integration allow us access to more developed forms of satisfaction. Without this type of integration of desires, we remain petty men, as Xunzi would say, or no better than reptiles, according to Neville. Furthermore, Neville argues that Xunzi fails to properly account for and address the possibility and significance of disruptions to the higher levels of ritual integration caused by the accumulated pressure in the lower levels. Neville argues that these disruptions inevitably occur and that "religious rituals connect otherwise incommensurate strategies of integration. They release pressures. They reestablish broken dances."[23] Using the insights of semiotics, Neville develops a powerful set of conceptual tools for understanding Xunzi's theory on the one hand and reveals a potential difficulty within the theory itself on the other.

Lee Yearley recognizes three levels of spirituality in Xunzi's writings. The first level involves the explication and defense of social ritual as a means for spiritual fulfillment, the level much discussed by Neville. The next level includes Xunzi's critiques and reinterpretation of religious ideas and actions that lead to what Yearley refers to as spiritual deformation. Finally, there is the level at which humans come into contact with numinous powers arising, to some extent, from within themselves. Although Yearley discusses all three of these levels, it is the third level that informs much of the substance of his essay and constitutes Xunzi's significant contribution to the study of ritual. Before turning to the level of the numinous, let us look briefly at the lower two levels.

As most of the authors in this volume point out, Xunzi does not distinguish between social ritual and religious ritual. Social and religious ritual instead constitute elements on a continuum, from the proper way of addressing one's elder to the lavish pageantry of a ruler's plowing of the first furrow to begin the planting season. For Xunzi, all rituals along this continuum potentially contribute to full spiritual fulfillment, the life of the *junzi* or sage. Similar to Neville's connection of ritual to semiotics, Yearley argues that "social ritual provides the forms by which culture makes possible a specifically human life."[24] Furthermore, from this understanding of the first level of spirituality, Xunzi derives criteria to critique the religious practice of his contemporaries. At the second level of spirituality, Xunzi attacks two types of religiosity, what Yearley labels technological and masochistic religiosity. Xunzi reinterprets or rejects various ritual practices in order to avoid these two types of religion—on the one hand avoiding the magical manipulation indicative of technological religion and on the other hand avoiding the complete submission to an external figure paradigmatic of masochistic religion. At this point in the essay, Yearley turns to discussion of the numinous, the highest level of spirituality.

According to Yearley, what Xunzi recognizes better than many ritual theorists is the depth and significance of human frailty in the face of both origins and terminations that they cannot control. The last sections of Yearley's essay are examinations of Xunzi's understanding of our human and ritual response to origins and endings. Xunzi argues that humans incur unrepayable debts to three primary origins: our ancestors, our rulers and teachers, and Heaven. Recognition of these debts requires some form of response. In each case, the need for a response creates the possibility of spiritual deformation as well as development. Ritual shapes the expression of gratitude such that it once again avoids the pernicious forms of spiritual deformation. By acknowledging our debt as unrepayable and expressing gratitude through ritual forms, ideally we contact the realm of the numinous, especially in relation to Heaven. Yearley argues that proper relation to the numinous for Xunzi involves a trained ignorance toward Heaven and its workings. Through ritual participation, we cultivate and express an attitude of reverence toward the numinous we recognize in these origins.

In order to explicate Xunzi's understanding of terminations, Yearley makes use of the notion of the primordial. The primordial, for Yearley, fits into a particular model of personal religious development, a model in which mature religiosity involves achieving a level of psychological integration at which the primordial no longer controls our responses to the environment. The danger with this type of religious development, a danger recognized by Yearley and Xunzi, lies in losing contact with the primordial within us.

> This danger is significant because our spiritual health demands that we continue to be animated by what the primordial presents that is of

> irreducible value. Indeed, we must be able to bring it into our ordinary life, sometimes by integrating it into that life, sometimes by seeing how it challenges the presuppositions of that life. In this view, then, we ought not simply grow beyond the primordial. We must also be able to return to it, to employ and be employed by it, because only in and through it can we be open to the numinous.[25]

Yearley explores this idea of the primordial and contact with the primordial in our everyday lives through Xunzi's explanation of death rituals. Death, both the deaths of loved ones and the contemplation of our own death that these events bring about, reanimates strong primordial reactions in human beings, reactions that must be controlled and shaped through ritual participation or else they would likely lead to both psychological and spiritual deformation. Yet, Xunzi recognized that ritual must shape and express these reactions without denying their power or "the significant religious reactions they potentially contain."[26] Part of this task is accomplished, according to Yearley, through the lived acknowledgment of the "necessary fiction" involved in ritual practice, performing the funeral rites "as if" the spirits were present. Although we must accept our frailty before the origins and terminations that frame all human life, ritual enables us to face the numinous and constructively shape the primordial without succumbing to destructive forms of religiosity.

As with Yearley, Mark Berkson discusses Xunzi's reinterpretation of religious practice. In fact, Berkson sees Xunzi's program of reinterpretation as a hermeneutic response to the contemporary challenges facing the Confucian ritual order. According to Berkson, we can best understand Xunzi's hermeneutic achievement if we consider three main elements: meta-level awareness and reflexivity, participant-observer consciousness, and symbolic realism. The essay proceeds to explicate and examine these three elements and does so through conversation with Western scholars of ritual such as Sigmund Freud, Roy Rappaport, and Robert Bellah. When brought together, Berkson argues, these elements reveal the sophistication and depth of Xunzi's ritual theory, a theory that should receive more attention in contemporary ritual studies.

Berkson conceives of meta-level awareness as the ability, fostered in Xunzi's conception of ritual participation, of the participant to reflect on ritual itself through their participation. "When ritual points in the direction of the sacred, it is always pointing, in part, to itself."[27] According to Xunzi, when serving the ancestors through death rituals, we also become aware of the ways in which participation in the rite shapes and expresses our own reactions to death as well as reconstitutes the bonds of community among the living and between the living and the dead. Death rites, Berkson argues, must accomplish a dual task. They must facilitate the passage of the deceased from the realm of the living to the realm of the ancestors—in the minds of the living—and in the process also enable the living to move from being nonmourners to mourners and back again. According to Berkson, Xunzi's ritual theory takes account of these multiple aspects of ritual participation to some degree because of its emphasis on the cultivation of a meta-level awareness.

This meta-level awareness is closely connected to the second element of Xunzi's hermeneutic achievement, participant-observer consciousness. Berkson prefaces his discussion of participant-observer consciousness with a brief discussion of Freud's challenges to religious practice. Ritual participants, according to Berkson, are stuck with a two-horned dilemma. Either they unreflectively participate in ritual and become obsessed with wish fulfillment as Freud argues, or they become detached observers, cognizant of the delusional nature of ritual participation and alienated from ritual practice. Berkson rightly recognizes that Xunzi was aware of this dilemma himself. Xunzi, like Freud, worries about the possibility of obsession, of being blinded by a small portion of the truth. But rather than advocating detached observation, Xunzi instead argues that we should develop what Berkson calls participant-observer consciousness. "[T]he employer of participant-observer consciousness is aware of the paradox but also of the necessity of it. Ritual participation can be seen, perhaps, as a form of sophisticated pretending or play, artificial and invented, yet necessary for conflicted and fragile beings such as ourselves."[28] Although difficult to achieve, this state of awareness while participating is partially enabled by development of a meta-level awareness of ritual practice, ritual participants recognizing the self-reflective nature of their practice. Berkson goes on to argue that the character of ritual for Xunzi allows us to hold together opposites such as being simultaneously both participant and observer. The "as if" quality of ritual participation combined with its affective and somatic properties make it ideal for allowing these opposites to be woven together.

Given the difficulty of cultivating the first two elements of ritual participation, one of the consequences of Xunzi's conception of ritual participation is that there will be a hierarchy of ritual participants. Those who have fully cultivated a meta-level awareness that enables them to develop a participant-observer consciousness will participate in ritual at the highest level. Berkson describes those participating at this level as symbolic realists, a concept that he borrows from Robert Bellah. "Xunzi tells us that the truth lies not behind the symbols, but *in* them; in fact, it cannot be expressed in any other way. The symbols do not hide or distort reality; they are often the only way to fully express, apprehend, or experience reality."[29] While recognizing that the symbols and signs of the ritual order are human constructs, Xunzi's ideal ritual participant also understands that these symbols constitute the human cultural order, more specifically the Dao. As Berkson summarizes, only when we come to understand how these three elements interrelate in ritual practice do we see the depth and beauty of Xunzi's ritual theory. By itself, any one element is insufficient to convey the compelling nature of ritual practice.

One characteristic of Berkson's analysis can help us to understand the nature of the last two essays. Berkson makes excellent use of Western ritual theory both to challenge and explicate Xunzi's conception of ritual participation. The final two essays in this volume go one step further. They employ an explicit comparative religious framework.[30] That is not to say that the other essays do not engage in comparative analysis. Indeed, all of them engage in some level of comparative study. It proves difficult to discuss ritual theory without some amount of comparative material. What sets these essays apart is the aim of their authors to elucidate new aspects of other theories through comparison with that of Xunzi. Good comparative works of this kind usually share several characteristics. The focus of the comparison tends to be quite narrow. Although the theories or texts being compared may be broad and complex, comparative analysis is most successful when it can be tightly focused on a given issue or limited set of issues within the broader theories. Given this narrow focus, comparison begins by finding apparent affinities or differences between the theories. However, it then proceeds to find differences within the similarities and similarities within the differences, revealing the ways in which apparent similarity and difference at one level of analysis may dissolve into their opposite at another. Finally, comparative analysis succeeds when it enables us to see new aspects of the objects of comparison revealed through the comparative process itself. In both essays in this final section, the authors argue that comparison provides us with a new way of seeing and appreciating the ritual theories in question.

James Robson's essay narrowly focuses on the connection among ritual, tradition, and the role of the teacher in both Xunzi and Dōgen's understanding of ritual practice. As Robson points out, rarely do scholars compare Japanese and Chinese theories of ritual, and even more rarely are Confucian and Buddhist theories compared. Nevertheless, the comparison of Xunzi's third-century-b.c.e. Confucian conception of ritual practice with that of twelfth-century Buddhist Dōgen uncovers interesting affinities between the theories, affinities that Robson argues help shed light on Dōgen's later work. Beginning with an examination of the nature of ritual, Robson reconsiders previous comparisons made between the conceptions of ritual found in Xunzi and Durkheim. He concludes that their conceptions of ritual differ in at least two important respects. First, for Xunzi, collective effervescence is *not* central to ritual practice. Ritual differentiates and creates hierarchy rather than joining all participants into an undifferentiated unity. Second, Xunzi does *not* recognize a split between the sacred and profane spheres of human activity. Ritual is not set off from everyday life but a ubiquitous feature of everyday life. These differences between Xunzi and Durkheim lead Robson to suggest that there are greater affinities between Dōgen and Xunzi than between Durkheim and Xunzi. Like Xunzi, Dōgen conceives of ritual as differentiating and hierarchical as well as a part of everyday practice. For Dōgen, "ritual conduct is the realization of the Way, and this should be realized at all times and in all places, whether one is alone or in the presence of others."[31]

Having argued for the affinities between Xunzi's and Dōgen's conceptions of ritual, Robson next considers the role of the teacher and tradition in both theories. For both Xunzi and Dōgen, the role of the teacher and a specific ritual tradition are central to the achievement of moral cultivation or realization through ritual practice. The teacher plays the role of guide and interpreter of the tradition. Rituals require interpretation to be understood and performed properly. It is in the role of the teacher that we see a difference in the similarity between the two theorists. For Xunzi, a teacher can be anyone who has cultivated himself through participation in the Confucian ritual order to the extent that he becomes a *junzi*. Dōgen is more exclusive about who counts as a legitimate teacher. Only the master who has received face-to-face transmission of the Dharma in direct line from the Buddha should be considered a true teacher. As Robson argues, it is here that the importance of tradition can be seen as well. For Xunzi, it is the tradition of the Zhou rites transmitted through Kongzi that legitimates the Confucian ritual order. For Dōgen it is the tradition of face-to-face transmission originating with the Buddha. In both cases, the teacher acts as a living embodiment and interpreter of the tradition. Ritual further connects to tradition for Dōgen in that "Dōgen situates his treatment of meditation in the context of his ideas about the ways that particular ritual actions link the practitioner to the lineage of patriarchs and past Buddhas."[32] Robson's comparison of Xunzi and Dōgen ultimately provides, he believes, a means to better understand Dōgen's focus on ritual and its role in the monastic community of Eiheiji. It helps us to see more clearly aspects of both Xunzi and Dōgen's ritual theories.

The last essay in this volume is T. C. Kline's comparative examination of Xunzi's conception of ritual and religion with aspects of Peter Berger's sociological theory of religion found in his book *The Sacred Canopy*. Both theories include sophisticated explanations of the relationship between any given individual and the social environment in which she lives, an environment consisting primarily of ritual as it was broadly understood by Xunzi. Berger and Xunzi agree that human beings are born unfinished. They must be socialized and learn how to become competent participants in their social environment. In addition, they agree that the social environment is entirely a human construction, comprised of the type of signs and sign-shaped behaviors discussed by Neville. Despite their agreement on these fundamental points, when examined more closely it becomes apparent that they hold very different beliefs about the proper relationship between human beings and their socially constructed environment. On Kline's view, this difference can be understood in terms of Jonathan Z. Smith's distinction between locative and dynamic religious systems, where the former stresses the importance of "fully inhabiting" one's social roles and the latter requires religious practitioners to go beyond those roles.[33]

In order to clarify these differences, Kline explains Berger's and Xunzi's conceptions of the ideal human life, which are sagehood for Xunzi and authenticity for Berger. An advocate of a dynamic religious system, Berger argues for the individual's need to break out of the social constructions of the worldview and stand naked before the chaotic cosmos. It is through moments of authenticity of this sort that the ideal religious practitioner recognizes the constructed nature of the social environment and simultaneously understands the necessity of such a sacred canopy to shelter human beings from the chaotic cosmos. Without these moments of authentic awareness, the individual remains trapped within the social constructions and exemplifies a form of bad faith. Xunzi, on the other hand, conceives of the ideal human life, that of the sage, as being one in which the individual becomes shaped in accordance with the ritual order to the extent that he is completely at home in it. The sage achieves a type of effortless harmony within the social order. There are no moments of rupture, or authenticity, as Berger understands them. According to Berger, the sage is living in bad faith, failing to occasionally break out of the social order and stand alone before the cosmos. Likewise, for Xunzi, Berger's authentic individual has failed to fully cultivate himself such that he can achieve the effortless harmony of the sage. He remains at odds with the social order that will provide him with the greatest level of human fulfillment.

Kline argues that these differences in the two theorists' conceptions of the ideal human life partially grow out of different conceptions of the nature of the cosmos. For Berger, the cosmos is fundamentally chaotic and human beings merely project order, in the form of a worldview, onto this underlying chaos. For Xunzi the cosmos contains order, though of a lower level than that achieved through the activity of the sages. As significant as these differences are, the most fruitful result of the comparison comes from examining the role that Xunzi's characterization of human nature as bad plays in his theory. Berger's theory posits that human nature itself is a constructed element of the worldview. Because of this claim, Berger has difficulty explaining the supposed fragility of the constructed worldview or how one could distinguish between authenticity and bad faith. Although Xunzi shares Berger's belief in the fragility of the socially constructed ritual order, he does not encounter similar difficulties when trying to explain this fragility. Xunzi's conception of human nature provides the basis for the explanation. Our innate dispositions, while capable of being shaped by the ritual order, do not originally direct us toward such ritual activity. Instead, human nature directs us away from just the type of socialization that would eventually enable us to achieve the highest level of human fulfillment, namely, the harmonious ease of the sage. As Kline argues, this shows that

Berger's theory would profit from a more explicit explanation of the inchoate conception of human nature that seems to be present in many of the theory's claims. Simultaneously the essay also makes a case for the inclusion of Xunzi's theory in contemporary discussion of religion and ritual.

Now that each essay has been briefly described, the overall scope and depth of this volume should be apparent. While we will not attempt to tie the insights of all eight essays together in such a short introduction, two points of commonality deserve mention. First, all of the authors affirm Xunzi's claim that ritual, broadly conceived, is central to human interaction. We cannot understand human interaction, and thus human society or even what is significant in individual human lives, without careful attention to the function and dynamics of ritual participation. Ritual gives meaning and depth to human existence. It enables us to become fully human creatures capable of expressing and participating in rich and powerful emotions in ways that create and maintain social bonds. We come to perceive the world and those around us in humane ways through proper ritual participation. Second, given the importance of ritual to the understanding of human flourishing and religious practice, more attention should be paid to Xunzi's understanding of religion and ritual. Although Xunzi develops his theory in order to defend the Confucian ritual tradition of the late Warring States period in China, his insights into ritual practice can be of use to us, twenty-first-century scholars outside of the Confucian tradition, in explaining and understanding our own lives and ritual practices. After a long period of neglect, there are signs that Xunzi's importance to ritual studies is gaining recognition. For example, one of the two epigraphs to Ronald Grimes's volume, *Readings in Ritual Studies*, consists of a long passage from the *Xunzi*. Yet we are far from seeing Xunzi as one of the world's great theorists in religious studies, as the authors of these essays would argue. This anthology begins to make a case for such a strong claim. Hopefully, it will be but a first step in this direction. Drawing Xunzi more fully into the contemporary conversation in religious studies will not only bring much deserved recognition to a great thinker but also enrich our discussion of ritual and religion.

Notes

1. See the beginning of the essay in this volume by Edward Machle, "Xunzi as a Religious Philosopher."

2. *Houhanshu* 後漢書 (Shanghai: Shangwu, 1927, reprint of 1739 ed.), *juan* 62.5b–6a.

3. The term 君子 *junzi* has been translated in a variety of ways, among them "superior person" and "gentleman." None of these translations seem to capture fully the meaning of the term, and often the translations inadvertently carry unwanted associations in English. For this reason we have left *junzi* untranslated.

4. For a clear and concise introduction to the Confucian tradition and conceptions of moral cultivation, see Philip J. Ivanhoe, *Confucian Moral Self Cultivation*, second ed. (Indianapolis, IN: Hackett, 2000).

5. The period of philosophical growth in early China, roughly the fifth to third centuries b.c.e., is remarkable. Numerous philosophical schools arose and joined the collective debate concerning how best to organize the state, live a good life, reunify China, and bring peace and prosperity to the people. There are several excellent books on this period of Chinese thought. See, for example, A. C. Graham, *Disputers of the Tao* (Chicago: Open Court, 1989); Heiner Roetz, *Confucian Ethics of the Axial Age* (Albany: State University of New York Press, 1993); and Benjamin I. Schwartz, *The World of Thought in Ancient China* (Cambridge: Harvard University Press, 1985).

6. For a clear and concise discussion of this point, see the opening section of Mark Berkson's essay in this volume.

7. Paul Kjellberg and David Nivison have both written about the relationship between Zhuangzi and Xunzi in illuminating ways. See Kjellberg, "Sextus Empiricus, Zhuangzi, and Xunzi on Skepticism," in Paul Kjellberg and Philip J. Ivanhoe, eds., *Essays on Skepticism, Relativism, and Ethics in the "Zhuangzi"* (Albany: State University of New York Press, 1996); and Nivison, "Xunzi and Zhuangzi," in T. C. Kline III and Philip J. Ivanhoe, eds., *Virtue, Nature, and Moral Agency in the "Xunzi"* (Indianapolis, IN: Hackett, 2000).

8. The competing conceptions of human nature offered by Mengzi and Xunzi have already been discussed in depth. See D. C. Lau, "Theories of Human Nature in *Mencius* and *Xunzi*"; Bryan W. Van Norden, "Mengzi and Xunzi: Two Views of Human Agency"; and David Wong, "Xunzi on Moral Motivation," all in T. C. Kline III and Philip J. Ivanhoe, eds., *Virtue, Nature, and Moral Agency in the "Xunzi"* (Indianapolis, IN: Hackett, 2000).

9. Xunzi's expressions of concern about Mengzi's misinterpretation of Kongzi's teachings marks an important moment in the development of a religious tradition. Both Mengzi and Xunzi recognize themselves to be part of the Confucian tradition. They agree on most of their positions. Their disagreement arises out of a debate about the proper understanding of the tradition as it is found in the original teachings of the founder, Kongzi. Xunzi accuses Mengzi of being a heretic, of developing what could be labeled a heretical interpretation leading followers away from the true Confucian Dao. This type of internal disagreement, in some important ways, signals the maturity of the Confucian tradition. Beginning with Xunzi, followers of the Confucian tradition continuously engage in debate about the proper interpretation of the tradition itself. For a discussion of some of the debate that occurs as the tradition develops through time, see John H. Berthrong, *Transformations of the Confucian Way* (Boulder, CO: Westview Press, 1998).

10. A. R. Radcliffe-Brown, "Religion and Society," in *Structure and Function in Primitive Society: Essays and Addresses* (Glencoe, IL: The Free Press, 1952), pp. 153–177. We had hoped to include this essay in the first section of this volume, but exorbitant permission fees have prevented us from including it here. Nevertheless, we briefly discuss the essay here in the introduction and encourage those who are interested to seek out the essay for further reading.

11. Radcliffe-Brown, "Religion and Society," p. 157.

12. It is interesting to note that Radcliffe-Brown does not use Xunzi or even Chinese religious practice as a case study but as a conceptual resource for developing a new approach to understanding religion and its relation to society. In 1945, during the height of functionalist approaches to religion, Radcliffe-Brown chose to use Xunzi as a source for explicating and legitimizing his own approach to the study of religion.

13. Radcliffe-Brown, "Religion and Society," p. 176.

14. Machle, chapter 1 of this volume, p. 21.

15. Thomas P. Kasulis, "Philosophy as Metapraxis," Frank Reynolds and David Tracy, eds., *Discourse and Practice* (Albany: State University of New York Press, 1992), pp. 169–195.

16. Machle has written extensively about Xunzi's conception of Heaven in his book-length translation and study of chapter 17: *Nature and Heaven in the "Xunzi": A Study of the Tian Lun* (Albany: State University of New York Press, 1993).

17. Machle, chapter 1 of this volume, p. 40.

18. Ivanhoe, chapter 2 of this volume, p. 47.

19. Ibid., p. 52.

20. Neville, chapter 3 of this volume, p. 65.

21. Ibid., p. 65.

22. Ibid., p. 72.

23. Ibid., p. 74.

24. Yearley, chapter 4 of this volume, p. 85.

25. Ibid., p. 96.

26. Ibid., p. 97.

27. Berkson, chapter 5 of this volume, p. 109.

28. Ibid., p. 120.

29. Ibid., p. 123–4.

30. We do not defend here the practice of comparative religious studies or even the more specific practice of comparative analysis of ritual theory. The essays themselves are left to speak in their own defense. Those who are interested in sophisticated and compelling defenses of comparative religion should read the essays collected in Kimberley C. Patton and Benjamin C. Ray, eds., *A Magic Still Dwells: Comparative Religion in the Postmodern Age* (Berkeley, CA: University of California Press, 2000). For examples of successful comparative religious studies, see Lee Yearley, *Mencius and Aquinas: Theories of Virtue and Conceptions of Courage* (Albany: State University of New York Press, 1990); Karen L. Carr and Philip J. Ivanhoe, *The Sense of Anti-Rationalism: Zhuangzi and Kierkegaard's Religious Thought*, revised second edition (Createspace.com, 2010); and Aaron Stalnaker, *Overcoming Our Evil: Human Nature and Spiritual Exercises in Xunzi and Augustine* (Washington, DC: Georgetown University Press, 2006).

31. Robson, chapter 6 of this volume, p. 146.

32. Ibid., p. 152.

33. For the source of this distinction, see Jonathan Z. Smith, "The Influence of Symbols on Social Change: A Place on Which to Stand," *Worship* 44 (1970), pp. 457–474.

Religious Vision

CHAPTER 1

Xunzi as a Religious Philosopher

Edward J. Machle

I

One of the widely acknowledged sides of Xunzi, the great Confucian philosopher of the third century b.c.e., is his work as a critic of religion. He subjected many religious currents of his time to philosophical criticism. Belief in ghosts, phrenology and similar superstitions, praying in order to cause rain, belief that natural calamities were divine punishments, and determining policies by augury all felt the edge of his attack. Even overweening interest in the secrets of nature moved him to analysis and rejection. It is then no wonder that he has commonly been pictured as a thoroughgoing secularist and enemy of religion, or, as Rosemont puts it, an "avowed atheist."

I have not found anything in the literature that could be called an attempt to deal with Xunzi not as a philosopher of religion but as a religious philosopher. Here and there one may find hints that this might be possible: Hughes, for instance, speaks of Xunzi's "spiritual" philosophy.[1] Yet the received interpretation has its almost complete way.

By "religious philosopher" I mean a thinker whose philosophizing has some guiding religious motivation. He is a philosopher rather than a theologian, because he speaks for the "reasonable man" of his culture rather than for some particular worshipping community, but like the theologian, he seeks to make sense of the received religious tradition as a way of continuing to be part of it. For the former reason, he does not shrink from criticizing dearly held practices or beliefs: for the latter, he holds not a purely rational goal of pristine clarity in analysis or neat consistency in system-building, but one of edification of himself and others.

A religious philosopher is not a prophet. By this I mean he does not, and cannot, add significantly to the religious materials available to his times. He draws on them, restructures them, reinterprets them, perhaps rejects many of them. When finished, he may claim, "This is what they always really meant." But he is essentially a renovator, not a regenerator.

Was Xunzi moved by religious concerns, to at least some extent? The received interpretations deny it. The Marxists claim him as a prime spokesman for the materialism implicit in the working-man's outlook, though they do argue over just how much his materialism contributed to revolutionary progress. The Chinese, impressed with the Western scientific outlook, have acclaimed his naturalism, and Western scholars have read his view of Nature as one of the closest approaches in all of Chinese thought to a thoroughly secular stance, affirming natural law and even mechanism. It is in connection with Xunzi that Liu Wu-chi remarks that "in the third century b.c. the Chinese lost their spiritual soul";[2] and Fung Yu-lan maintains that Xunzi never rises above the merely moral and hence falls short of what he calls "the spiritual."[3]

There are many roots for this position. Modern Chinese scholars are the heirs of Neo-Confucian scholarship, which read Xunzi out of the Confucian party, most apparently because he rejected Mengzi's views on human nature and moral energy, which Neo-Confucianism took as its basis for affirming a spiritual continuity between man and the highest sphere of "Heaven-and-Earth." His rejection of this basis for their belief led them to see him as crass, antispiritual, and two-dimensional, guilty of what Niebuhr has called "self-satisfied finitude." Bringing to flower what had been living within Confucianism all along, the faith in the moral continuity between Nature and human nature, they were ill-disposed to believe they had any alternative to Mengzi.

More recently, the picture changed. As Yang tells us:

> In the twentieth century, when the dominance of Western influence brought contempt for superstition and magic as the very sign of national backwardness, a new generation of Chinese scholars, such as Chang T'ai-yen, Liang Ch'i-ch'ao, Ch'en Tu-hsiu, and Hu Shih, came forth to defend the dignity of Chinese civilization not only by stressing the rationalistic view of the Confucian doctrine but also by claiming that the dominance of Confucian orthodoxy had helped develop China into a "rationalistic society" where there was neither a powerful priesthood nor protracted struggle between religion and the state.[4]

Such scholars, stressing the secular and rational character of Confucian thought, could hardly treat Xunzi, the left-wing Confucian, as anything but their antireligious and proscientific ally. Western sinologists, reading into Chinese cultural history Western Enlightenment biases regarding the relationships of science, nature, reason, ritual, and religion, tended to go along with the trend. Once again, Xunzi was celebrated for agnosticism and naturalism.

One difficulty all along has been the lack of a consistent tradition of interpretation from the earliest days. It is noteworthy that Sima Qian, writing of Xunzi scarcely a century and a half after the philosopher's death, says nothing of his religious views but implies that he was apparently against "attending to magic and prayers, and believing in omens and luck."[5] Since this is the only real biographical source we have regarding him, we cannot go much beyond the guess that his views on religion were not a lively topic of discussion in the second century b.c.e. His texts were collected around 76 b.c.e., but there seems to be no trace of any continuing or systematic study of his work for nine hundred years thereafter. The received tradition of serious study dates from Yang Liang in 818, who seems to have had no previous Xunzi scholarship on which to draw. We are thus really left with the text itself, general background knowledge, and scholarship of a far later age.

The grounds for painting Xunzi as antireligious seem to be: (1) his criticisms of widespread beliefs as superstitious; (2) his apparent denial of the existence of spirits, particularly spirits of the dead; (3) his treatment of ritual as "mere ornament" which nevertheless had some educational function in molding men's emotional life; (4) his apparent denial of an anthropomorphic Heaven-deity; (5) his belief that man is evil by nature, implying that the Nature that gives man human nature is itself evil, or at best morally irrelevant; (6) his suggestions that nature may be technologically exploited rather than revered; and (7) his widespread, often dominating concern with matters political, economic, legal, and educational.

These must be set over against the fact that Xun Qing aimed at being and claimed to be nothing but the best possible Confucian, and whatever "Confucianism" has been down through the centuries, it has always been in some sense *religious* even when not a religion. To quote Yang again, "Modern students of China who maintain the purely rationalistic view of Confucianism are not able to explain away the religious aspects of the doctrine without distorting the meaning of the original texts."[6] It is striking that discussion of the preceding seven points revolves around relatively very few loci in the *Xunzi* corpus, often without relating them to whatever contrary evidence there may be. Some of these loci are important, certainly, and merit much discussion. The chief issue is whether they are to be given an interpretation which then controls our reading of the entire corpus, or whether they are to be considered as a few items among many, all needing mutual interpretation.

II

The task of reexamining the established position has two steps: we must show both that the received view is without adequate foundation and that there is a viable alternative to it. The former enterprise requires analysis of the grounds for the received view, an analysis that itself provides the basis for calling it into question. Only if the received view is shaken can the presentation of an alternative be a serious gesture. Fortunately, attacking one view often suggests, of itself, an alternative.

We pointed out the seven points upon which the idea that Xun was anti-religious, or at least irreligious, rests. One of these, his absorption with political, economic, legal, and educational matters, can be set aside quite simply, since religious leaders from Moses to Martin Luther King Jr. have shown their most extensive concerns often to be such matters. The decision whether these are also religious concerns must be decided in light of the particular man's religious orientation, which is what is here at issue. Such interests do not of themselves count for or against the existence of such an orientation, particularly, one might add, in a Chinese thinker.

Another of these frequently appealed to points, Xunzi's "technological" or "scientific" interest, I believe to be based on an unfortunate collocation of misreadings and Western scientific biases. Since I am developing an argument on this point elsewhere, let it suffice here to point out its dependence upon another point, namely, Xunzi's so-called naturalistic view of Heaven. Without this latter claim, the claim of a technological vision on his part would have no foundation.

Still another of the alleged grounds may be quite summarily reduced. That he gives a psychological account of ritual, when speaking of ritual in nonritual contexts, would be reduction only if his psychology is reductionistic. Though this has been claimed quite blandly, I have found in the literature no worked-out case for it as over against alternatives. If an author's own psychology is itself religiously reductionist, or if on the basis of other things, such as his view of the evil of human nature, an author assumes Xun's psychology to be so, this argument might gain some apparent force. But many a devout handbook of religious discipline is full of psychologizing, even about sacred matters. The interpretation of Xun's psychological treatment of ritual is part of the question of his religious motivations, not an independent ground on which to support an answer.

Likewise, his view of man's natural or innate evil may be set aside for the present. Although it does set him against Mengzi and the religious affinities of the latter's followers, only an investigation of the other points can make it clear whether this is a religious opposition, in some sense, rather than an opposition to religion. That later followers of Mengzi took it to be a rejection of "the principle of sublime transcendence" means only it was a rejection of *their* principle, no more.

We are thus left, at least in the main, with two areas that count independently for a nonreligious interpretation of Xunzi: his critiques of superstition (including belief in spirits) and his "naturalistic" view of nature. We shall take these up in order.

III

When we turn to his criticisms of superstition, we find two quite different sorts of cases. In the one, there is no disagreement as to what he is attacking, or how, or why. He overthrows physiognomy and related fortune-tellings, for instance, by amassing counterexample after counterexample to show their untenability. His reason for attacking them is not scientific, but moral and practical, since evaluating men by their appearance cannot conduce to a moral, and hence, responsible and successful administration. As he puts it,

> to physiognomize a person's appearance is not as good as to consider his heart; considering his heart is not as good as to select his principles. . . . When a person's principles are upright and his heart obeys them, although his physiognomy be repulsive, yet if his heart and principles are good, his physiognomy will not hinder him from being a superior man.[7]

Physiognomy is not merely empirically false, it usurps the place of proper moral evaluation.

Such moral criticism of superstition, of course, is not of itself irreligious; it can as easily reflect a critical but deeply religious mind.

Were all his positions as clear-cut as that against physiognomy, this article would have no reason to exist. Consider the following celebrated passage:

> You pray for rain and it rains. Why? For no particular reason, I say. It is just as though you had not prayed for rain and it rained anyway. . . . But it is not as though you could hope to accomplish anything by such ceremonies. They are done merely for ornament. Hence the gentleman regards them as ornaments, but the common people regard them as supernatural. He who considers them ornaments is fortunate; he who considers them supernatural is unfortunate.[8]

This is Watson's translation. The following alternative translation points up the problem of deciding just what he did say:

> When we sacrifice for rain, it rains. Why? I say, there is nothing to ask "why?" about. It rains even though we don't sacrifice. . . . This isn't something to be regarded from the point of view of obtaining something we seek, but from a cultured standpoint. Consequently,

> although the gentleman looks on it as a matter of humane culture, the lower gentry see it as a matter of dealing with spirits. Regard it as a matter of humane culture and good fortune follows; regard it as a matter of dealings with spirits and misfortune follows.[9]

Though this passage is often cited as evidence that Xunzi denied the existence of spirits, that is certainly not what he is doing. The matter of belief that he concerns himself with is belief in the efficacy of rituals to effect some change in events *independent* of their place in the total lives and development of the people involved. It is the business of men to deal with nature only according to 禮 *li*—that is, only through the proper development of their characters and institutions, two things intimately connected in his view. It pertains to man to be related to Heaven wholesale, not piecemeal; as a human world focused in the equality with Heaven that characterizes the Sage. Anything else is counter-productive, and produces just those unfortunate consequences that the vulgar view ritual as the means to avoid.

Compare the passage just quoted with another well-known one.

> A man, having contracted a chill from the dampness, proceeds to beat a drum and make offering of a pig in hopes of effecting a cure. He wears out the drum and loses a pig in the process, that is certain, but no blessing of recovery follows as a result.[10]

Both passages deny the physical efficacy of rituals. The first, however, deals with rituals that Xunzi *approves*, rituals which add to the enrichment of communal human life. Such rituals produce in his eyes, as far as we can tell, no ill effects *as rituals*, whatever the materials they consume. Ill effects come not from their celebration, but from the expectation of particular effect, which encourages confusion regarding the proper separation of what is human and what is Heaven.

In the second case, however, two evil results are presented as accruing: ineffectiveness and the waste of the ritual materials. Apparently the folk ritual for illness cannot have the humanizing effect that a prayer for rain may have. One may suspect that Xun distinguishes two sorts of rituals; rituals which are not part of *li*, but merely of folklore, are superstitious; rituals which are part of *li* are a proper part of the *Dao* of man, though not to be considered part of the *Dao* of Heaven.

It is worth noting that the example of the man with the chill occurs in a context arguing that men's judgments are unreliable when swayed by emotion. The story is preceded by, and explicitly associated with, the following tale:

> There was a man . . . who lived south of Xiashou. . . . One night he was walking in the moonlight when, glancing down and seeing

> his shadow, he took it for a crouching ghost. Looking up, he caught sight of his own hair and took it for a devil standing over him. He whirled around and starting running, and when he reached his home he fell unconscious and died. Is this not sad? Always when people see ghosts, it is at times when they are aroused and excited, and they make their judgments in moments when their faculties are confused and blinded.[11]

Apparently he is maintaining that, were the first man well, he would know better than to believe that a drum-and-pig ritual would cure a chill. Sick, he confuses what is of man and what is of Heaven, and so makes a fool of himself. The point being made is that people's judgments, even their perceptions, are impaired when they are emotionally upset. To make this point Xun must take for granted that his readers will already agree that claims to have seen ghosts are very questionable claims, whose dubitableness need not be established. He is not arguing the falsity of the superstitions; he is using an already established belief in their falsity to make another point. Evidently the process that Modi objected to so much earlier, that men were giving up their belief in ghosts that punish, had proceeded a long way before Xun's time. What this shows us is that however else Confucianism in his day was still religious, it did not find need for belief in retributive spirits. Nor did it have to. It is already quite clear in Mengzi that the good man does right because it is right, and for no other reason; Modi's need for belief in such spirits was already undercut.

If this be sound interpretation, we do not find Xunzi actively denying that spirits exist. Instead, he accepts what appear to be widespread doubts regarding the 鬼 *gui*, the dark, disorderly, and at times hungry and vengeful spooks. Here, however, the expectation that his readers share these doubts simply shows he took his place within an already existing tradition of doubt. Similarly, the word for the magical powers of diviners and spooks—靈 *ling*—occurs in his writings only in proper names, in noticeable contrast to the *Laozi* and the *Zhuangzi*. In this, however, he simply agrees with both Kongzi and Mengzi, and apparently stands well within their tradition.

IV

What then did Xunzi maintain regarding spirits? A proper place to begin the discussion of the place of spirits within Confucianism is with the famous remark of Kongzi in the *Analects* 6:20, "To respect spiritual beings (鬼神 *guishen*), maintaining a proper distance in one's relations with them, may be called wisdom." "Maintaining a proper distance" is a question of *li*, of ritual or propriety. Xunzi here clearly follows his master's example, although probably going beyond it in holding that the expectation of particular results does not accord with *li* and brings about misfortune. Both men would surely hold that truly following *li* brings about only good.

A further note may be sounded. Kongzi uses the phrase *guishen*, "spooks and spirits" or "*yin*-spirits and *yang*-spirits," to stand for the whole realm of spiritual powers under Heaven. *Gui* and *shen* are never associated in the *Xunzi*, or for that matter in the *Mengzi* or the *Great Learning* (*Daxue* 大學). Distinction between them is most striking in the *Xunzi*, where *shen* is used nearly forty times, but *gui*, outside of quotations, only four times. Moreover, these four times are all of them highly pejorative in tone, while *shen* appears in contexts of the very highest approval.

It is understandable that the pejorative passages speaking of *gui* are widely quoted to show the sage's rejection of both *shen* and *gui*. But although *shen* may perhaps be used to include both *gui* and *shen*, I know of no instance where *gui* embraces both. We may conclude that Xun's opposition to superstitions involving *gui* is not so easily extended to beliefs and practices involving *shen* as many have taken it to be.

An instance of this occurs in his treatment of funeral rites. Contrasting high culture with lack of sophistication, he says,

> The sage understands them, the gentleman finds comfort in carrying them out, the officials are careful to maintain them, and the common people accept them as custom. To the gentleman they are a part of the way (道 *Dao*) of man, to the common people they are something pertaining to the spirits (*gui*), (literally, "ghost-serving").[12]

When he is speaking seriously about the meaning of the rites, however, he says,

> At the internment one reverently lays his form away; at the sacrifices one reverently serves his spirit (*shen*); and by means of inscriptions, eulogies, and genealogical records one reverently hands down his name to posterity.[13]

This sounds as if ordinary folk are superstitious, and think of the rituals as a serving of the *gui* (鬼事 *guishi*), while the sophisticated gentleman speaks of serving (worshipping, or acknowledging) the *shen* of the departed (事神 *shishen*) as part of the true *Dao* of man. (That common folk would also acknowledge *shen* is, of course, true but unimportant here.)

We have a problem, however. In the funeral rites, it is part of man's *Dao* to serve the *shen*, but it is superstition to think one is serving *gui*. In the case of sacrifices for rain, it is superstition to think one is serving *shen*, for the gentleman knows such rites are rather a matter of 文 *wen*, or humane culture. What is one to make of this?

It might be answered: the essay on ritual was written earlier than the one on Heaven, and the author's thought developed in the interim. From viewing only *gui*-ritual as superstitious, he moved to viewing all reference to spirits as superstitious. This could be a solution, right enough, but a purely fiat one. There seems to be no way whatever to establish which essay was written first. Regarding the dates of composition, about all we can say is that the somewhat pejorative reference to the king Chu in the essay on Heaven was probably written while Xun Qing was not a resident of Chu. That indicates nothing of the relative priority of the essays. In the absence of a firm chronology of Xunzi's writings, theories about his intellectual development can only be projections of our own assumptions.

Verbal solutions do not help, either, such as the suggestion that the word "*shen*," in the one case, excludes *gui*, while in the other case, includes them. This is undoubtedly so, but unless *shen* in chapter 17 includes *only gui*, which is most unlikely, nothing is solved. Likewise, nothing can be made out of the point that in one case the contrast is between *serving gui* and *serving shen*, in the other, between a supernaturalist attitude and a humanist attitude. That merely restates the problem, no more.

The most promising resolution would seem to be this. Funeral rituals deal with the alteration of a close personal relationship, already defined within the rules of propriety. For whatever analogy there may be between one's relation to a loved-one living and the same loved-one dead, there is also a profound difference. Xunzi's whole approach calls attention to the passing from one to the other. The relation to the living is defined by the 孝 *xiao* of family life, that to the dead, in terms of honoring and reporting to the *shen* of one's ancestor, presenting him no more in the flesh, but as resident in the ancestral tablet. Truly humane living requires not only that this transition be lived through, but that it be lived through expressively. The psychology of such living-through can be described, and Xun's essays do that. But effectively to produce the described results, the ritual, and its ritual references, must be *believed in*. Otherwise, one cannot be sincere about the whole transaction, and for Xun, as for any Confucian, sincerity is fundamental.

In the case of prayers for rain, or other rituals directed toward nature, there is no such alteration of the relationship involved. The relation of man to Heaven is constant. Xunzi takes for granted that this constancy can be expressed and celebrated in ritual ways. He never criticizes the imperial rites addressed to Heaven and the royal ancestors, or the feudal nobles' sacrifices to the gods of the soil. Prayers for rain, however, are another thing altogether: particular desires and aims intrude into that relationship. This would constitute an imposition upon the powers of nature, an attempt by man to interfere in what belongs to Heaven. Man's place in dealing with drought, Xunzi makes clear, is to so administer his own affairs that he has sustenance enough no matter what Heaven in its mysterious ways sends down.

This also has its reverse side. For coping with drought, there are appropriate administrative technologies, and it is the task of the educated official to acquaint himself with those and to develop sound judgment in applying them. To do anything less is to violate the *Dao* of man, seeking shortcuts that do not fulfill the pattern of *li*. It is this pattern of *li* which constitutes the highest possibility of man's relation to the cosmos, the achievement of a harmonious triad with Heaven and Earth. To depart from it is to regress, to violate it is to cause confusion, to substitute private or local ends for it is obscene.

The outcome is, then, that serving the spirit of the dead has a humane function—it embodies the cosmic *li* in the particular human life. Its ultimate ritual function is to bring the fact of a particular death into the cosmic wholeness. As such, it is a part of *wen*: whatever else it may do is irrelevant. Hence it can be done with that wholehearted seriousness called 敬 *jing*, "reverence." Prayers for rain cannot be so done, for they are, as it were, prayers against wholeness. They refuse to accept the drought Heaven has sent. Xunzi mentions three times those who are "resentful of Heaven," and in chapter 4 he says, "He who understands himself is not resentful of men; he who understands the decrees (命 *ming*) is not resentful of Heaven." Lack of rain is not something that lies with man, only with Heaven; he who cannot accept it does not really understand the decrees. This is a mark of the "petty man," the man who is lacking in proper intention.

In saying this, have we done more than to apply to Xun Qing's scene Malinowski's distinction between magic and religion? The noted anthropologist writes,

> This difference will serve us as a *prima facie* distinction between magic and religion. While in the magical act the underlying idea and aim is always clear, straightforward, and definite, in the religious ceremony there is not purpose directed toward a subsequent event. . . . The native can always state the end of the magical rite, but he will say of the religious ceremony that it is done because such is the usage, or because it has been ordained, or he will narrate an explanatory myth.[14]

The common people "hope to accomplish something," for they see sacrifices as magic. The gentleman claims no specific efficacy for them, they are just "humane culture," a part of *li* or proper rituals. Although Xun discusses in chapter 19 the "historical antecedents" (禮之所起 *lizhi suoqi*) of *li*, their three roots, and their general functionings, he insists that their significance is cosmic, their meaning deep, great, and lofty, and only the Sage can understand them—language surely closer to religious myth than to secular explanation.

The opposition he maintains, then, is not one between sacrifices to *gui* and those to *shen*, but between sacrifices directed toward particular ends (which Malinowski would call "magic"), and those which are simply part of the profound expressive whole he calls *li*, which is for him not merely the pattern of elegant behavior, but the ground of human organization and happiness and the key to man's place in the cosmos.

So much for the problem of sacrifice. What else does Xunzi say about spirits? Some of his uses of *shen* are of little concern to us here. Two of these are quotations from the *Odes*; one is a textual error, long corrected by Chinese commentators. Two instances merely refer to psychic functions:

> When man's body develops and his spirit (*shen*) is produced, then love and hate, delight and anger, sorrow and joy find lodging in him.[15]

> A drunken man will try to leap a ditch a hundred paces wide as though it were a narrow gutter, or will stoop to enter a city gate as though it were a low doorway. This is because wine has disordered his spirit (*shen*).[16]

Similarly, oblique to our study are most cases wherein *shen* or 如神 *rushen* ("like a god") is used as a figure of speech, as in

> The people esteem him as a god, exalt him as Heaven, love him as parents, are in awe of him as of the manifestation of a spirit.[17]

> People are converted to Dao as though by a *shen*.[18]

> Make your speech precious, make it rare, make it laudatory, make it *shen*.[19]

Possibly also oblique are those few instances in chapter 15 wherein *shen* indicates charisma that demands respect: "Therefore it is his *shen* that commands respect for (or in?) his soldiers," and "Where he is present, he commands a godlike respect." This second passage, however, is of some special interest, since the identical wording occurs within a very different context in *Mengzi* 7A13. There Legge translates it, "Whatever he abides, his influence is of a spiritual nature," while Lau renders it, (he) "works wonders where he abides."[20] The two contexts are too similar to demand differing translations—except that one is in *Mengzi* and the other in *Xunzi*.

Among the remaining occasions of *shen*, however, there are some that are revealing, though not definitive:

> There is no greater godliness (*shen*) than to transform yourself with the Way.[21]

> There is nothing more godlike (*shen*) than to learn to love one thing alone.[22]

> The life of a man of perfect sincerity is godlike (*shen*).[23]

> With sincere mind preserve 仁 *ren*, and it will become outwardly evident; outwardly evident, it will become a spiritual power (*shen*); being a spiritual power, it will have the ability to transform.[24]

These suggest Xunzi had sense of spirituality, one quite typically Confucian, stressing the possibilities of going even beyond *ren* to a transformed and transforming unity of some sort. Language about transformations and unities is seductive, and one ought to maintain a suitable diffidence toward giving it a specific content. Here we note its occurrence and look further for more definitional statements.

Luckily, Xun twice approaches definitions of *shen*. In one we read,

> The stars in their course make their rounds, the sun and moon shine in their turns . . . and the myriad things properly receive each its own nourishment so as to reach maturity. We see the efficacy of the entire process while not seeing its actual workings, and so we call it *shen*. Everyone knows the final outcomes, but no one knows the formless antecedents, and so we call it Heaven.[25]

Xunzi's phrase here, 之謂 *zhiwei*, is his usual definitional one. He is not saying as I read him, "Folks don't know what it is, so they read a ghost into nature"—though many interpreters, especially the Marxist ones, take him to do so. When he says *zhiwei* he is ordinarily giving a definition; he is presenting a usage he himself owned to. He is saying, in effect, "Nature is properly called spiritual, since, though we see the effects, we don't see the workings; it is properly called Heaven, since, though we know the outcomes, we can't know the invisible causes." This is as close to a definition of "spirit" as a cosmic category as we can find.

In the other definitional statement, he is discussing rather the makeup of man, but of that perfectly developed man, the sage or "holy man" (聖人 *shengren*). Of him he says,

> This Dao of his proceeds from his unity. What do we mean by unity? The answer is: laying hold on *shen*, to be firmly established. What do we mean by *shen*? Exhausting goodness and cherishing orderliness is to be called *shen*. To be perfectly established is for there to be no thing in the world sufficient to subvert one. To be *shen* and firmly established is to be a sage.[26]

We may have here the outline of Xunzi's view of spirituality. The first quasi-definition given above indicates that in his eyes, spirit in the natural world is chacterized by:

1. invisibility in its source or prime workings but productiveness of visible results
2. the inclusion in these results of remarkable but orderly transformations into higher states of fulfillment.

So far, these characteristics would not go beyond his use of *shen* to mean man's biological life; they do not seem to limit him to merely that.

The second quasi-definition, dealing with spirit in human affairs, adds these further traits:

3. the power to transform morally both individuals and whole populations.
4. a character exhausting all goodness and supportive of true orderliness.

and associates closely with the idea of *shen* still another:

5. the presence of an ongoing unity that cannot be subverted by things.

It is apparently in reference to the first of these "definitions" that Chan says of Xun, "What he called spirit is but cosmic change and evolution"; it is in reference to the second that Watson speaks of his making *shen* "a quality of moral excellence."[27] In what they affirm, these statements are true enough, but both carry a private element, the first, explicitly and the second, implicitly. Xun surely does call "cosmic change and evolution" *shen*, but clearly does not limit *shen* to that. He does make *shen* "a quality of moral experience," but how this relates to religious sensibilities is not readily apparent. Nor, for that matter, is it quickly settled that his "cosmic change and evolution" is devoid of more-than-secular or more-than-moral significance.

An interesting conclusion follows when we set the preceding five characteristics associated with *shen* alongside other general aspects of Xun's thought. For him, evil consists of disorder, and the primal flaw in man lies in his susceptibility to being turned toward disorder by *things*, as objects of desire or aversion. Since this flaw is characteristic of man *by nature*—but it is typical of the man who lays hold on *shen* that there is no *thing* that can subvert him—*shen* must be, in human affairs, the contrary to 性 *xing*, or human nature. Since *shen* is in this sense contrary to nature, superior to it, and supervenient upon it, it would not be unjustifiable to call it "supernatural," even though it is not set over against Nature (in another sense). This possibility is in itself a challenge to much current interpretation of Xun's whole system of thought.

V

As indicated, *shen* is often associated with the figure of the Sage. The Sage receives many characteristics in the *Xunzi*, and we can only summarize here. He is one who perfectly follows *Dao* and who is wholly beautiful doing so (chapter 18); he has complete mastery of all moral principles (chapter 21); he is altogether skilled in *li* (chapter 26); his emotions are at rest in *li* (chapter 2); he is the acme of the *Dao* (chapter 19); his thoughts are joyous (chapter 21); he transforms his own human nature (chapter 23); he attains equality with Heaven (chapter 25). He transforms whole populations, but could not do this if he did not embody the 誠 *cheng* ("sincerity") which Heaven and earth exhibit (chapter 3, possibly not authentic). A full paragraph in chapter 8 eulogizes him. One striking characteristic which appears again and again is that of unity. It is not just that he has the ability to unify a people; this ability is but the outer aspect of his unique inner unity. He is never of two minds (chapter 21), but more than that, he has a distinctive goodness which is a single whole. He has unified his loves (chapter 1); he cannot be fooled, for he finds in himself the true standard (chapter 5); in his self-cultivation he completes the efficacy of Heaven (chapter 17). His unity seems intimately related to the ultimate artistic unity, for

> When form and meaning, and emotion and practical use, are treated as the inside and outside or the front and back of a single reality and are both looked after, then rites have reached the middle state. . . . He who dwells in (this state), who wanders widely and masters all its corners and gradations, is a sage. . . . [H]is enlightenment is the mastery of ritual.[28]

Some of the passages relating to the Sage and his unity are more obscure. In chapter 25, Malmquist translates as follows:

> The thoughts will then become refined: this is the flowering of one's purpose. If one cares for it well and unifies it, one's spirit will thereby become accomplished. When the essence (of one's thought) and the spirit blend one with another, when they become unified and inseparable, one will have become a sage.[29]

The passage certainly presents difficulties, and one may, with all due respect for Malmquist's expertise, doubt if he has really succeeded in making sense of it. It does at least affirm that Sagehood is achieved by a unity of "spirit" (*shen*) and "essence" (精 *jing*), whatever that is. (The same word is also translated "refined" in the first line. I suspect that it should be read in light of its use in the "Neiye" book of the *Guanzi* 管子, where it means "the essence of things that gives them life.")[30]

In light of the difficulties of the passage, too much may not be made of any one reading of it. Let us therefore go on. In chapter 19 we find a passage translated by Watson as follows:

> Only when nature and conscious activity combine does a true sage emerge and perform the task of unifying the world.[31]

When we compare this with Dubs' translation it becomes apparent that the text hardly requires Watson's reading. Dubs has

> When original nature and acquired characteristic unite in character-development, then only the name of Sage becomes inseparable from that man: and therefore the benefit of the whole empire comes to him.[32]

Chai translates along the same vein,[33] but Hughes has

> It is not until there is the harmony of nature and the acquired that the terms "sage" and "man" become one, for this is the way in which the virtue of the Great Society is completed. ("The Great Society" is Hughes's rendering of 天下 *tianxia*, "world" or "empire.")[34]

The issue is partly one of punctuation. The standard Wang text gives no punctuation within the passage; Liang punctuates before 一 *yi* ("one" or "unify"),[35] the Harvard-Yenching text after it,[36] indicating no firm tradition in the matter. We suggest the following reading:

> Once nature and what may be acquired come into accord, thereafter "One" is the proper term for the complete Sage-man, and it is from him that the ability of the (social) world to operate effectively derives.

It does not seem inappropriate to consider this a wry Confucian caricature of the Daoist view of *Laozi* 老子 chapter 42: "Dao gives rise to 'One,' 'One' gives rise to 'Two,'" as if Xun is saying, "The Confucian Dao gives rise to 'One,' the Sage, and the Sage divides, makes distinctions, and makes human life in society possible."

Yet another such passage deserves attention. In chapter 9, we find a passage on which Watson remarks that it "is couched in highly mysterious language, and the translation . . . is tentative."[37] He offers,

> His understanding is of godlike clarity (神明 *shenming*)[38] and breadth, and yet of the finest simplicity. Therefore it is said, he whose every move is founded on unity is a sage.[39]

Duyvendak would have it,

> Although his intelligence is wise and just, yet he is very simple. Hence it is said: By one principle he unifies the whole. The man who acts in this way is called a Sage.[40]

Hughes, however, translates the last two sentences,

> The upshot is the One communicating oneness (*i.e.,* unity) and so being A MAN. That is what I mean by a sage-man.[41]

The first two words, 故曰 *guyue*, may mean "thus it is said" or, following the Mohist logicians, "hence I affirm." The last four words are no problem: 謂之聖人 *weizhi shengren* is simply Xun's usual definitional formula applied to the word "sage": "this is what 'sage' properly means." As for the rest, 一與一是為人者 *yiyuyi shi weirenzhe*, Hughes is certainly closest to a word-for-word rendition, for better or for worse. I believe it justifiable to translate it:

> On these grounds I affirm; he is the One who bestows unity. He it is who truly acts as a Man. This is what "sage" properly means.

To "truly act as Man" may go slightly beyond the text, but hardly. It suggests something Xun mentions several times, man being an equal copartner with Heaven and Earth, the ideal of Confucian religion.

The deepest problem of native Chinese religion may be stated as follows: given the ultimacy of nature (which includes ancestral spirits), wherein does the key to unity therewith lie in human life? So far we have found Xunzi's answer to be a denial of localized or piecemeal sacredness, such as superstitious attempts to control rainfall, coupled with an apparent affirmation of wholeness or unity, expressed in the Sage's character and in the *li*, which both spring from that character and lead to it. It is as if even the sacrificing to one's ancestors owes its sacredness to its participation in *li*, the ordering and unifying structures that find their source in the Sage's own unique unity, the one locus in the whole cosmos wherein nature and moral perfection coincide.

VI

So far, he who denies a religious motif to Xunzi could still agree. Watson says of the philosopher's definition of human spirituality that it makes of *shen* "a quality of moral excellence,"[42] just as Fung Yu-lan says Xunzi "never rises above the merely moral."[43] The unity of nature and high culture, at least in the Chinese milieu, could be religious only if nature, that is, "Heaven," retains the transcendent dimensions it shows, in different ways, in Kongzi, Mengzi, the *Zhongyong*, Modi, and the Daoists. Or these cannot be maintained if nature is as desacralized in the *Xunzi* as the received interpretations claim. We can here only outline an argument to show that he may well have had more "natural piety" than he has been credited with.

Xunzi rejects "knowing Heaven" as a proper desire or pursuit of man, except for that "knowing" which consists of developing human potentialities to their fullest. He nowhere gives any clear enunciation of his view of Heaven; even his essay entitled "A Discussion of Heaven" turns out to be an extended exposition of the importance of distinguishing between Heaven's ways and man's ways and of largely excluding the former from our concern. I find it ironic that his resolute refusal to present a theology of Heaven has been turned by interpreters into a full-fledged antitheology. Thus Chinese philosophers on the mainland affirm that Xunzi's "Heaven" "has no will nor consciousness,"[44] two denials I have been completely unable to find in his works.

Rather than make the futile move of arguing from what he does *not* say, let us note some aspects of his actual talk. In the first place, the received interpretation must treat many of his comments as rhetorical flourish. Consider the following:

1. . . . rites serve Heaven above and earth below.[45]
2. The Son of Heaven alone performs the suburban sacrifice to Heaven. . . . In this way rites distinguish and make clear that the exalted should serve the exalted.[46]
3. The very existence of Heaven and earth exemplifies the principle of the higher and lower.[47]

4. The drum is surely the lord of music, is it not? Hence, it resembles Heaven.[48]
5. The fate of a man lies with Heaven; the fate of the nation lies in ritual.[49]

and perhaps

> The Kings have Heaven for their first ancestor.[50]

It is significant that every one of these occurs in a context speaking of ritual, and it is here that Xunzi's heart lies. In fact he claims,

> How can *li* not be considered wonderful! Through it Heaven and earth join in harmony, the sun and moon shine, the four seasons proceed in order, the stars and constellations march, the rivers flow, and all natural things flourish.[51]

The perfection of the cosmic *li* has its moral dimension, since it is reflected, in a distinctive human way, in the superior man, for

> Heaven has its constant way, earth has its constant dimensions, the gentleman has his constant deportment. The gentleman follows what is constant.[52]

That Heaven supplies a model for men to follow seems quite obvious to Xunzi, as could be shown from other passages.

Loci such as the preceding are frequently discounted, probably on the basis of the following:

> Heaven's way of acting has consistency. It did not act as Yao's security nor as Jie's destruction. . . . If you encourage agriculture and are frugal, Heaven cannot make you poor. . . . if you follow Dao and are not of two minds, Heaven cannot send you misfortune. . . . but if you neglect agriculture and spend lavishly, Heaven cannot make you rich.[53]

and again,

> Are order and disorder from Heaven? I reply, the sun, moon, stars, planets and other heavenly auspices were the same under both Yü and Jie. Yü produced order and Jie chaos. Order and chaos are not from Heaven.[54]

The latter does not conflict at all with Jesus's remark that God sends his rain upon the just and the unjust, but the former states Heaven's *inability* to perform its traditional rewarding and punishing role. It is this assertion of inability which seems to underlie the widespread belief that Xunzi completely deanthropomorphized Heaven. Surely a purely blind, impersonal, and amoral "heaven" would function as he describes. But so would a thoroughly moral but transcendent Heaven, so long as its *Dao* or *li* did not include the function of rewarding and punishing. In the latter case, Heaven's "inability" to reward or to punish would be its unwillingness to overstep the bounds of its proper *Dao*.

That this is not a fantastic interpretation can be shown through another passage. In chapter 23, we find:

> Why is it, then, that everyone is not able to accumulate good acts in the same way? I would reply: everyone is capable of doing so (可以 *keyi*), but not everyone can be made to do so (可使 *keshi*). The petty man is capable (*keyi*) of becoming a gentleman, yet he is not willing (肯 *ken*) to do so; the gentleman is capable (*keyi*) of becoming a petty man but he is not willing to do so. . . . Hence, it is correct to say that the man in the street is *capable* (*keyi*) of becoming a Yu but it is not necessarily correct to say that he will in fact find it possible (能 *neng*) to do so. But although he does not find it possible (*neng*) to do so, that does not prove that he is incapable (*keyi*) of doing so.[55]

Xunzi here distinguishes two kinds of impossibility: the abstract impossibility of incapability and concrete impossibility of being unable to bring oneself to choose what he is abstractedly perfectly capable of doing. Thus the gentleman *cannot* become a petty man, no matter how capable he is of doing it; his moral character does not permit him to do so.

One cannot simply take this distinction neatly and transfer it to the essay on Heaven. It can be argued, however, that it does two things: (1) we cannot treat "Heaven cannot make you poor," as if there is no ambiguity regarding the precise force of the "cannot," and (2) when Xun needed to distinguish "will never take the occasion to do *x*" from "does not have the capability of doing *x*," he used *neng* (or its negation, 不能 *buneng*) for the former and *keyi* (or 不可以 *bukeyi*) for the latter. When we look at the passage ascribing to Heaven the inability to reward and punish, we find he uses *buneng* exclusively. This at least allows the reading that this inability is not a matter of abstract incapacity but *a consistent pattern of responding to situations*. The gentleman will not consent to becoming a petty man; Heaven will not consent to using flood and drought, heat and cold, as punishments. Such things arrive, but they are not special acts of Heaven directed to special ends; they are Heaven steadily following out its own ritual, its *li*, its *Dao*.

This coheres perfectly with Xunzi's insistence that the crucial problem is not Heaven's action but men's responses—but the proper response to ritual action is a ritual response. Xunzi includes all proper responses to Heaven's action under his rubric of *li*, which is surely better translated with *ritual* than any other one term. A ritual response to natural initiative is surely in some proper sense *religious*.

This interpretation seems to me eminently consistent not only with his rejection of looking on rituals as ways of obtaining local and particular benefits, but also with the central Confucian belief in what Munro calls "model emulation." In the ideal state, men are moved not by hope of reward or fear of punishment but by the attractive example of the perfect Sage king. As Xunzi argues elsewhere, men are moved toward the goodness they know they themselves lack. How could such a sagely leader be an equal of and copartner with Heaven and Earth unless they, too, operated on the basis of unity, beauty, and profundity of *li* rather than on the basis of reward and punishment?

In sum, then, I have argued that the widespread treatment of Xunzi as a nonreligious, even antireligious, philosopher is based in part on the biases of Neo-Confucianism and of twentieth-century Westernizers, in part on his rejection of superstition, and in part on his appearance of demythologizing Heaven. I have presented grounds for not extending his denial of *gui*-worship to *shen*, for taking his interpretation of *shen* to be something more than mere naturalism, and for rejecting the interpretation of passages attributing inability to Heaven as denials of Heaven's moral supremacy or religious significance. The picture that emerges is one of a Xun Qing who is trying to protect the religious substance of Confucianism from dangers on many sides: from the superstitious who seek to use rituals to obtain special favors or to escape the results of their own foolishness, from Mohists who appeal to heavenly reward and retribution to correct social ills, from Daoists who would downgrade or abolish all *li* as artificial and unresponsive to Nature and substitute disciplines of self-culture which would contribute nothing to high culture and would turn statecraft over to the Legalists; and indeed from followers of Mengzi who rely so much on natural processes to produce moral goods that they threaten the Confucian discipline itself.

From his concern for both the consistency of Heaven and the consistency of his own thought, and for the joint primacy of *li* on the one hand and human effort on the other, he was led to deny that the continuity between Heaven and human sanctity lay in the natural processes of production, a principle held by Mengzi and the Daoists. Those who could relate men to Heaven only through such a continuity were constrained to find him irreligious. It would be more fruitful to discern his own sense of the sanctities of men and Heaven, and his own principle of their continuity through *li*. This article is intended to be a step in that direction.

Notes

1. Ernest R. Hughes, *Chinese Philosophy in Classical Times* (London: Dent, 1960), p. 226.

2. Liu Wu-chi, *A Short History of Confucian Philosophy* (Baltimore, MD: Penguin Books, 1955), p. 96.

3. Fung Yu-lan, *The Spirit of Chinese Philosophy*, E. R. Hughes, trans. (Boston: Beacon, 1962), p. 81.

4. C. K. Yang, *Religion in Chinese Society* (Berkeley and Los Angeles: University of California Press, 1970), p. 245.

5. Sima Qian, *Shiji* 史記, *SBBY* ed., vol. 6, LXXIV, p. 46.

6. Yang, *Religion in Chinese Society*, p. 256.

7. Homer H. Dubs, *Hsüntze Works, from the Chinese* (London: Probsthain, 1928), p. 67; *Xunzi* K 5.1, 5/17/11–13.

8. *Xunzi* 85, K 17.8, 17/82/6–8.

9. Regarding the translation of *wen* as "humane culture," see *Xunzi* 125, K 21.4, 21/103/8, where 文 *wen* is precisely what Mozi does not understand.

10. *Xunzi* 135, K 21.8, 21/106/15–16.

11. *Xunzi* 134–135, K 21.8, 21/106/12–14.

12. *Xunzi* 110, K 19.11, 19/98/2–3.

13. *Xunzi* 105, K 19.7b, 19/5/17–18.

14. Bronislaw Malinowski, *Magic, Science, and Religion and Other Essays* (Garden City, NY: Doubleday, 1954), p. 38.

15. *Xunzi* 80, K 17.3a, 17/80/9.

16. *Xunzi* 134, K 21.8, 21/106/4–5.

17. *Xunzi* K 16.2, 16/75/13–14.

18. *Xunzi* 146, K 22.3e, 22/110/2.

19. *Xunzi* K 5.8, 5/20/8.

20. James Legge, *The Four Books* (Shanghai: Commercial Press, n.d.), p. 331; D. C. Lau, *Mencius* (Baltimore, MD: Penguin, 1970), p. 184.

21. *Xunzi* 16, K 1.2, 1/1/9.

22. *Xunzi* 26–27, K 2.4, 2/6/10.

23. *Xunzi* K 14.3, 14/67/1.

24. *Xunzi* K 3.9a, 3/11/5.

25. *Xunzi* 80, K 17.2b, 17/80/5–7.

26. *Xunzi* K 8.7, 8/31/3–5. Cf. the rendering in Hermann Köster, *Hsün-tzu ins Deutsche übertragen* (Kaldenkirchen: Steyler, 1967), p. 79: "Was aber ist Geist? (Antwort:) Vollkommenes Gutsein, das die ganze, öffentliche Ordnung erfasst."

27. Wing-tsit Chan, *A Source Book for Chinese Philosophy* (Princeton, NJ: Princeton University Press, 1972), p. 121; Watson, *Hsün Tzu*, p. 8.

28. *Xunzi* 96, K 19.3, 19/92/22–93/4.

29. *Xunzi* K 25.20, 25/121/2–3. Göran Malmquist, "The Cherng Shianq Ballad of the Shyun Tzyy," *Bulletin of the Museum of Far East Antiquities* 45 (1973), p. 71. Köster offers a different interpretation (p. 325) which is no more felicitous. I have found no other Western translations. Neither Bruno Belpaire, *Les Plus Belles Pages du Philosophe Chinois Suen-tse* (Brussels: Editions de l'Occident, 1060) nor Dubs translates this *pian*. In

fact, both misunderstand its title, though differently. See Belpaire, p. 8, and Homer H. Dubs, *Hsüntze: The Moulder of Ancient Confucianism* (London: Probsthain, 1927), p. 45.

30. *Guanzi, SBBY* ed., xvi, 49, 1a7, 2a9, 2b10. Translated in W. Allyn Rickett, *Guanzi* (Hong Kong: Hong Kong University Press, 1965), pp. 158, 159, 160. Rickett dates the section as older than the *Xunzi* and as probably from the same Jixia academy that Xun was associated with for a number of years.

31. *Xunzi* 102–103, K 19.6, 19/95/2.

32. Dubs, *Hsüntze: The Moulder of Ancient Confucianism*, p. 234.

33. Ch'u Chai and Winberg Chai, *The Humanist Way in Ancient China* (New York: Bantam, 1965), p. 249; Köster, *Hsün-tzu ins Deutsche übertragen*, p. 253, is similar.

34. Hughes, *Chinese Philosophy*, p. 252.

35. Liang Ch'i-hsiung, *Xunzi jianshi* (Taibei: Commercial Press, 1973), p. 270.

36. *A Concordance to Xunzi: Harvard-Yenching Institute Sinological Index Series, Supplement No. 22* (Taibei: CMRASC, 1966), p. 73.

37. Watson, *Hsün Tzu*, p. 74n.

38. The term *shenming* undoubtedly is relevant to our discussion, but the problems of interpretation it raises (see Köster, *Hsün-tzu ins Deutsche übertragen*, p. 4n11) seem not to have received much attention. I have not yet found any evidence that in Xun's day it simply meant "perfectly clear," though that use does appear later.

39. *Xunzi* 47, K 9.16c, 9/39/24.

40. J. J. L. Duyvendak, "Notes on Dubs' Translation of Hsün-tzu," *T'oung Pao* 24 (1932), pp. 1–42.

41. Hughes, *Chinese Philsophy*, p. 247.

42. Watson, *Hsün Tzu*, p. 8.

43. Fung Yu-lan, *The Spirit of Chinese Philosophy*, E. R. Hughes, p. 81.

44. For example, Li Deyong, *Xunzi, gongyuanqian sanshiji zhongguo weiwuzhuyi zhexuejia* 荀子，公元前三世紀中國惟物主意哲學家 (Shanghai: Renmin, 1959), p. 18, and Zhou Fucheng, "Xunzi," *Zhongguo qingnian* 11.1 (1956), p. 21.

45. *Xunzi* 91, K 19.2a, 19/90/21–22.

46. *Xunzi* 91, K 19.2a, 19/91/2.

47. *Xunzi* 36, K 9.3, 9/35/22.

48. *Xunzi* 118, K 20.4, 20/100/20–101/1.

49. *Xunzi* K 16.1, 16/75/9, and 86, K 17.9, 17/82/12.

50. Dubs, *Hsüntze: The Moulder of Ancient Confucianism*, p. 220fn, but compare the different interpretation in *Xunzi* 91, K 19.2a, 19/91/1. Perhaps the difference in interpretation is not as great as it seems at first reading.

51. *Xunzi* 94, K 19.2c, 19/92/4–5.

52. *Xunzi* 82, K 17.5, 17/81/1.

53. *Xunzi* 79, K 17.1, 17/79/16–19.

54. *Xunzi* 82, K 17.4, 17/80/21–22.

55. *Xunzi* 167, K 23.5b, 23/116/17–22; parentheses are my own additions.

CHAPTER 2

A Happy Symmetry

Xunzi's Ecological Ethic

Philip J. Ivanhoe

Introduction

Xunzi (c. 310–219 b.c.e.), the second great representative of the Confucian tradition, disagreed with his eminent predecessor, Mengzi (c. 391–308 b.c.e.), over one of the most widely contested and philosophically important issues in Chinese ethical philosophy: the true character of human nature.[1] Xunzi is notorious among Confucians for arguing against Mengzi and for the view that human nature is basically bad.[2] This aspect of Xunzi's thought has had the unfortunate effect of leading many contemporary scholars to neglect his work as being outside the Confucian mainstream.[3] It also has led some to compare him with Thomas Hobbes, and at least in some respects this comparison is neither unwarranted nor unhelpful.[4]

Both Xunzi and Hobbes believed that human nature was essentially bad and that if left unrestrained it would lead us to pursue lives that were, in Hobbes's memorable phrase, "solitary, poor, nasty, brutish, and short." To avoid this unappealing fate, both proposed restraining human nature, but in different and distinctive ways. Hobbes proposed what David Gauthier rightly describes as a political—as opposed to an ethical—solution, offering a strict social contract combined with the absolute authority of the monarch.[5] Xunzi advocated a genuinely ethical solution in the form of a program of spiritual training that had as its core the practice of Confucian ritual and the mastery of its textual tradition. Unlike Hobbes, Xunzi believed that we could train ourselves out of the state of nature from which we all begin. We could reform the crooked timber of humanity to fashion ethically straight arrows which would never miss their mark.[6] The Confucian "Way" (道 *Dao*) led to a life that was not just the best strategy to pursue in a game in which the odds were against one. It offered an enhanced way to live, a self-consciously fashioned, genuinely human form of life.

Another important way in which Xunzi differs from Hobbes is in recognizing that human nature needs to be restrained not only to protect one human being from another but also to protect the rest of the natural world from being destroyed by unregulated human exploitation. The Confucian Way not only made peace among human beings, it located them in a greater, harmonious natural system. This grand ecological ethic went well beyond warnings about the danger of wasting and despoiling our natural resources. Like much of Xunzi's ethical philosophy, it was not just prudential advice. Xunzi believed that the Confucian *Dao* showed human beings the unique way to cooperate with Heaven and Earth for the fulfillment of all three. This ecological aspect of the Way is an important yet often under-appreciated feature of Xunzi's philosophy. However, it is the key to understanding other important parts of his system of thought. For example, it helps us to understand what he meant by his teaching that the gentleman "forms a triad with Heaven and Earth." The ecological aspect of his thought also helps us to see why Xunzi believed that the Confucian rites expressed "patterns which do not change" and why he expressed nothing less than religious reverence for the Way.[7]

Xunzi's Ethic

Xunzi argued that without the control and guidance of the rational parts of the human mind, human nature would drive us to engage in a continuing struggle of all against all in which none would realize satisfaction. In such a state, each of us would be in competition with every other human being, seeking to maximize the satisfaction of as many of our individual desires as we possibly could. According to Xunzi, such unrestrained competition is in no way healthy. Not only does it cut off the important possibility of developing tastes and inclinations for higher types of satisfaction, it does not even result in the satisfaction of our basic natural desires. In fact it inevitably leads to deprivation, danger, and anxiety.

The Way provides us with an avenue leading out of this sad state. The rites and norms which describe the Way limit the extent and the means of the search for satisfaction of our basic desires and provide us with the best way to fulfill them. They redirect, regulate, and refine our natural desires, embellish the search for satisfaction, and ultimately enhance the satisfaction we are capable of experiencing. Because the rites prevent disorder, lead to the satisfaction of our desires, and extend and enhance our satisfaction, they clearly have great instrumental value. However, Xunzi insists that as one cultivates a deeper understanding of the Way, one begins to see it as intrinsically valuable, worthy of profound respect and complete devotion. At the highest stage of moral awareness, the Confucian Way becomes an end unto itself.[8] One's primary source of motivation and satisfaction is pursuing the ideal described by the Way. This degree of dedication is characteristic of only a few individuals, true sages.

The rites reflect and support a hierarchical structure, traditional Confucian society, in which goods are unevenly distributed according to one's station. Given such a society, composed of various specialized roles, each with its own function and obligation, it is easy to see why specific and distinct needs would be thought to accompany the different roles. In order for things to run smoothly, each person would have to be supplied with those goods and services needed for her or his role within the greater social scheme. For example, according to Xunzi, society requires the special services of a king and in order to fulfill this critical role effectively, the king needs the special accoutrements and deference associated with his station.

> What is meant by "differentiations"? I say: It is for noble and lowly to have their proper ranking, for elder and youth to have their proper distance, and for poor and rich, humble and eminent each to have their proper weights. And so, in the Grand Chariot of the Emperor there are cushions, as a means to nurture his body. On the sides are carried sweet-smelling angelica, as a means to nurture his nose. In front there is a patterned yoke, as a means to nurture his eyes. The sounds of the attached bells match the tunes Wu and Xiang when proceeding slowly, and they match the tunes Shao and Hu when proceeding quickly, as a means to nurture his ears. There is a dragon pennant with nine tassels, as a means to nurture his ability to inspire trust. There are insignias of a crouching rhinoceros and kneeling tiger, serpent-decorated coverings for the horses, silk curtains, and dragon patterns on the chariot hooks, as a means to nurture his awe-inspiring authority.[9]

This inequality in both goods and treatment is seen as necessary in order for society to function, and given Xunzi's view of the state of nature, almost any social system is preferable to none. The Confucian rites, though, offered much more than a way out of the state of nature. Xunzi believed that if properly followed they would produce the best possible society, one clearly superior to any of the other contemporary options.[10] Confucian society not only ensures that the needs of all will be met, it offers the richest array of goods and satisfactions available to human beings, and it alone accords and harmonizes with the structure of the universe itself.

Xunzi does not allow the elite members of society to have absolute freedom to pursue the satisfaction of their basic desires. The Confucian rites accomplish a quite different end. They bring about an attenuated damping of the basic goods enjoyed by each social class. The elite members of society in particular have certain definite limits placed upon their wealth, power, and privilege, and their attention is directed toward other, more noble ends. The most humble members of society are protected from the ravages of unrestricted competition and unrestrained power or privilege, ensured a comfortable and decent life, and encouraged to pursue the cultivation of virtue.[11]

Why, though, might the powerful and crafty, those best able to secure for themselves the lion's share of desired basic goods, agree to follow the Way? Xunzi provides a variety of arguments in order to persuade such individuals to embrace Confucianism. First, those who live outside the Way cannot avoid suffering the fear and anxiety of knowing that whatever they have acquired they might lose, either by having someone else snatch it from them or by being eliminated from the competition.

> In such a case, a man may be confronted by all the loveliest things in the world and yet be unable to feel any gratification. Even if he should feel a moment's gratification, he could never completely shake off his anxieties and fears. Hence, although he confronts all the loveliest things in the world he is overwhelmed with worry, and though he enjoys all the benefits in the world, he knows only loss.[12]

Another reason Xunzi offers for believing that the state of nature can never provide true satisfaction, even for the powerful and crafty, concerns the nature of basic desires themselves. He argues that without the mind to set a limit on the search for satisfaction, the search itself has no chance of ever reaching a conclusion. Some appetites, like hunger, are bounded physiologically; they abate when sated. However, even such desires tend to excess and the search for ever greater and more refined means of satisfaction has no clear terminus. Though sated, such desires can never be fully satisfied. There are also many desires which have no natural bounds, such as the pursuit of wealth, power, or privilege. In general, Xunzi describes our basic desires as blind engines of consumption, incapable of experiencing contentment. Without the mind to declare a limit, the desires will compel us to embark on a never-ending and ultimately futile quest for satisfaction.

While we are as much physical and emotional as we are intellectual, it is clear that we can only know what we are through our minds. We can only judge our overall success and contentment by deciding this issue in our minds, and in order to do this, we must possess a set of criteria for making such a judgment. We require some definite and compelling ideal of human life to serve as a standard for such considerations. The Confucian Way offers just such an ideal, a way of life that allows one to satisfy most of one's basic desires—without incurring the liabilities which plague those in the state of nature—while opening up new and profound sources of satisfaction, sources which are available only to those who are inside and committed to the project of the Confucian Way.[13]

It is important to appreciate the difference here between Xunzi's view and that of Mengzi. Xunzi offers a more radically naturalized justification for the Way. What the mind enables us to do is to perceive, enjoy, measure, and weigh a wide range of satisfactions which accompany our broad and rich capacity to appreciate different goods, activities, and states of affairs. Some of these satisfactions need to be developed through dedicated practice—for example, the satisfaction associated with successfully composing a work of music—but they are all grounded in our particular nature as human beings. The mind is not disposed toward or capable of detecting special, preexisting moral qualities, as Mengzi claims it is. According to Xunzi, the most important values that the mind comes to perceive and appreciate do not exist in the presocial state of Nature. They are intentional human creations. Mengzi's theory of human nature claims that our most distinctive and important feature is our moral sense as revealed in the spontaneous responses of our Heavenly endowed "four sprouts" (四端 *siduan*).[14] In contrast and deliberate disagreement, Xunzi singles out the mind's ability to make distinctions of difference and rank as our most important and distinguishing feature.

> However, that by which humans are human is not because they are special in having two legs and no feathers, but rather because they have distinctions. Now the ape's form is such that it also has two feet and no feathers. However, the gentleman sips ape soup and eats ape meat. Thus, that by which humans are human is not because they are special in having two legs and no feathers, but rather because they have distinctions. The birds and beasts have fathers and sons but not the intimate relationship of father and son. They have the male sex and the female sex but no differentiation between male and female. And so among human ways, none is without distinctions. Of distinctions, none are greater than social divisions, and of social divisions, none are greater than rituals, and of rituals, none are greater than those of the sage kings.[15]

Because we are endowed with the ability to make careful distinctions, weigh, and evaluate the relative value, advantage, and liability of different actions, practices, and states of affairs, we are able to give shape to our social organization and through this, our own lives. This ability enabled a series of gifted human beings to devise the system of rituals and social norms which led to the ideal Confucian society. The possession of these social norms and the rites which embody them distinguishes human beings as the unique creatures that they are.

> Water and fire have 氣 *qi* but are without life. Grasses and trees have life but are without awareness. Birds and beasts have awareness but are without standards of righteousness. Humans have *qi* and life and awareness, and moreover they have standards of righteousness. And so they are the most precious things under Heaven. They are not as strong as oxen or as fast as horses, but oxen and horses are used by them. How is this so? I say it is because humans are able to form communities while the animals cannot. Why are humans able to form communities? I say it is because of social divisions. How can social divisions be put into practice? I say it is because of standards of righteousness. And so if they use standards of righteousness in order to make social divisions, then they will be harmonized. If they are harmonized, then they will be unified. If they are unified, then they will have more force. If they have more force, then they will be strong. If they are strong, then they will be able to overcome the animals. And so they can get to live in homes and palaces. Thus, that people can order themselves with the four seasons, control the myriad things, and bring benefit to all under Heaven is for no other reason than that they are able to get these social divisions and standards of righteousness.[16]

For Xunzi, traditional Confucian rites, norms, and general social practices are precious cultural artifacts, as much a part of the sages' legacy as are the glorious bronzes which one can hold and admire. The sages brought these cultural patterns and practices to a state of perfection through a long and arduous process of trial, error, and critical reflection, just as a potter learns to fashion bowls, develops, and passes on the art of pottery.

> In every case, ritual and the standards of righteousness are produced from the deliberate effort of the sage; they are not produced from people's nature. Thus, when the potter mixes up clay and makes vessels, the vessels are produced from the deliberate efforts of the craftsman; they are not produced from people's nature. Thus, when the craftsman carves wood and makes utensils, the utensils are produced from the deliberate efforts of the craftsman; they are not produced from people's nature. The sage accumulates reflections and deliberations and practices deliberate efforts and reasoned activities in order to produce ritual and standards of righteousness and to establish proper models and measures.[17]

Thus Xunzi argued that human nature is bad in the sense that if untrained it will lead us rapidly to bad states of affairs. We are not inclined toward morality by any special features of our original endowment. Moral values are not special, preexisting features of the natural landscape. They arise out of a sustained and difficult process of human discovery and invention. Human social norms are artificial yet good because they lead us to the most complete and satisfying lives available for creatures like us.

The role played by the rites is played within certain definite limits. On the one hand there is human nature. The form, number, relative strength, and relationships among the natural desires of human beings is a given which the rites directly address. The mind is able to know the various aspects of human nature, but it cannot fundamentally alter or efface them. This is an explicit and central feature of Xunzi's view of human nature. However, with enough training of the right sort, the mind can learn to be satisfied before the senses are sated. It can learn to turn away from sensual pleasures as its primary concern, once it comes to appreciate other, deeper sources of satisfaction.

> If the mind is calm and at ease, then even beauties that are less than mediocre will gratify the eye, even sounds that are less than mediocre will gratify the ear. A meal of vegetables, a soup of boiled greens will gratify the mouth; robes of coarse cloth, shoes of coarse hemp will give ease to the body; a narrow room with rush blinds, a straw carpet and a table and mat will give comfort to the form.[18]

If one remains committed to the moral life, the mind can come to see the Way as its first choice, primary aim, and deepest motivation.

> The gentleman knows that whatever is imperfect and unrefined does not deserve praise. And so he repeatedly recites his learning in order to master it, ponders it over in order to comprehend it, makes his person so as to dwell in it, and eliminates things harmful to it in order to nourish it. He makes his eyes not want to see what is not right, makes his ears not want to hear what is not right, makes his mouth not want to speak what is not right, and makes his heart not want to deliberate over what is not right. He comes to the point where he loves it, and then his eyes love it more than the five colors, his ears love it more than the five tones, his mouth loves it more than the five flavors, and his heart considers it more profitable than possessing the whole world. For this reason, power and profit cannot sway him, the masses cannot shift him, and nothing in the world can shake him. He lives by this, and he dies by this. This is called grasping Virtue.[19]

In order for the Way to be so effective, compelling, and profoundly satisfying, it must do more than regulate and order the desires of human beings, it must present a plan for universal harmony and flourishing. This is precisely what it does. The Way balances human needs and desires with the capacities, limitations, and needs of the non-human realm. In fashioning the rites and norms of Confucian society, the ancient sages took into account the Natural realm as well as human nature. They understood how Nature worked and brought its workings into harmony with human needs and desires. The sages saw that Nature produces its bounty in different quantities and qualities and that its production of things follows discernable seasonal patterns and natural cycles. Xunzi's sages did much more than take stock of the demands described by human needs and desires, they carefully examined and took into account the details of Nature's ability to supply the goods required to satisfy these needs and desires. Only by proceeding in this way were they able to bring human needs and desires and Nature's products, patterns, and processes into a harmonious and mutually beneficial balance, the happy symmetry which is the Way.

Xunzi emphasizes the need for such a happy symmetry in the opening section of the chapter "Discourse on Ritual."

> From what did ritual arise? I say: Humans are born having desires. When they have desires but do not get the objects of their desire, then they cannot but seek some means of satisfaction. If there is no measure or limit to their seeking, then they cannot help but struggle with each other. If they struggle with each other then there will be chaos, and if there is chaos then they will be impoverished. The former kings hated such chaos, and so they established rituals and the standards of righteousness in order to allot things to people, to nurture their desires, and to satisfy their seeking. They caused desires never to exhaust material goods, and material goods never to be depleted by desires, so that the two support each other and prosper. This is how ritual arose.[20]

According to Xunzi, Confucian ritual had as one of its explicit aims the protection and support of Nature. The rites sought to bring human beings and Nature into balance with one another and led to the common flourishing of Heaven, Earth, and humanity. Enlightened rulers took an active role instituting and enforcing restrictions and regulations in order to protect Nature and enhance the operation of Natural processes.

> These are the regulations of a sage king: When the grasses and trees are flowering and abundant, then axes and hatchets are not to enter the mountains and forests, so as not to cut short their life, and not to break off their growth. When the turtles and crocodiles, fish and eels are pregnant and giving birth, then nets and drugs are not to enter the marshes, so as not to cut short their life, and not to break off

> their growth. Plow in the spring, weed in the summer, harvest in the fall, and store in the winter. These four activities are not to miss their proper times, and then the five grains will not be depleted, and the common people will have a surplus to eat. Be vigilant in the seasonal prohibitions concerning ponds, rivers, and marshes, and then turtles and fish will be fine and plentiful, and the common people will have a surplus to use. Cutting and nurturing are not to miss their proper times, and then the mountains and forests will not be barren, and the common people will have surplus materials. This is the way a sage king operates: He observes Heaven above, and applies this knowledge on Earth below. He arranges completely everything between Heaven and Earth and spreads beneficence over the myriad things.[21]

Xunzi's perspective on the role of the rites was nothing less than universal. The sage needed to view things in such a manner in order to attain his grand vision of universal harmony. Only such a comprehensive and systematic approach could take account of and bring into balance the myriad constituents, various considerations, and diverse aspects of the Way. The Way served not only humans but Heaven and Earth as well.

> When human nature and reflective activity unite, then all under Heaven is ordered. For Heaven can give birth to creatures, but it cannot enforce distinctions among creatures. Earth can support people, but it cannot order people. In the world, all members of the myriad things and the human race must await the sage, and only then will they be appropriately divided up.[22]

For Xunzi, the Way extended far beyond society. It united the human and Natural realms into a single seamless web. In this aspect of his thought we see clearly the influence of Daoist thinkers and in particular Zhuangzi. In contrast to most thinkers of his time, Zhuangzi saw the *Dao* not as the best possible "way" to organize human society but as the underlying patterns and processes of the universe itself.[23] Xunzi, though, disagreed with Zhuangzi over the role and value of our abilities to make distinctions and fashion culture. Zhuangzi saw these as the source of all the world's problems. Our tendency to make distinctions carves up and disfigures the original unity of the Way; human cultures obscure the natural Heavenly *Dao* and lead us to live alienated and perverse lives. In stark contrast, Xunzi saw these distinctively human abilities as offering the only possibility for universal harmony and flourishing. Once one understands and masters the Way, things fall into place on a universal scale. The Way protects one from all harm, offers one every benefit, and brings peace, order, and prosperity to the entire world.

> By ritual, Heaven and Earth harmoniously combine,
> By ritual, the sun and the moon radiantly shine,
> By ritual, the four seasons in progression arise,
> By ritual, the stars move orderly across the skies,
> By ritual, the great rivers through their courses flow,
> By ritual, the myriad things all thrive and grow,
> By ritual, for love and hate proper measure is made,
> By ritual, on joy and anger fit limits are laid.
>
> Use it in being a subordinate, and you will serve smoothly, use it in being a superior, and you will be enlightened; the myriad things will undergo their changes and there will be no disorder. But deviate from it and all is lost. Is not ritual perfect indeed! It establishes a lofty standard which is ultimate of its kind, and none under Heaven can add to or subtract from it.[24]

This paean to and praise of the Way is not an isolated occurrence in Xunzi's writings. The Way inspired profound respect, awe, and nothing less than reverence in those who understood it. They alone realized that through the Way the sages joined human intelligence with the vast, complex, and staggering power of Nature to produce a harmonious and magnificent result. Xunzi described the carrying out of this grand project as human beings "forming a triad" with Heaven and Earth.

> Wherever the sky stretches and the Earth extends, there is nothing beautiful left undiscovered, nothing useful left unused. Such goods serve above to adorn good and worthy men, and below to nourish the common people and bring them security and happiness. This is what is called a state of godlike order. . . . Heaven and Earth are the beginning of life. Rites and social norms are the beginning of order, and the gentleman is the beginning of rites and social norms. . . . Heaven and Earth produce the gentleman and the gentleman brings order to Heaven and Earth. The gentleman forms a triad with Heaven and Earth; he is the controller of all things, the father and mother of the people. Without the gentleman, Heaven and Earth will lack order and rites and social norms will lack unity.[25]

In these and other passages, Xunzi manifests a religious reverence for the Way. Such an attitude seems appropriate to those who appreciate that the Way sets the standard and offers the means to set all things right. It enables human beings to put not only themselves but the entire universe into "a state of godlike order."

Xunzi believed that the Way strikes a perfect balance between human needs and desires and what the world can supply. It takes into account and addresses the needs of all things and facilitates their flourishing and fulfillment. This promise of universal well-being is an important part of why the Way is something worthy of complete commitment. However, as we know, the world changes. Populations expand and increase the demands placed upon Nature. Natural resources dwindle and squeeze the supply. Technologies and new ideas are developed which alter and put pressures on both sides of Xunzi's happy symmetry. If balance and mutual well-being between human beings and Nature are to be maintained, the rules which govern this relationship, the rites and norms which human beings are to follow, would require at least regular adjustment and modification if not periodic, large scale, and radical revision.

Xunzi did not see things this way. Though he believed that the rites went through a process of evolution, he also believed that this process had reached its conclusion in the rites of the Three Dynasties.[26] The sage rulers of this golden age worked out and perfected the roles, practices, and norms needed to establish and maintain an ideal society. Those who came after them were to study and emulate the model which they had established. While some rites might need to be adjusted because our understanding of what was done in the past is not fully accurate and some might need to be fine tuned in order to deal with novel or unforeseen situations, Xunzi did not entertain the possibility that the traditional rites would ever need radical alteration or modification.

> When they (the rites) are properly established and brought to the peak of perfection, no one in the world can add to or detract from them.[27]

> Music consists of unchanging harmonies, rites are unalterable patterns.[28]

The traditional rites faithfully if not perfectly stand for and guide us to the Way and,

> The Way is the proper standard for past and present. He who departs from the Way and makes arbitrary choices on the basis of his own judgment does not understand wherein fortune and misfortune lie.[29]

In terms of his belief in the immutable truth of the Confucian Way, Xunzi was very much like his rival Mengzi. However the reasons for this agreement serve to distinguish these two thinkers. The difference can more easily be appreciated if we imagine how each would have reacted to conditions of extreme stress. For example, what if human beings had to live their lives in a harsh and unforgiving environment, one in which it was regularly the case that during the winter months food would inevitably run short and not everyone could survive? Under such conditions, what would become of the practices and norms which express the virtue of filial piety? Could it ever become acceptable or right to establish and follow the practice of allowing, perhaps even aiding, one's aged parents to voluntarily sacrifice themselves in order to save the community?[30]

It seems that, in principle at least, Xunzi could not only find this acceptable, he could advocate it as the right thing to do. Were he to embrace such a practice, he would of course seek to embellish this difficult task. He would not deny the natural feelings of remorse which one would experience carrying out such a wrenching obligation, for these are part of human nature and cannot be effaced. However he might argue that part of this feeling is simply the expression of the deep feelings of grief one experiences whenever one's parents die, while part of it is one's profound sense of admiration and gratitude for their remarkable sacrifice. Those who helped their parents carry out this act of self-sacrifice would not be regarded or feel in any way unfilial. To the contrary, those who failed to help their parents would be regarded as and feel severely unfilial.[31] Those who understood the true function and aim of this rite would appreciate how it perfectly balanced human needs and desires with the demands and capacities of Nature. This final act of parental nurture and sacrifice fit with and completed the universe in a way which ensured that all things flourished. Seen in such a light, this rite might well be cherished as much as, perhaps more than, any other.

Mengzi presents a very different case. Regardless of how different the surrounding environment might be, he could never regard such a practice as right or even acceptable. For Mengzi, the forms of filial piety manifested in the rites are not something "welded onto me from outside."[32] They directly manifest an essential aspect of human nature. One has an overriding obligation to provide for, protect, and love one's parents, and one is endowed with a nature which inclines toward these attitudes and behaviors. Were the world a very different place, Mengzi might well allow for different expressions of one's basic filial tendencies. He recognized that one sometimes had to bend or suspend the rites in extraordinary circumstances.[33] However, because Mengzi grounded the Confucian Way in a set of specifically moral reactive attitudes and tendencies, he simply could not endorse radical changes in such fundamental aspects of the tradition. Mengzi would insist that one simply cannot develop a moral "taste" for leaving one's parents to die. It simply cuts too deeply against the grain of inborn natural tendencies. One has an innate, visceral repugnance for harming one's parents. If faced with the proposed hypothetical scenario, Mengzi would insist that the filial child sacrifice him or herself rather than allow his or her parent to die.

Mengzi believed that the Way was the refined expression of the most basic and essential elements of human nature. The Confucian Way was encoded into and manifested the underlying structure of the human "heart and mind" (心 *xin*). His method of self cultivation required one to observe and engage the spontaneous reactions of one's heart and mind, for only in this way could one develop the ability to discern and follow the Way. Traditional practices, the proper teacher, and a nurturing environment helped one develop one's moral sprouts, but one came to understand and find the motivation to follow the Way primarily through a process of introspection.

However, for Xunzi, human beings came to understand the *Dao* primarily by way of a thorough and critical inspection of the world.[34] There was no internal moral code or preset value detector within the self. One was not hunting for special moral qualities to guide one's behavior. The rites and norms of the Confucian way were established as the rational minds of a series of gifted individuals sought to bring peace, prosperity, stability, and order out of the dangerous chaos of the state of nature. Morality was forged through experience and refined through a long process of experimentation and reflection in the course of which the sages fashioned that form of life which, all things considered, offered human beings the greatest satisfaction and fulfillment. Had the sages contemplated a substantially different world, it seems they not only could have but necessarily would have devised appreciably different rites and norms.

As mentioned earlier, Xunzi did not believe that the world could change to such a radical extent. His universe and hence his conception of the Way was much more stable and enduring. The fundamental structure and operation of the world was open to inspection and discernable. There were patterns on Earth as there were in the Heavens, and those who dedicated themselves to studying and reflecting upon them could find the proper place and purpose for human beings.

Hu Shih recognized this aspect of Xunzi's thought. In the following passage, he criticizes Xunzi's view, but in a way which seems a bit off the mark and which may have led him to fail to appreciate important aspects of its value.

> Xunzi's philosophy was a denial of the theory of evolution and progress. Throughout his writings we find an explicit belief in the uniformity of nature. It is the application of this conception of the uniformity of nature that led him to deny the reality of progress.[35]

We must understand Hu Shih's comments about "the uniformity of nature" to mean the idea that nature remains stable over time and not that it is everywhere the same. He seems to be criticizing Xunzi for not taking into account the force of biological evolution. However, if Xunzi's theory needs modification, it is more in need of a recognition of how cultural practices and technological advances—rather than the force of natural selection—tend to disrupt the happy symmetry which he envisaged. It would also have to recognize that there might well be more than one set of rites and norms which could produce a state of stability and mutual flourishing between human needs and desires and the rest of the natural world. Working out how Xunzi's theory might accommodate such changes is well beyond the range of the present work. However, there seem to be resources within his view that allow for such modifications. In any event, his insight that there is a need to find a way to realize a happy symmetry between human beings and the rest of the natural world, that realizing such a goal offers us a profound sense of satisfaction with the society within which we live and the lives that it affords us, would be unaffected by these proposed changes.

Conclusion

Xunzi's ethical theory sought to establish an order among human beings that led them to avoid the devastating and mutually destructive competition characteristic of the state of nature, allowed them to satisfy their natural needs and desires, and that refined and extended the range of satisfactions available to them. At the same time, his ethical theory took as one of its explicit and central aims the protection of Nature from potential devastation by unregulated human exploitation. When the Way was realized, it established a perfect balance, a happy symmetry, between human beings and the rest of the natural world. The rites and norms of the Confucian Way functioned to protect, enhance, and order both society and Nature and bring them together into a homeostatic union. Through the Way, human beings formed a "triad" with Heaven and Earth and all things flourished in "a state of godlike order."[36]

Mengzi shared with Xunzi a concern for Nature, but for Xunzi this concern served as one of the foundations of his ethical philosophy.[37] Part of what marks the *Dao* as the right way for human beings to live is the fact that it fits them into the greater scheme of Nature in a harmonious and beneficial way. We can appreciate this difference between Xunzi and Mengzi by considering another concern common to both, their allegiance to the traditional rites and norms of the Confucian tradition. They differ rather dramatically in terms of the warrants that each provided to justify his advocacy of the Way. Mengzi grounded his defense of the Way in human nature itself. The goodness of Confucian rites and norms was a reflection of the fundamental goodness of human nature. We come to see and appreciate the value of the Way by relying on our innate, though nascent, sense or taste for moral values. This good aspect of our nature was established by Heaven, and by understanding and developing our nature, we come to understand and serve Heaven.[38]

Xunzi saw the rites and norms of traditional Confucianism as the only means for restraining and reforming our fundamentally bad nature in a way that would protect us from our own worst tendencies and that would lead us to realize the happy symmetry of the Way. The rites and norms that describe the *Dao* were not in any direct way a manifestation of human nature. The sages who created these precious cultural artifacts were not led to them by following an internal moral sense but by study of and reflection on the world and human behavior. Heaven did not endow us with a special morality detector nor did it establish or sustain special moral qualities in the world. There was nothing sacred about any part of human nature or the world prior to the process which eventually yielded the Way.

Once we appreciate the ecological dimension of Xunzi's thought we can understand what he meant by his teaching concerning how the sage forms a "triad" with Heaven and Earth. This in turn can help us to appreciate the distinctive reverence which he expressed for the Way. Only the rites and norms of the Confucian tradition could bring about the universal harmony and mutual flourishing of Heaven, Earth, and human beings. The *Dao* and only the *Dao* offered the possibility of this happy symmetry.

Notes

An earlier version of this essay was published under the same name in *Journal of the American Academy of Religion* 59.2 (1991), pp. 309–322. It is republished by permission of Oxford University Press. While my main line of argument remains unchanged, I have substantially revised and expanded the earlier essay for this volume. I thank Eric L. Hutton and T. C. Kline III for helpful discussions of the central ideas and arguments in this essay and suggestions for its improvement.

1. The dates I cite for Xunzi's life are from the work done by John H. Knoblock's "The Chronology of Xunzi's works," *Early China* 8 (1982–1983), pp. 29–52. Those for Mengzi follow David S. Nivison's "Meng-tsu," in Mircea Eliade, ed., *The Encyclopedia of Religion*, vol. 9 (New York: Macmillan, 1987), pp. 373–376.

2. What Xunzi meant by his claim that human nature is bad is a topic of considerable debate. The Tang dynasty scholar Han Yü (768–824) regretted that Xunzi argued for such a view. He considered it a flaw in an otherwise commendable collection of writings and expressed his desire to excise it from the *Xunzi*. In the Ming Dynasty, Wang Yangming (1472–1529) explained Xunzi's view as focusing only on the impure "human mind" as opposed to the original, pure "mind of the Way." The Qing dynasty scholar Wang Xianqian (1842–1918) insisted that Xunzi did not really hold that human nature is bad. He argues that Xunzi was moved to express such a pessimistic view as a reaction to the ethically debased age in which he lived but that this was not his considered opinion. Modern scholars have tended to try to explain away the difference between Mengzi and Xunzi. For a review of the most influential modern treatments of this issue, see my "Human Nature and Moral Understanding in the *Xunzi*," in T. C. Kline III and Philip J. Ivanhoe, eds., *Virtue, Nature, and Moral Agency in the "Xunzi"* (Indianapolis, IN: Hackett, 2000), pp. 237–247. (This volume also contains Lau's seminal article on this topic, which I discuss.) Han Yü's views can be found in his essay, "Reading Xunzi" *Du Xun* 讀荀 in *Han Changli quanji* 韓昌黎全集 (*SBBY*) 11.15b. Wang Yangming's discussion of Xunzi's view of human nature is found in his *Chuanxilu* 傳習錄. For a

translation, see Wing-tsit Chan, trans., *Instructions for Practical Living and Other Neo-Confucian Writings by Wang Yang-ming* (New York: Columbia University Press, 1963), pp. 236–237. For Wang Xianqian's comment, see the preface to his "Collected Explanations of the *Xunzi*" *Xunzi jijie* 荀子集解.

3. Mengzi's philosophy was regarded as the orthodox view by almost all Neo-Confucians, and this reading of the Confucian tradition has been accepted by many contemporary scholars, resulting in comparatively less work on the *Xunzi*. However, recently, philosophers and scholars of religious studies have begun to pay more attention to Xunzi's work, and to good effect.

4. For example, see Antonio S. Cua, "The Quasi-Empirical Aspect of Hsun-Tzu's Philosophy of Human Nature," *Philosophy East and West* 28.1 (1978), pp. 3–19.

5. This point was first noted by David Wong. See his "Xunzi on Moral Motivation" in Philip J. Ivanhoe, ed., *Chinese Language, Thought, and Culture: Nivison and His Critics* (Chicago, IL: Open Court, 1996), p. 204. For Gauthier's view, see David Gauthier, *Morals by Agreement* (Oxford: Clarendon Press, 1986), pp. 162–163.

6. The importance of this point cannot be overstated. Most contemporary ethicists and political philosophers (most of whom are poorly camouflaged ethicists) assume that the most basic needs and desires of human beings are fixed. Given this assumption, figuring out what to do is best understood as a kind of gaming situation. Xunzi believed that we can transform our basic nature and reorient ourselves in ways that lead to greater satisfaction. He thus differs not only with Hobbes but with such influential thinkers as Kant and Freud as well.

7. Xunzi's most fundamental standard for proper action is the "Way" (道 *Dao*). The Way was embodied and expressed in a system of traditional rites which Xunzi believed captured the most important features of the Way. (I discuss the issue of the degree to which the rites require or admit of modification below.) It is important to keep in mind that Mengzi's ultimate standard for proper action is "Heaven" (天 *tian*). While Xunzi used the same word for "Heaven" in his writings, he always meant by this the "heavens above" and their various celestial phenomena.

8. Some scholars claim that Xunzi recognized three distinct levels of moral awareness, the "scholar" (士 *shi*), "gentleman" (君子 *junzi*), and "sage" (聖人 *shengren*). See, for example, Burton Watson, trans., *Hsün Tzu: Basic Writings* (New York: Columbia University Press, 1963), p. 19n7. However, Fujii Sennei points out that there are actually four such levels, the fourth being the morally unaware masses. He also notes that Xunzi employs a variety of different terms for each of these levels. See Fujii Sennei, "Junshi" 荀子 in *Shinshaku Kanbun taikei* 新釈漢文大系 5 (1966), p. 31.

9. From *Xunzi*, chapter 19, "A Discourse on Ritual." Translation by Eric L. Hutton in Philip J. Ivanhoe and Bryan W. Van Norden, eds., *Readings in Classical Chinese Philosophy*, second ed. (Indianapolis, IN: Hackett, 2006), pp. 274–275. *Xunzi* 90, K 19.1c, 19/90/10–14.

10. There was a wide variety of social and political theories in play in Xunzi's time, among them the leveled society of the "agriculturalists," the state-centered consequentialist society of the Mohists, and the primitive, agrarian utopia advocated in works like the *Daodejing*. Xunzi's primary objection to such alternatives is that they are fundamentally unworkable, and yet he also criticizes them for failing to appreciate the full range of goods which human beings are capable of enjoying.

11. Henry Rosemont Jr. has argued persuasively that Xunzi saw the hierarchical society of traditional Confucianism as the only way to ensure a minimum of goods for even the weakest members of society. Important in this regard is Rosemont's observation that Xunzi advocated a welfare system as part of this social scheme. See Henry Rosemont Jr., "State and Society in the *Xunzi*," in T. C. Kline III and Philip J. Ivanhoe, eds., *Virtue, Nature, and Moral Agency in the "Xunzi,"* pp. 1–38.

12. From *Xunzi*, chapter 22: "On Correct Naming." Translation by Watson, *Xunzi* 155, K 22.6 d, 22/112/12–13. Xunzi believes that many of the most important goods that one can experience in life are "internal" to the practice of the Way, both in the sense that one cannot find them in any other endeavor and that one cannot appreciate them without being a committed practitioner of the Way.

13. For the notion of goods being internal to practices, see Alasdair MacIntyre, *After Virtue* (Notre Dame, IN: University of Notre Dame Press, 1984), pp. 187–191.

14. For a brief description of this aspect of Mengzi's theory, see my *Confucian Moral Self Cultivation* (Indianapolis, IN: Hackett, 2000), pp. 18–19.

15. From *Xunzi*, chapter 5, "Against Physiognomy," in Ivanhoe and Van Norden, eds., *Readings in Classical Chinese Philosophy*, p. 266. *Xunzi* K 5.4, 5/18/16–18.

16. From *Xunzi*, chapter 9, "The Regulations of a True King," in Ivanhoe and Van Norden, eds., *Readings in Classical Chinese Philosophy*, p. 267. *Xunzi* 45–46, K 9.16a, 9/39/9–13.

17. From *Xunzi*, chapter 23, "Human Nature Is Bad," in Ivanhoe and Van Norden, eds., *Readings in Classical Chinese Philosophy*, p. 300. *Xunzi* 160, K 23.2a, 23/114/8–11.

18. *Xunzi* 155, K 22.6e, 22/112/18–20. Cf. *Analects* 1.14.

19. From *Xunzi*, chapter 1: "An Exhortation to Learning," in Ivanhoe and Van Norden, eds., *Readings in Classical Chinese Philosophy*, pp. 260–261. *Xunzi* 22, K 1.14, 1/4/16–20. Compare *Mengzi* 3B2.

20. From *Xunzi*, chapter 19: "Discourse on Ritual," in Ivanhoe and Van Norden, eds., *Readings in Classical Chinese Philosophy*, p. 274. *Xunzi* 89, K 19.1a, 19/90/3–8.

21. From *Xunzi*, chapter 9: "The Regulations of a True King," in Ivanhoe and Van Norden, eds., *Readings in Classical Chinese Philosophy*, pp. 268–269. *Xunzi* 47, K 9.16b–16c, 9/39/18–23.

22. From *Xunzi*, chapter 19: "Discourse on Ritual," in Ivanhoe and Van Norden, eds., *Readings in Classical Chinese Philosophy*, pp. 281–282. *Xunzi* 103, K 19.6, 19/95/3–4.

23. This greater, universal perspective on the *Dao* is the primary reason that thinkers like Zhuangzi were referred to as *Dao*-ists. They enlarged the sense of this term until it embraced everything. This dislocated the more human-centered perspective of most early Chinese thinkers.

24. From *Xunzi*, chapter 19: "Discourse on Ritual." Adapted from Hutton in Ivanhoe and Van Norden, eds., *Readings in Classical Chinese Philosophy*, p. 276. *Xunzi* 94, K 19.2c, 19/92/4–8.

25. Adapted from Watson. *Xunzi* 44–45, K 9.14–15, 9/38/17–39/4.

26. The Three Dynasties refer to the Xia, Shang, and Zhou dynasties. Xunzi took the Zhou as the clearest example of the Way (because it was the most recent). This idea can be traced back to Kongzi. See *Analects* 2.23. For Xunzi's view, see *Xunzi* K 5.4–5, 5/18/13–19/15. Later Confucians elaborated on the idea that the rites went

through a process of evolution. Perhaps the most notable thinker to put forth such a view is Zhang Xuecheng (1738–1801) who was deeply influenced by Xunzi. In his essay "On the Way" (*Yuan Dao* 原道), Zhang reveals himself to be a kind of Chinese Hegel. However, for him, what came into being was *Dao*, not *geist*, and the process reached its conclusion in the Zhou dynasty, not the Prussian state. For Zhang and his philosophy, see David S. Nivison, *The Life and Thought of Chang Hsüeh-ch'eng* (Stanford, CA: Stanford University Press, 1966).

27. 立隆以偽極，而天下莫之能損益也。 *Xunzi* 94, K 19.2c, 19/92/8.

28. 且樂也者，和之不可變者也。禮也者，理之不可易者也。 Adapted from Watson, *Xunzi* 117, K 20.3, 20/100/14.

29. 道者，古今之正權，離道而內自擇，則不知禍福之所託。 *Xunzi* 153, K 22.6b, 22/112/2.

30. This hypothetical case has of course been the practice of a variety of cultures at different times. A dark and beautiful film which explores many facets of such a practice is Shohei Imamura's *The Ballad of Narayama* (Japan, 1983).

31. A similar argument could be made that, under certain conditions, helping parents to successfully euthanize themselves might be an expression of filial piety. In such cases, the primary good would probably be that of the parents, though relieving severe burdens upon their descendants could also be a conceivable motivation.

32. *Mengzi* 6A6.

33. Mengzi did allow that even strong taboos such as the prohibition against physical contact between men and women could, under extraordinary conditions, be suspended. For example, see *Mengzi* 4A18. However, such cases do not entail adding to or abandoning a standing traditional practice.

34. I have argued that these different perspectives of Mengzi and Xunzi represent two distinct philosophical trends which later run throughout and beyond the Confucian tradition. See my "Thinking and Learning in Early Confucianism," *Journal of Chinese Philosophy* 17.4 (1990), pp. 473–493.

35. Hu Shih, *The Development of the Logical Method in Ancient China* (New York: Paragon, 1963), p. 155.

36. We can see in this aspect of Xunzi's thought the beginnings of a trend that would wax full and inform much philosophical thought in the succeeding Han dynasty. Chinese thinkers sought to provide detailed and systematic accounts of both the underlying structure and processes of Nature and the corresponding human practices needed to accord and harmonize with Nature. Dong Zhongshu 董仲舒 (circa 179–104 b.c.e.) is one of the most remarkable examples of this tendency, which Hsiao Kung-chuan describes as "Heaven-Man Correlative Thought." See Hsiao Kung-chuan, *A History of Chinese Political Thought*, trans. F. W. Mote (Princeton, NJ: Princeton University Press, 1979), pp. 484–530.

37. I explore and compare the ecological aspects of both Mengzi's and Xunzi's philosophy in my "Early Confucianism and Environmental Ethics," in Mary Evelyn Tucker and John Berthrong, eds., *Confucianism and Ecology: The Interrelation of Heaven, Earth, and Humans* (Cambridge: Harvard University Press, 1998), pp. 59–76.

38. See *Mengzi* 7A1.

Ritual Theory

CHAPTER 3

Ritual and Religion

A Lesson from Xunzi for Today

Robert C. Neville

That Xunzi was marginalized in the tradition of Confucianism framed by Zhu Xi's edition of the Four Books had a worse result than relative neglect by East Asian and Western scholars.[1] The genius of his original philosophy has not yet had the impact it deserves on framing the contemporary philosophic discussion.[2] The scholarly neglect is being remedied with great efficiency at the present time, building on the modern edition and translation into English of Xunzi's works by John Knoblock and exemplified by a burgeoning commentarial literature, not the least of which is the present volume and its predecessor.[3] The purpose of this essay is not to contribute to the scholarly retrieval of Xunzi but rather to his philosophical retrieval.

After some initial remarks on themes in Xunzi, I shall develop three main points of contemporary interest to which Xunzi has much to contribute. The first is an intriguing connection between ritual theory (especially in Xunzi) and semiotics. The second relates ritual to the proper formation of desire. The third addresses the question of diversity and integration of desires and relates this question to a religious thesis about ritual connecting the "depths" with civilization and joy.

Initial Considerations of Ritual in Xunzi

Ceremony is one of the meanings of ritual for Xunzi, as for the rest of the Confucian tradition. Ceremonies fall into five sorts in Xunzi's thought, as Knoblock has pointed out:

> those dealing with such auspicious occasions as sacrifice and marriage; those dealing with inauspicious occasions such as mourning and the loss of the state; rites of hospitality involving tribute offerings and appearances at court; usages involving warfare, especially the display of weapons, types, and decorations of chariots, and the use of banners; and festivities, notably serving elders, showing respect for the aged, making offerings, presenting gifts, and giving daughters in marriage.[4]

Late-modern societies have versions of all these ceremonies, if you count retirement parties as "respect for the aged" and back off from "giving away" modern daughters in marriage (paying for the wedding is still a custom, if not a ceremony, even when daughters do not want their father to give them away). Modern democratic societies may have more ceremonies for political transitions than Xunzi's Chinese states had because of frequent formalized elections of officials. Late-modern societies observe a sharp distinction, lacking in Xunzi's culture, between political or court ceremonies (secular) and religious ceremonies, based on the modern Western division between public and private spheres of life.

Ritual (禮 *li*) means far more than ceremony, however, for all of Confucian thought. Knoblock points out that in Xunzi's thought it includes "the highest sense of morality, duty, and social order as well as the most minor rules of good manners, the minutiae of polite forms, and insignificant, it seems to us, details of costume and dress."[5] I have developed a more elaborate spectrum of meanings of ritual as convention, starting with penumbral conventions such as eye contact, posture and movement, semiotically coded signs such as language and gesture, sign-shaped behavior the very exercise of which constitutes social institutions, manners regarding the playing of socially defined roles, the cultivations of personal relationship, and the practices of etiquette, and then explicit ceremonies themselves.[6] This list obviously can be subdivided and extended, reaching to all thought and practice shaped by learned conventions.

The clue to the broad extension of ritual in Xunzi is his conception of human nature and what is added to its biological givens, as Edward Machle has pointed out.[7] Heaven and Earth (nature) provide human beings with their bodies, their various senses, a range of emotions, and a mind capable of governing the natural elements and relating them to external things such as food.[8] Simply as given by Heaven and Earth, these elements are too underdetermined for human life. Given the range of possible postures, for instance, people can stand with their feet parallel (the ritual way in East Asia) or with the toes angled a bit to the side (the European way). Given the senses, everything is a cacophony, a "blooming, buzzing confusion," in William James's celebrated phrase, without learned discrimination and a sensibility as to what is important.[9] Emotions as given have little or no measure and no intrinsic connection with proper objects. Conventionally learned signs and sign-shaped behaviors are required to determine the naturally underdetermined givens of nature in order for human life to be possible.

I take ritual (*li*) to encompass all conventions, all learned signs and sign-shaped behaviors. For Xunzi, these human-building conventions are what need to be added to Heaven and Earth in order for human life to be possible and, as constituting the human, they complete the potentials of Heaven and Earth. This is Xunzi's version of the Trinity of Heaven, Earth, and the Human.[10]

The importance of the ancient kings and sages of old is that they hand down the conventions that determine human nature so as to make civilized human life possible. Lacking a strong evolutionary view of nature and society, Xunzi and many of his sophisticated colleagues avoided supernaturalistic explanations. The popular culture, perhaps, within which Xunzi worked, had a supernatural view of the culture-building imagination of the ancients: the rituals had to originate from somewhere. In any historical situation, the rituals need to be given and learned. Xunzi did not conceive a sharp boundary between the merely natural and the elementary human. He said, "The inborn nature of man is certainly that of the petty man."[11] Without tutoring, such a petty man will be selfish and contribute to chaos. Even selfishness requires a modicum of internal organization and regulation, and capacity to relate to things outside. So he would admit that a purely unritualized or untaught person would be impossible. But sageliness requires learning the sophisticated rituals and learning them well. "The sage purifies his natural lord, rectifies his natural faculties, completes his natural nourishment, is obedient to the natural rule of order, and nourishes his natural emotions and thereby completes nature's achievement."[12] Not just individual perfection but civilization itself depends on ritual mastery in the sense that humaneness cannot arise unless there are ritual social habits that allow for its expression. Without ritual there is no family life, only procreation, no division of family responsibilities, only the desire to get free as soon as possible, no political life, only strong-man rule, no loyalties to a political entity larger than proximate community (e.g., the nation or empire/emperor), only clan-based self-serving. Civilization involves the move from face-to-face (usually clan) organization to more nearly universal role-based behavior, which means ritual. The great Confucian contribution to contemporary philosophy is calling attention to the moral weight of rituals that undergird every other sense of the social meaning of moral actions.

Our own late-modern science is very different from Xunzi's, emphasizing evolution and biological continuities up through sign-shaped behavior and language.[13] Nevertheless, his point is well taken, namely, that the causal processes of interpreting signs are different from causal processes that are merely natural and do not have signs, to put the point a modern way. Many human processes are mixtures, with some elements best understood in terms of chemical reactions, say, and others in terms of signs. Human life is a kind of biopsychic dance. Chemical states cause the stomach to contract and growl, stimulating thoughts of food, purposeful eating, pleasurable digesting, and chemical metabolic nourishment; most meals also involve social interaction. Any explanation or understanding of this process that leaves out the chemical patterns of causation or the semiotic ones is stupidly reductive. Insofar as semiosis is involved, there is an element of Xunzian ritual.

Ritual and Semiotics

Rituals across the spectrum are conventions. Conventions are not innate but are signs that need to be learned. The upshot of this is that semiotics, the study of signs, should be brought in to the paideia of religious studies in an important way. The semiotic theory most attuned to the ritual point is that of Charles S. Peirce, for whom it is closely connected with his pragmatic theory of engaging the world and also with his metaphysics of nature.[14] Implicit in my argument here and drawn out elsewhere is that religious symbols serve to engage us with realities where otherwise we would have no handle. Other theories of signs take them to be distancing substitutes for addressing the realities. The chief distinction between Peirce's semiotics and that of the European tradition associated with Saussure is that whereas the latter takes the interpretation of texts to be paradigmatic, Peirce takes the interpretation of nature to be paradigmatic. For Peirce, interpretation is the process of engagement with realities. The interesting question, then, is not so much the decoding of signs within semiotic systems, the European preoccupation, as the analysis of how signs arise within semiotic systems, how they take on definiteness, and sometimes lose definiteness. The reasons for this "genetic history" of signs have to do with pragmatic concerns for their roles in engaging realities, that is, whether they make proper discriminations for the contexts and purposes of interpretation.[15] That signs "grow" within semiotic systems illustrates Peirce's metaphysics, according to which there is a cosmic propensity for growth of connection and relationship, which is what signs produce. All of this resonates with the contextualism of Xunzi's theory of ritual that marks its conventionality. For instance, ritual for him was seasonable; he adjusted periods of mourning to the station and importance of the deceased, as well as to the resources of the family.[16] He knew there were alternative calendars and different classifications of social merit, all conventional distinctions but articulating something real.

Peirce's semiotic theory introduces many distinctions that are obscure or wholly nonexistent in Xunzi's theory of ritual. Peirce said there are three main topics of semiotics.[17] One is the analysis of signs themselves in their meanings relative to one another; Xunzi does some of this, as in 19.7a–7b. A second topic is the context within which signs are used. The context determines the respects in which the signs stand for objects, thus what is taken to be important in the context. Context connects what is important in the object with what is important in the purposes and values of the interpreters. Xunzi is massively brilliant in analyzing the appropriateness of ritual behaviors for particular situations, dealing on the one hand with the objective occasion for ritual and on the other with the nature and contexts of the participants. The entire Confucian tradition has important contributions to make to this theme of contextual interpretation, so important to the pragmatic tradition. The theme was particularly important for John Dewey, and the fact that he failed to address the connection with Confucian culture was a significant missed opportunity.[18]

The third main topic of semiotics, according to Peirce, is reference, and he distinguished at least three kinds, conventional (which he called symbolic), iconic, and indexical. Conventional reference means that signs refer according to the ways their semiotic systems define, the way language does. Any kind of sign that can be talked about is at least conventional. Iconic reference takes reality to be like what the sign says. Simple iconic reference is like an isomorphism between the form of the thing and the form of the sign, as a cross is an icon of Jesus's crucifixion (to use Peirce's example). More complicated kinds of iconic reference go all the way to descriptions in which the words paint a picture, if you will, or present a theory, of the way the referent is supposed to be. Xunzi recognizes iconic reference in saying, for instance, that the cost and elaborateness of funerals should be in proportion to the importance of the deceased: "The funeral of the Son of Heaven affects all within the four seas and brings together the feudal lords. . . . The funeral of a castrated criminal does not involve uniting his family and neighbors, but brings together only his wife and children. . . . As soon as his body is interred in the earth, everything ends as though there had never been a funeral."[19] In his discussion of music, Xunzi relates instruments to great themes. The general idea of correlative thinking in ancient Chinese, especially Confucian, thinking is a kind of iconic reference.

Indexical reference, the third kind, is most important for Confucianism. Signs can refer by pointing, which is to say they can establish a causal relation between the object and the interpreter like getting the person to turn and look. More significantly, many signs refer by requiring deep and important changes in the interpreter. This is especially significant for religious signs upon which people meditate or that guide religious practices: only long practice can transform the person enough to properly engage the object as the sign would require. The Confucian theme of the rectification of names should not be understood as an attempt to get the right icon or description but as the attempt to get the right index.[20] The right index causes the interpreter to be properly comported toward the object, treating it according to its true nature and worth. A description might be involved in a rectified name, but then again the descriptive or iconic elements of the "right name" might be quite fanciful, plainly false if interpreted literally. Chad Hansen's "Daoist" interpretation of language can be seen as rightly emphasizing the indexical, as opposed to iconic, character of reference, according to Peirce's categories.[21] With this distinction in hand, a major new research project opens up for extending the Confucian analysis of the rectification of names.

Perhaps the most important connection of Xunzi's theory of ritual with semiotics has to do with ritual performance and semiotically shaped behavior. Speech act theory, derived from Austin and Searle, distinguishes the performative function of speech acts from cognitive statements, questions, and so forth.[22] Peirce's pragmatic semiotics treats all speech and sign-shaped acts as performatives, functioning to engage the interpreter or actor with the realities interpreted in one way or another. Distinctions between kinds of engagement, some quite physical and others purely contemplative with a vast array in between, are made on Peirce's theory in terms of considerations of meaning systems, interpretive contexts, and dimensions of reference. Sign-shaped behaviors are analyzed as habits whose guiding principles are interpretive signs that can be understood semiotically and objectified in consciousness as a thought conceived as a thought. Xunzi's spectrum of rituals across all kinds of conventionally shaped actions and thought lend themselves to a Peircean analysis of performatives rather than a speech act analysis that distinguishes performatives from other locutions. Like Peirce's theory, Xunzi's supposes and manifests a unity of thought and action characteristic of Confucianism and pragmatism alike.[23]

One final point needs to be made about the semiotic character of ritual theory, which is that rituals as sign-shaped behaviors are vague and require individuation or specification in their performance. As Xunzi pointed out, there is a dancelike quality to rituals.[24] The dances have formal "steps" that integrate many people's movements and those steps can be learned. Since they are vague, however, each performer has to make them specific to individuated actions. Underdetermined human nature can be determined greatly by the conventions of sign-shaped behavior; but that determination is still vague and needs individuation. Whereas individuation in Western philosophy has often been interpreted in terms of matter, or the haecceity of actualization, Xunzi's approach is through the analogies of music. Tones are entirely specific, and the major tone in a song sets all the other relations. Moreover, for Xunzi, specific cooperation in integrating society does not come only from laws or precepts, though surely from them as well, or even from just the modeling of a life, but from the ruler being like a singing master who provides the tune so that others actualize an appropriate harmony.[25]

Ritual and Desire

Xunzi opened his essay on ritual principles with the question of the origin of ritual, by which he meant its founding utility as well as its historical origin: what is ritual basically good for? He answered by pointing out that people are born with desires, which prompt action to achieve their satisfaction. The action of seeking satisfaction has no measure, he said, leading people to fight over the means to satisfy their desires. That fighting leads to disorder, which in turn leads to the impoverishment of the society. The Ancient Kings abhorred disorder and wanted their people to have satisfaction in their desires. So they invented ritual regulations that appropriately related desires to the goods that might satisfy them. "In this way, the two of them, desires and goods, sustained each other over the course of time."[26] Note that desires are not bad. Nor is the fact that the pursuit of their satisfaction is unmeasured bad in itself. The drawback of unmeasured pursuit of desires is that it leads to conflict that diminishes wealth so that the desires cannot be satisfied—poverty is bad for the satisfaction of desires. The rebalancing of Xunzi's ill-founded reputation as a dour misanthrope who thinks human nature is bad requires this point to be emphasized. Desires are often good and should be limited by ritual only so that their satisfaction might be maximized. Discussing music as ritual, Xunzi puts the point even more positively: music is joy and leads to joy.[27] Moreover, being full of joy, a person will start singing and dancing, exercising the ritual forms of music and dance.

The problem Xunzi recognized with desires is that they are inchoate, powerful, and underdetermined, to continue the point made earlier. With our evolutionary biological understanding we can see this as the problem of stimulus-response organization. Animals have evolved so that complex defensive, aggressive, or appetitive responses are triggered by specific immediate stimuli like a flash of light or sudden sound that makes one jump. Reptilian brains are triggered to fight, flight, devour, or copulate by basic stimuli with relatively little mediating interpretation. Amphibians, for instance, lack the mental capacity to rotate a visual image in the mind's eye so as to imagine the backside of prey or predator; a frog on a lily pad flicks its sticky tongue at tasty bugs in its field of vision but cannot imagine creeping up behind one (and is not built to creep). Human beings have old "reptilian" brains, but these are overlaid by many other organs of the brain that mediate kinds of data that can suggest alternative modes of response to fighting or fleeing; we do not eat everything that looks good (after about the age of two) nor copulate on impulse. The frontal and temporal cortices, in fact, have evolved to readiness for semiotic interpretation with capacities for extraordinary mediation according to long-range personal and social values. Contemporary science is a long way from clearly demarcating the "merely biological" from the semiotic elements in the biopsychic dance, though we understand that there are a great many human functions in which basic biological or chemical interactions are ordered at a higher level by semiotic considerations. Stomach contractions register as hunger pangs that in turn motivate people to stop work and go to lunch, debating whether to have Chinese or Turkish food.

Wherever the semiotic organization of behavior reaches down into the biopsychic dance, Xunzi's point about ritual obtains. Without the culturally learned signs, the behavior cannot take on the kind of organization that signs allow. Hence desires can be only immediate responses to stimuli rather than interpreted responses that take the stimuli to stand for states of affairs beyond themselves. Xunzi commonly described human nature as that which people are born with, in contrast to what they subsequently learn.[28] Like babies they are selfish and irritable. "The inborn nature of man is certainly that of the petty man."[29] He described the natural human faults as adult vices such as aggressiveness, greediness, envy, and hatred; natural desires are crudely sensuous.[30] The characteristic of all these faults is lack of semiotic (*li*) ordering, like a baby. A person who grows up to exhibit the adult faults remains a baby in the failure to learn the rituals that allow proper mediating reference to others and to the real goods and evils of the social and natural world apart from immediate stimuli; Xunzi called this lack of deference, or inattention to the nature of other things.

Mengzi's mistake, according to Xunzi, was to believe that desires could grow their needed semiotic focus from within. Because Xunzi believed that the semiotic or ritual elements derive from human contributions (e.g., the Ancient Kings) rather than the biological impulses given by Heaven and Earth, he rejected Mengzi's theory of internal exfoliation of virtue as simply wrong. Moreover, by expecting people to become rightly related to others and nature simply by letting their natural impulses grow uncorrupted, Mengzi's theory in practice would lead to adult babies, selfish and aggressive, envious and hateful. Or it would smuggle in ritual training disguised by romantic posturing. At any rate, to Xunzi, Mengzi was literally irresponsible, failing to recognize the responsibility to acculturate desires ritually or semiotically so that they can attain their right objects and focus of activity. Only ritual can allow one to desire dancing with desirable others in a dance of civilized beauty.

Today we recognize that the biological is not prior to the semiotic in any simple sense. Only because primitive human ancestors had rudimentary signs could they evolve with *Homo sapiens* brains and thus develop even more complex signs so as to desire civilized ways of life and satisfaction. The ancient Chinese did not conceive of the interaction of semiotics and biology in evolution. Nevertheless, Xunzi is right over against Mengzi about the movement from primitive desire as response to immediate stimuli on to authentically human and civilized desires, relating our capacities for sensation to their best proper objects. That movement requires human learning, especially ritualization into conventional organization that mediates immediate stimuli to larger human meanings. The moral, as obvious to us late moderns as to Xunzi himself, is that failure to pay attention to ritual and teach it intentionally results in merely "natural" behavior that falls short of the human.

Ritual, Integration, and Religion

The notorious problem with desires is that they conflict and lead to such disorganized behavior that even those whose fulfillment is possible and easy are unfulfilled. This problem is as bad when the individual desires are clearly articulated with regard to sophisticated identification of their real fulfillment as when they are foolishly immediate. Xunzi, of course, was late in a long line of philosophers, East and West, who have recognized this point, for instance Plato in his discussions of eros. What parent of an adolescent can miss the difficulty?

The tempting response to the problem is to find a theory or overall pattern by which the many desires properly suitable to a person and community can be integrated. Patterns are usually conceived to be static however, with the result that appetitive behavior is forced into fixed forms that are inattentive to the constant shifts in the natural and social environment, as well as to the psychological and physical development of the individuals. The better response is to conceive of the integration as a ritual dance, with the competing desires all having their roles to play according to appropriate timing and reactions with other desires, the desires of other people, and the shifting terrain for the human performance. A healthy and properly deferential individual has a rich internal ritual life that allows the measured satisfaction of all important desires required for personal fulfillment and social obligation.

From our evolutionary standpoint we can sort levels of ritual integration that Xunzi might recognize as ready to handle his examples. We have already noted the very primitive ritual level that integrates basic posture and movement with "styles" of determining the underdetermined biological potential. Closely related to this are the ritual dances imposed to clamp down on the immediate fight, flight, devour, and embrace responses. Likely this is not a happy dance but, as Freud pointed out about learning physical and impulse control, closely akin to forcing oneself to withhold or expel feces contrary to impulse. As Plato said, elementary as well as sophisticated discipline is the application of one's aggression to oneself.[31] As Xunzi said, no one would undertake this naturally but needs to be taught with tough lessons.

Beyond impulse control the affective life of an individual needs to be organized so as to constitute an integrated personal style, a personality. This is done while yet a further level of integration is learned, namely, the roles the individual plays in the larger family. The Greeks, like the Confucians, stressed the back-and-forth movement between learning to play roles in the family and learning to integrate personal style. Just as immediate impulses need to be forced into a dance that allows for personal integration, one's personal interests need to be forced into a dance that allows for family functioning, which in turn defines personal interests. The Confucian ritual problematic of filiality, as important for Xunzi as for others, traces the development of personal and familial integrating rituals.[32]

The fortunes of families themselves are not naturally integrated in a larger community and need a further level of ritual integration. Left to themselves, competing for short resources, honor, and dominance, families feud, and a civil society with a king is needed. Civil ritual cannot be reduced to law imposed by the royal army alone. It is a function of a learned dance that acknowledges authority and subordinates the designs of families for their own blood to the needs of the trans-family whole. The ritual dances of public society are never without a supplementary police force, however much Confucius himself hoped they might be. Xunzi was never in doubt about the point. Public rituals need enforcement. No good king would tolerate the crude public policies of Mozi; the Way of the King is music![33]

Perhaps there is an even higher level of integration than that of public life, namely, the exquisite beauty of the arts. As mentioned, Xunzi praises music for its sheer joy, punning on a homophone for music, joy, and delight. Music and the other arts call for the special organization of public life to support them, and they in turn shape public life. Our category of "art" is too narrow for the ancient Chinese conception, and for the reality too. Living, doing, making, and enjoying things that are intrinsically valuable and appreciable is a kind of perfection of civilized life, and this requires a further complex of rituals or socially shared and exercised conventions.

Although the image of levels of integration is artificial, belying many causal and ritual crossings from one level to the next, it does make a powerful point about human life that Xunzi would acknowledge quickly. Each level achieves a ritual integration and intensity by weaving a pattern on the lower level. But that is a kind of force, a constriction. The lower levels pay a price by being integrated into the dance of the higher levels. Brute impulses are constricted for the sake of personal integration; personal interests are subordinated to family integration; family interests are limited by public order; public order is given shape and justification by the goods and ways of life most nearly appreciable for their own sake. The ritual dances order their components by keeping them under pressure. When things work well, the pressure is released in the performance of the higher level. Or at least the pressure is managed. Confucians generally, and Xunzi in particular, have known that human life is organized with pressure and control. If Confucians have seemed a bit stiff and forced to Daoists, it is because they know and are willing to pay the price for impulse control, personal discipline, family flourishing, public order, and the high arts. Daoists generally count on Confucians paying the price for them, or pay themselves by shifting into a Confucian mode. The price is generally thought worthwhile because each level of integration brings a richer level of personal or civilizational satisfaction.[34]

But things rarely go perfectly well for long. The economy gets tight and the public schools cut out the arts budget. A crisis in public confidence causes representatives of private families to vote for school vouchers rather than public schools. Then children rebel against the family attempting to force its version of the social microcosm upon them. Untaught they are defeated by their own impulses and wallow in selfish, aggressive, envious, hateful, and narcissistically immediate desires. Cut off on the freeway, even the patriarch burns white-knuckled with road rage, a velociraptor in a Volvo. The reptile erupts through all the levels of civilized ritual meaning and accomplishment. What most sets Xunzi apart from Mengzi is that he knew this:

> Thus a warped piece of wood must first await application of the press-frame, steam to soften it, and force to bend its shape before it can be made straight. A dull piece of metal must first be whetted on the grindstone before it can be made sharp. Now, since human nature is evil, it must await the instructions of a teacher and the model before it can be put aright, and it must obtain ritual principles and a sense of moral right before it can become orderly. Nowadays, since men lack both teacher and model, they are prejudiced, wicked, and not upright. Since they lack ritual principles and precepts of moral duty, they are perverse, rebellious, and disorderly.
>
> In antiquity the sage kings took man's nature to be evil, to be inclined to prejudice and prone to error, to be perverse and rebellious, and not to be upright or orderly. For this reason they invented ritual principles and precepts of moral duty. They instituted the regulations that are contained in laws and standards. Through these actions they intended to "straighten out" and develop man's essential nature and to set his inborn nature aright. They sought to tame and transform his essential nature and to guide his inborn nature with the Way. They caused both his essential and inborn natures to develop with good order and be consistent with the true Way.[35]

This sums up Xunzi's view that the normative Way of being human, that which the *Zhongyong* says is Heaven-sent, is not given in Heaven and Earth's biological or "natural" donation but in what the sages have learned about the conventions or rituals that humanize. The Way for humans is conventional but not arbitrary in the sense of being the result of capricious will. For Xunzi the ancients figured out how rituals make the achievements of human life and civilization possible and developed rituals that do this; his moral crusade, like that of Confucius, was to recover those rituals so as to restore the possibility of high civilization. Whereas we take a more evolutionary view as to the development of those rituals or signs, we can accept the main point: without ritual semiotics, we are not human, more like reptiles.

Whereas Xunzi would resonate with the analysis of ritual as organizing desires to be attuned to proper objects, and also as organizing different levels of integration and achievement from the merely biological to high civilization, he seems not to have addressed the breakdown of the levels and the eruption of the pressures of the lower through the higher. He would not know what to do with the velociraptor in the Volvo nor would his tradition generally. The traditions of West Asia, Judaism, Christianity, and Islam have been more sensitive than the Confucian to the situation of the pressures of life's hierarchical organization.

The situation, I have argued, is twofold. On the one hand, human life at each level feels the pressures of the lower levels. Cumulatively this is felt as guilt, the layers of prices paid to achieve higher organization. Rarely if ever is this guilt personally culpable, and hence it fails to register in the Enlightenment mentality. But one's impulses pay a price to be integrated into a personal style, which pays a price to live within a family, which pays a price to function in a public society, which pays a price to bear a high culture. To be a human being at all in a high society is to be a great expense for other things and the feeling of that price paid is guilt. Christianity carries this idea furthest in its idea of original sin. Xunzi himself held that a sage could harmonize all these elements, but I think that for him harmony includes holding things in tension, balance under pressure. Although I have developed his ideas in a contemporary language shaped by Freudian and Nietzschean sensibilities, obviously anachronistic in a sense, I suspect that part of the Neo-Confucian wariness of Xunzi came from an accurate apprehension of high pressure beneath his correct manner.

On the other hand the reaction to the pressure, doubled by the feelings of guilt, is destructive disruption of the levels of ritual organization in individuals and society, usually violent evil. Confucians generally have attempted to account for human evil by saying that it is the result of selfishness obstructing what otherwise would be naturally appropriate responses to things. Xunzi weighed these things differently from the Mencian tradition in Confucianism. He said first that selfishness is not a learned vice but the natural state of untutored desire that has only an immediate responsiveness. Failure to tutor the desire with ritual leads to infantile selfishness lasting into adulthood. But then Xunzi recognized that the ritual tutoring of desire itself puts infantile desire under pressure. Learning involves work, force, and control. When it fails, those infantile desires under pressure can explode. Xunzi does not go so far as to describe evil in this explosive way, although he does appreciate the pressure that ritual education applies to the merely natural and always remains suspicious of the natural alone and its threat to civilized life.

Ritual has a religious dimension that Xunzi and the ancient Confucians may not have fully recognized. If one imagines layers of ritual dance organizing horizontal levels of biopsychic human reality, one also can imagine vertical rituals that weave up and down through the horizontal levels. My hypothesis is that religious rituals connect otherwise incommensurate strategies of integration.[36] They release pressures. They reestablish broken dances. They acknowledge disruptions, tragedies, collapses of entire dimensions of human life. They rewind and set the clock so that things can go again. The paradigmatic religious ritual is the sacrifice in which something's or someone's lifeblood is drained and body parts rearranged as if rearranging some broken personal, social, or cosmic body. Emperors and parents function as priests to perform the humanly healing sacrifices and other religious rituals that realign the levels of semiotically meaningful human reality.

Of course Xunzi did not have this late-twentieth-century, psychoanalytically and anthropologically oriented theory of ritual. But he did understand the role of the Son of Heaven, the chief sacrificer, to be to order the human world and fulfill Heaven and Earth, integrating both horizontally and vertically.[37] The emperor's diet, constituting his life and endurance, has abundant meat from the sacrificial animals.[38] Sacrifices were offered to the legendary sage emperors who invented the rituals that harmonized society (by creating hierarchical relations).[39] Few Chinese thinkers in the Confucian tradition had as much sensitivity as Xunzi to the ways by which the best laid rituals might slip. Whereas Mengzi would say that people with uncorrupted human nature unfolding throughout life would employ ritual as the external expression of internal humaneness, Xunzi would warn that rituals need to be taught, imposed, and enforced for humaneness to develop at all out of the chaos of desires.[40] The perceived threat of a collapse back into personal and social chaos led some of Xunzi's followers to legalism, a move Xunzi steadily declined. But I would not be surprised if his insistence on returning to ritual in the threat of chaos did not have some hope in the purgative and restorative powers of sacrifice.

To distinguish a religious dimension from others within ritual is anachronistic in reference to Xunzi and his milieu. Nevertheless, to bring Xunzi into the contemporary discussion where that distinction is indeed very important is to play to his strength relative to other Confucians. For Xunzi, in contrast to the Mencian line, the virtues of humaneness are achievements of harmonious determination of underdetermined human nature by ritual broadly conceived and are fragile as their ritual medium is fragile. Where Mengzi would interpret the social collapses in Rwanda, Congo, Zimbabwe, Yugoslavia, India/Pakistan, and Ireland as failures of inadequate ritual to allow the proper expression of humaneness that would otherwise naturally unfold, Xunzi would see those collapses as preventing the formation of humaneness out of inchoate immediate and aimless desires. Moreover, Xunzi would recognize, and approve as necessary, the pressures required to bring the desires to order and integration. But he would expect, and lament as tragic, occasional explosions of ritual organizations under those very pressures, thereby deconstructing the very essence of the human. In the face of this threat, Xunzi advocated ever more rule and control by the government.[41] But this should not be exercised by military strength, he said, only by strengthening the king's personal inner and outer power, accomplished through ritual.[42]

Ritual should not be overstressed in Xunzi so as to make it seem as if he lacked the Confucian commitment to humaneness or doubted that human nature derives from Heaven. But he did insist that the normative civilization made possible through ritual derives from Heaven only indirectly in ways requiring the creative discernment of the sages, not in what Heaven contributes to human biology, which includes "a bundle of 'unlovely' desires and impulses."[43] So for him, as for many contemporary thinkers, semiotics is required to understand how the human organism becomes a human being.[44]

Notes

1. I am pleased to thank T. C. Kline III for many helpful suggestions and criticisms of an earlier draft of this essay. For a general narrative of the Confucian story by a scholar sympathetic to Xunzi, see John H. Berthrong's *Transformations of the Confucian Way* (Boulder, CO: Westview Press/HarperCollins, 1998), especially the introduction and chapter 7.

2. Confucianism developed through what might be called the Mencian line has indeed become a major player in the global philosophic conversation. Perhaps this is because of the increasing importance of the students of Chinese expatriates in Taiwan in the second half of the twentieth century, such as Mou Zongsan, who carefully related Western philosophy to the Confucian tradition interpreted through Mengzi and Zhu Xi/Wang Yangming. I discuss this line of interpretation, compared with a reinterpretation giving Xunzi a central place, in *Boston Confucianism* (Albany: State University of New York Press, 2000), especially chapters 1, 3–5.

3. John Knoblock, *Xunzi: A Translation and Study of the Complete Works*, 3 volumes (Stanford, CA: Stanford University Press, 1988–1994). The predecessor of this volume is *Virtue, Nature, and the Moral Agency in the "Xunzi,"* ed. T. C. Kline III and Philip J. Ivanhoe (Indianapolis, IN: Hackett, 2000). An outstanding monograph on Xunzi that figures in my reflections here is Edward J. Machle's *Nature and Heaven in the Xunzi: A Study of the Tian Lun* (Albany: State University of New York Press, 1993).

4. Knoblock, *Xunzi*, vol. 3, p. 52.

5. Ibid., vol. 3, p. 49.

6. See my *Normative Cultures* (Albany: State University of New York Press, 1995), p. 166ff; *Boston Confucianism*, pp. 123–125.

7. See his *Nature and Heaven in the Xunzi*, especially pp. 90–104.

8. *Xunzi* 80–81, K 17.3a, 17/80/9–15.

9. Paul Weiss's *Privacy* (Carbondale: Southern Illinois University Press, 1983) is the most thorough and sensitive treatment I know of the learned character of sensation and taste; see especially its introduction and first two chapters.

10. *Xunzi* 80, K 17.2a, 17/80/1–3. Xunzi might have been the originator of this idea, although some earlier scholars had dated the *Great Learning and the Doctrine of the Mean* prior to Xunzi. The idea itself has frequently been likened to Christian ideas of the Trinity, hence the common translation. The notion could just as well have been translated as the "triad" of Heaven, Earth, and the Human. Surely superficial differences in the agendas of Confucians and Christians exist regarding the Confucian notions and

the Christian Father, Son, and Holy Spirit. By "Earth" Confucians never meant anything as specifically epitomizing and paradigmatic for ways of life as Christians have meant by Jesus. Nevertheless, Confucians have closely related categories for articulating the epitomes of humanity that need to be appropriated and internalized the way Christians talk about attending to the "mind of Christ." Moreover, the metaphysics of more than one primordial principle is something that Confucians and Christians have in common. The term "Trinity" therefore demarcates a common ground regarding a problematic that runs from obvious phenomena to deep metaphysics.

11. *Xunzi* K 4.10, 4/15/14–15.

12. *Xunzi* 81, K 17.3a, 17/80/13.

13. See Terrence W. Deacon's *The Symbolic Species: The Co-Evolution of Language and the Brain* (New York: Norton, 1997) for a somewhat speculative but excellent summary and explanatory theory of the biological evolution of thinking. It is closely related to Peirce's theory of semiotics, to which I relate Xunzi's theory later.

14. Peirce was the greatest of the American philosophers, heir to the New England traditions of Transcendentalism, science, and the wilderness experience and to the dialectic initiated by Emerson of distinguishing the American from the European traditions of thought. Those not acquainted with his thought should see Joseph Brent's *Charles Sanders Peirce: A Life* (Bloomington: Indiana University Press, 1993). The standard edition of Peirce's philosophical writings, now outdated, is edited by Charles Hartshorne and Paul Weiss, *The Collected Papers of Charles Sanders Peirce*, volumes 1–6 (Cambridge, MA: Harvard University Press, 1931–1936) and by Arthur Burks, volumes 7–8 (Cambridge, MA: Harvard University Press, 1958). Peirce wrote on semiotics and signs in nearly all of his papers; the greatest concentration is in volume 2 of the *Collected Papers*, especially book 2, "Speculative Grammar." The greatest concentration of his discussions of pragmatism are in volume 5; volume 6 focuses on his metaphysics and contains the great paper "A Neglected Argument for the Reality of God" that combines his best statements of semiotics, theory-construction, and pragmatism (and a little theology). A briefer but more available collection of Peirce's philosophical papers is *The Essential Peirce: Selected Philosophical Writings, Volume 1 (1867–1893) and Volume 2 (1893–1913)*, Nathan Houser and others, eds. (Bloomington: Indiana University Press, 1992, 1998). These two volumes stress the chronological development of Peirce's ideas about semiotics. A good general introduction to Peirce, stressing his semiotics and metaphysics, is Robert S. Corrington, *An Introduction to C. S. Peirce: Philosopher, Semiotician, and Ecstatic Naturalist* (Lanham, MD: Rowman & Littlefield, 1993). See also Corrington, *A Semiotic Theory of Theology and Philosophy* (Cambridge, England: Cambridge University Press, 2000). For more specialized studies, see *Peirce's Approach to the Self: A Semiotic Perspective on Human Subjectivity* (Albany: State University of New York Press, 1989). On the metaphysical connection of thought and action, see Michael L. Raposa's *Peirce's Philosophy of Religion* (Bloomington: Indiana University Press, 1989). My own integrated interpretation of Peirce is stated briefly in *The Highroad around Modernism* (Albany: State University of New York Press, 1992), chapter 1.

15. On the relation of Peirce's semiotics to that of Saussure and Husserl, see Jacques Derrida, *Of Grammatology*, trans. Gayatri Chakravorty Spivak (Baltimore, MD: Johns Hopkins University Press, 1976), pp. 44–52. Derrida consistently misunderstands Peirce's emphasis on science and the engagement with nature and reduces his semiotics

to what registers in the European tradition. Umberto Eco, *A Theory of Semiotics* (Bloomington: Indiana University Press, 1979) is better, discussing Peirce throughout; Eco distinguishes between codes and sign production, noting Peirce's emphasis on the process of forming and deforming signs but still downplaying the interaction with natural reality that shapes the process.

16. *Xunzi* 100–102, K 19.5b, 19/94/8–21; 105, K 19.9a, 19/96/4–8.

17. On the analysis of semiotics into the topics of meaning, context, and reference, see my *The Truth of Broken Symbols*, which analyzes and extends Peirce's theory, giving the detailed citations to Peirce. The extension of Peirce's theory is supposed in what follows as a Peircean semiotic.

18. Do *not* see *John Dewey: Lectures in China, 1919–1920*, ed. and trans. Robert W. Clopton and Tsuin-Chen Ou (Honolulu: University of Hawaii Press, 1973), which shows Dewey at his scientistic worst. But *do* see Roger T. Ames and David L. Hall, *The Democracy of the Dead: Dewey, Confucius, and the Hope for Democracy in China* (Chicago: Open Court, 1999), which brilliantly relates Dewey's thought to the themes of continuities of thought and action, and of individual and communal experience, in Confucianism.

19. *Xunzi* 97–98, K 19.4b, 19/93/13–17.

20. For Xunzi on the rectification of names, see *Xunzi* chapter 22.

21. See Chad Hansen, *A Daoist Theory of Chinese Thought: A Philosophical Interpretation* (New York: Oxford University Press, 1992). The proper employment of Peirce's distinction between iconic and indexical reference is a vast help in clarifying much fustious confusion about Chinese aesthetic sensitivity versus Western propensities for scientific description. Although the claim that the East is sensitive and the West utilitarian is an old cliché, something like that point has been developed with extraordinary subtlety by the late David L. Hall and his Sinologically expert colleague, Roger T. Ames. See the adroit discussion in Hall and Ames, *Thinking Through Confucius* (Albany: State University of New York Press, 1987), especially chapter 3. See also their contrast between Chinese and Western cultures in *Anticipating China* (Albany: State University of New York Press, 1993).

22. See John Searle's *Speech Acts* (Cambridge, England: Cambridge University Press, 1969).

23. Wang Yangming is the representative of Confucianism most noted for stressing the continuity of thought and action, though the theme is expressed one way or another in most Confucians. It is no accident that Antonio Cua, who wrote the fine study *The Unity of Knowledge and Action: A Study in Wang Yang-ming's Moral Psychology* (Honolulu: University of Hawaii Press, 1982) is also the author of *Ethical Argumentation: A Study in Hsun Tzu's Moral Epistemology* (Honolulu: University of Hawaii Press, 1985). See also his fine *Moral Vision and Tradition: Essays in Chinese Ethics* (Washington, DC: Catholic University of America Press, 1998) for his reading of the breadth of the Chinese tradition, including Daoist sources. Other basic studies of Wang Yangming stressing the continuity of knowledge and action are Julia Ching's *To Acquire Wisdom: The Way of Wang Yang-ming* (New York: Columbia University Press, 1976) and Tu Weiming's *Neo-Confucian Thought in Action: Wang Yang-ming's Youth (1472–1509)* (Berkeley: University of California Press, 1976). See also Philip J. Ivanhoe's *Ethics in the Confucian Tradition* (Indianapolis, IN:

Hackett, 2002) and *Confucian Moral Self Cultivation*, second ed. (Indianapolis, IN: Hackett, 2000), chapter 3. True, Wang and his tradition identified with Mengzi rather than Xunzi. So the anachronistic reading of "continuity of thought and action" from its slogan status with Wang to Xunzi is doubly precarious. It surely is anachronistic to transfer it from its sixteenth-century slogan status to pre-Han antiquity, and Wang and the Neo-Confucians thought mainly about Mengzi. But it applies to Xunzi just as well. He cannot be read out of the Confucian camp on this issue!

24. *Xunzi* 110–111, K 19.11, 19/98/3–10. See also *Xunzi*, chapter 20.

25. *Xunzi* K 18.1, 18/83/11–14. See my analysis of individuation of ritual or practical reason in *Normative Cultures*, chapters 7–8.

26. *Xunzi* 89, 19.1a, 19/90/5.

27. *Xunzi* 112, K 20.1, 20/98/14.

28. *Xunzi*, chapter 23.

29. *Xunzi* K 4.10, 4/15/14–15.

30. *Xunzi* 157, K 23.1a, 23/113/3–6.

31. He argued this in the *Republic*, especially books 2–4, in distinguishing the functions of the spirited (aggressive) from the appetitive and rational parts of soul. Nietzsche picked up the theme in the second essay of *On the Genealogy of Morals*.

32. Tu Weiming's *Centrality and Commonality: An Essay on Confucian Religiousness*, revised and enlarged ed. (Albany: State University of New York Press, 1989) is a brilliant study of filiality as the central virtue for creating a fiduciary community, explicating the text of the *Zhongyong*. Tu interprets filiality as the learning of 仁 *ren*, humaneness. Tu's own book, however, can be interpreted as the learning of family rituals—sign-shaped behaviors—relating parents, children, siblings, friends, figures and institutions of public life, and the emperor so that *ren* is possible and itself learned for expression in civilized relations. This is the interpretive take on Tu's north of the Charles Boston Confucianism from south of the Charles; see his foreword to my *Boston Confucianism*, pp. xvi–xix.

33. *Xunzi*, chapter 20, especially 117–120, K 20.4–5, 20/100/19–101/22.

34. See the analogous points made by Joel Kupperman and David Nivison in their essays "Xunzi: Morality as Psychological Contraint" and "Xunzi and Zhuangzi," respectively, in *Virtue, Nature, and Moral Agency in the "Xunzi."*

35. *Xunzi* 157–158, K 23.1b, 23/113/9–12. Knoblock follows the traditional translation from Burton Watson and Wing-tsit Chan, for instance of 惡 *e* as "evil," in the phrase, "human nature is evil." The English word "evil" has connotations of culpable wickedness that are not entirely appropriate for Xunzi's meaning. Xunzi means something more like human nature being unformed (like unstraightened wood) and disconnected, so that it does bad, selfish things and misses doing the good it could. I have followed Edward Machle's stress on ritual as providing the connections that allow human nature to be formed and properly engaged. See my defense of Xunzi relative to Mengzi in discussing Tu Weiming's position in *Boston Confucianism*, 102ff.

36. This hypothesis generalizes the thesis of René Girard about sacrifice and social guilt. See his *Violence and the Sacred*, trans. Patrick Gregory (Baltimore, MD: Johns Hopkins University Press, 1977) and *The Scapegoat*, trans. Yvonne Freccero (Baltimore, MD: Johns Hopkins University Press, 1986). Whereas Girard writes mainly of socially constructed guilt, my hypothesis locates the beginning of guilt in biological evolution, in

the biopsychic dance. I have explored it at greater length in the discussion of Levitical and New Testament atonement theories in *Symbols of Jesus: A Christology of Symbolic Engagement* (Cambridge, England: Cambridge University Press, 2001).

37. *Xunzi* 44–45, K 9.15, 9/39/4–6.

38. *Xunzi* K 18.5c, 18/86/18; see Knoblock's notes to this discussion of sacrifice.

39. See Knoblock, *Xunzi*, vol. 2, p. 6.

40. On ritual as the external expression of internal humaneness, interpreted in terms of Mengzi over against Xunzi, see Tu Weiming's *Humanity and Self-Cultivation: Essays in Confucian Thought*, reprint (Boston: Cheng & Tsui, 1998), pp. 5–34. I have responded to his argument on Xunzi's behalf in *Boston Confucianism*, pp. 92–96.

41. *Xunzi* 36–39, K 9.3–5, 9/35/22–36/20.

42. *Xunzi* 39–45, K 9.7–15, 9/36/23–39/7.

43. The quoted phrase is from T. C. Kline III, who also comments: "Xunzi does not believe that Heaven cares one way or the other about human beings. He has taken on the Daoist impersonal vision of a Heaven that treats all 'like straw dogs.' " Xunzi is more consistent than many Confucians in depersonalizing the high god Shangdi into mere Heaven; many Confucians find a highly personal "mandate" in Heaven.

44. A different version of this chapter appears in a separate collection of my essays, *Ritual and Deference: Extending Chinese Philosophy in a Comparative Context* (Albany: State University of New York Press, 2008), chapter 3.

CHAPTER 4

Xunzi

Ritualization as Humanization

Lee H. Yearley

Introduction

Certain thinkers, but only certain great thinkers, resemble mountains of forbidding but appealing grandeur that normal humans try to climb. The majesty and diversity of the mountain both draw climbers and provide them with compelling experiences. Any climber, however, ascends up but a small section of the mountain and therefore knows well only one small part of it; the whole is never adequately grasped.

Xunzi is such a monumental figure, and that helps explain why he is often portrayed as a pragmatic thinker who rejects all that cannot further the sensible demands sensible people make. His complex and profound spiritual vision can, that is, be overlooked by even the most talented climbers. We all may, moreover, find congenial such inattention because Xunzi forces us to face questions about our own ability to approach his level of spiritual understanding, particularly when we see ourselves described, in an incisive but unflattering way, in his portrait of the lower levels of human fulfillment. (Examining his spiritual vision also involves problems of another sort: technical problems about the authenticity of parts of the text, the coherence of his thought, and the meaning of certain cryptic terms or passages.) Nevertheless, the attempt produces, I think, important results.

One result is understanding that Xunzi's religious ideas are among the most subtle in the whole Confucian tradition as befits someone who probably is the most theoretically subtle of all the classical Confucian thinkers. Moreover, Xunzi's ideas about religion often reflect a consciousness closer to our own than do most traditional Chinese thinkers, and therefore he may have much to teach us. Finally, Xunzi's inquiry into religion, like that found in some modern thinkers, combines descriptive and normative concerns. He is a theorist about the phenomenon of religion as well as a constructive thinker who argues for the truth of a specific religious vision. Let us turn, then, to examine Xunzi's spiritual vision, especially as it is focused in his ideas about ritual.

Three levels of spirituality appear in Xunzi, if I may be permitted a brief, schematic formulation of his position. The first is Xunzi the explicator and defender of the spiritual fulfillment that comes from social rituals. These rituals often resemble our "etiquette," but they are, for him, the potent operations of a humane community. The second level is Xunzi the critic and reinterpreter of those religious ideas and actions that bring spiritual deformation if improperly understood and spiritual growth if properly understood. Finally, we reach that mysterious level of spirituality where humans contact numinous powers present in or working through the mind.[1]

These three levels interact, of course, with each other. Social ritual's full meaning, for example, becomes evident only when religious rituals are also understood and the highest level both informs and draws from the others. Nevertheless, such a scheme helps us to analyze the different strands in Xunzi's spiritual vision just as briefly sketching out, in what follows, his basic picture of the human self and of ritual's forms helps us to approach our more complex topics.[2]

Xunzi's Basic Picture of the Self and Treatment of Ritual

Many of Xunzi's spiritual ideas operate from, and even rest on, his understanding of the self's character, a situation that I believe is true for most religious thinkers. We will examine later some of the more complex, and religiously significant, features of his model of the self, but let us focus now on its more evident features.

In broad outline Xunzi's picture of the self presents us with a model that resembles models with which we are familiar. That is, he believes a fundamental division, a duality, characterizes the human self. (The idea that the self is divided, incidentally, more accurately captures his ideas than does his famous formula that human nature is evil or bad.) He thinks people spontaneously move toward certain satisfactions, but they also can entertain ideas that can modify those spontaneous movements and guide their action.[3]

Human beings, then, are characterized on the one hand by certain especially strong and persistent dispositions, for example, my disposition to feel hunger or to desire other people's appreciation. These dispositions and the feelings they generate are simply self-regarding, they are basically and often foolishly selfish. They manifest neither a notion of wider obligations to others nor a notion of the self's own long-range good. Another element is present in human beings however: the capacity for conceiving ideas that modify these simply self-regarding desires. I may, for example, desire food but give it to an elderly person either out of respect for her or from my own wish to be so treated when I am elderly.

Human beings are divided, then; their "desire" and their "judgment" are often in conflict. People have reactions that drive them to simply self-regarding actions; that is their nature (性 *xing*). But people also have the capacity to entertain ideas about goals, to choose them, to enforce that choice in a way that guides actions, and even (over time) to create new habits from which they act. That is their "conscious activity" (偽 *wei*), and it makes harmonious social life and personal flourishing possible. This understanding of the self's dual character informs many notions, but most important here is the context it provides for Xunzi's ideas on ritual.

"Ritual" is probably the most adequate of the multitudinous translations for the character 禮 *li*.[4] In the classical Chinese context, however, the single notion of ritual covers two activities that most contemporary Westerners think are quite different. One is solemn, explicit religious activity, such as Christian baptismal services. The other activity is what we call etiquette or, more accurately, those reasonable and humane learned conventions that make up the ethos of a culture. Ritual covers, then, everything from the solemn performance of an elaborate ceremony to the "excuse me" after a sneeze.

Religious rituals, our main concern in the latter part of this chapter, usually manifest one of two things. They manifest either one's grateful responses to what makes possible one's life—one's family, for example—or one's response to the movement from one to another state, from having a living parent to having a dead parent, for instance. In either case, the focus is on people facing "thresholds," situations where people move to a new state or respond to what lies beyond their ordinary routine.

Social rituals, in Xunzi's treatment, resemble some features of religious rituals, and we need to examine that resemblance in order to address the suspicion that Xunzi's connecting of them manifests an unsophisticated kind of thinking that fails to differentiate what can and should be separated. Social and religious rituals resemble each other because social rituals are more that just pedestrian social facts. Both are sacred ceremonies that express and foster a spontaneous coordination rooted in reverence. Moreover, both exemplify learned, conventional behavior that manifests distinctly human rather than simply animal-like actions. Both, then, promote human qualities and respond to human needs.[5]

Features of the close relationship between religious and social rituals can be illustrated by two examples from contemporary American culture. In many Christian rituals a series of acts expresses a picture of the world and manifests an ethos in which forgiveness, repentance, and reconciliation interact. An American's smile on meeting a stranger, however, also expresses a view of the world and manifests a concomitant ethos. The smile, that is, manifests the notion that people should meet with openness not suspicion because everyone can and should be friendly with one another. The distinctiveness of the American view and ethos becomes painfully clear when Americans travel to a country that lacks the ritual and sees such a smile as an example of silly naiveté or unbecoming forwardness.

Religious activities (the Christian ritual) and social activities (the American's smile) are, then, parts of one ritualistic continuum. Ritual exemplifies, therefore, "locative religiosity," the kind of religiosity where crucial features of true flourishing consist in properly locating one's self within a complex social order thought to have sacred qualities.[6] That means, for Xunzi, all activities can have a religious quality, can reflect a wider order and pattern of meaning.

In Xunzi's locative world no fully independent social realm exists, but he does distinguish between two kinds of social rituals. The first covers individual acts of etiquette such as my offer of a seat to an elderly person. The second covers relatively stylized and long-lasting social occasions such as my elaborate dinner party, or in one of Xunzi's own examples, a village ceremony that involves formalized drinking, music, and speeches.[7]

The boundaries among all these kinds of ritual are, of course, blurred. Simple acts of etiquette will always be present in each, and certain especially complex social ceremonies may resemble full-fledged religious rituals. If we think, for example, of a presidential inauguration in the United States, the formal swearing-in ceremony resembles a religious ritual; the inaugural ball resembles a stylized social ritual; and various individual acts of etiquette will occur in both those activities. Let us now turn to a further consideration of social rituals, focusing on Xunzi's response to certain of the most significant criticisms of his ideas.

Xunzi's Possible Responses to Criticisms of His Idea of Social Rituals

Critics of Xunzi's ideas can say that social rituals (even perhaps all rituals) limit individual expression and undercut spontaneity. They undermine or debilitate, then, those very qualities that undergird individual integrity and produce truly autonomous action. Moreover, these critics can also argue that such rituals reflect social conventions and therefore validate arrangements that basically benefit only those groups who control a society. Finally, the fact that social rituals (in Xunzi's treatment) receive religious justifications both enforces damaging social controls and leads people to think deleterious rituals ought to not be modified. Social rituals (especially when defended in the way Xunzi defends them) produce, that is, damaging illusions that impede the creation of truly flourishing people and a truly ethical society.

Considering these criticisms allows us, I think, to penetrate more deeply into Xunzi's rationale for social rituals than we otherwise might because it forces us to sketch out the theoretical framework on which it rests. Xunzi's basic response to these criticisms rests, I believe, on the idea that social ritual provides the forms by which culture makes possible a specifically human life. Human nature (in contemporary language, our instincts or biological endowment) cannot guide us toward full human actualization. Indeed, it often either leaves us without guidance or guides us to imperfect or even dangerous actualizations. Humans need, then, those "social conventions" that rituals provide if they are to flourish.

Examples from American culture can illustrate this point. One example concerns how we leave someone with whom we have been talking. We have few formal rituals of leave-taking (we do not bow, for example), but we do not just abruptly turn on our heels and leave. Rather we utilize a whole repertoire of ritual forms: we employ a smile, a parting word, or perhaps some physical contact. If we fail to utilize these rituals, our leave-taking appears to be too abrupt, and it can even be seen as disrespectful or at least as awkward.

Another if more complicated example of how ritual functions as a necessary humanizing activity appears in the activity of making new friends. The activity, that is, has its own set of ritual forms. If we are adept at making friends, we know when and how to smile, to make small talk, and to use physical contact. We are clear about when to show an exaggerated sensitivity to the other person's needs and about how much time should elapse before we attempt to reestablish contact. People who fail to grasp these rituals will have difficulty making friends, and we have various labels to identify their failures: they are called, for instance, pushy, standoffish, or overly curious.

These rituals unquestionably rest on and express conventions: leaving a person or making new friends is done in various ways in different cultures, a fact of which we can become acutely aware when we live in a foreign culture. But the ability to function successfully in a culture requires that we both understand and master these rituals. To be fully human is not simply to follow our natural inclinations. It requires that we live within the rituals of a specific culture because they alone enable us to express our humanity.

These rituals, it is true, will inevitably inhibit both the immediate gratification of many feelings and the clear expression of certain personal characteristics. Some desires to hit or to help, to confront or to confess, to yell with joy or to scream with anger will be inhibited by ritual. Nonetheless, rituals do not destroy people's ability to express either their individual characteristics or the distinctiveness of the particular situations they encounter. With an elaborate dinner party, for example, skillful people modify the form according to the needs of the participants. Indeed, the ability to improvise defines a good host or guest just as its lack defines a stuffy or punctilious one. If skillfully performed, then, ritual actions are deeply textured and can therefore express the individuality of both people and situations.

This expression can occur because ritual gestures can manifest a variety of attitudes within a basic form. In the military, for example, ritual demands that one salute an officer. But the salute can be executed in a great variety of ways, and those ways express one's attitude to the officer: one's respect, disrespect, hostility, or indifference. Indeed, the salute illustrates well how distinct messages come through at different levels, if (and only if) the actors in ritual dramas are familiar with and sensitive to the forms they use. Preservation of the formal response can combine with clarity about the individual message.

Skillfully performed rituals, then, allow for a significant degree of improvisation and can communicate highly individualized messages while also preserving a modicum of social harmony. A less ritualized form may well communicate the message more directly. But it can also exact a substantial price both by increasing social disharmony and by failing to give people adequate guidelines for various kinds of human interactions. Ritual forms, then, do limit and direct many relationships and gratifications, but the ability of the skillful performer to improvise can give a deep texture to the acts.

Nevertheless, the criticisms noted earlier are surely not adequately treated by just this point. To face them more directly we need, I think, to examine three closely related subjects: First, what are the differences between actions guided by rules and actions guided by skills? Second, what is the general relationship between moral actions and ritual actions? Third, and most significant, how do we establish criteria by which to judge the worth of social rituals?

Xunzi's response to the first question is relatively simple and foreshadowed in the subject we just discussed. To perform a ritual correctly, in Xunzi's view, is not merely to follow simple rules. Rather it involves the skillful entry into the spirit of a situation. This kind of skill is surely absent in the rustic who fails to know the ritual form. But it is also absent in the unimaginative conventionalist who knows the form but fails to possess the proper adaptive spirit that skillfulness generates.

Indeed, skillfulness is so important that skilled and unskilled people who perform the "same" ritual receive and give different things. A ritual act of respect to an elderly person, for instance, will generate different reactions in the elderly person and contribute different things to the agent depending on the level of skill of the person who performs the act. An inflexible or a stuffy person expresses and receives something quite different from a person who acts with the ease and flexibility born from skill.[8]

Xunzi believes, then, that often we should think in terms of social skills to be nurtured and exercised rather than in terms of moral rules to be followed. The claim is significant and can be best understood if we view guides for actions as appearing on a continuum with moral directives on one end and customary directives on the other end. Actions that fit on either end of the continuum are clear: for example, conscientious objection to a war my society is fighting and my use of one rather than another eating utensil.

Most significant human activity, however, occurs in the middle part of the continuum and distinctions in that area can be difficult to make. Many actions, that is, are inappropriate but escape any clear labels; they are neither immoral nor just violations of custom. Consider, for example, my belching loudly at dinner, my not greeting you with a smile, or my being inattentive when you talk about a topic of great importance to you. Many of our actions fall within a sphere the guidelines of which manifest neither clearly moral nor clearly conventional norms but that enable us to relate quickly, easily, and humanely with one another. This crucial class of actions, for Xunzi, falls within the sphere of ritual.

Indeed, Xunzi thinks that often only ritual forms enable us to apply moral rules well. A person may desire to act humanely and assent to rules that reflect the desire. But if ritual forms are either missing or unknown, the humane desire cannot take correct form and become effective. Ritual provides the map, for instance, that makes benevolence (仁 *ren*) possible; it allows a person to show respect, give help, or make friends. Social ritual is, then, what allows benevolence to flower and many other features of the religio-cultural system of this locative religion to thrive.

We may find Xunzi's defense of social rituals compelling or at least plausible and perhaps even attractive. Nevertheless, the question remains of how we are to find criteria to evaluate the appropriateness of social rituals in order to change them if that is necessary. We can, that is, be swayed by many of Xunzi's arguments for the importance of social rituals. We may realize that impulses to benevolence will always need embodiments understandable by and acceptable to people in the community. We may agree that most moral rules need ritual forms if they are to be sensitively applied. We may believe that only rituals can give appropriate guidance in all those delicate areas of human interaction that constitute much of the fabric of normal social life. We may even agree that only through ritual can social harmony be preserved and chaos avoided.

Nevertheless, even if we grant all this, we must still address the question of how to find standards to evaluate, and then possibly to change, social rituals. Only if we have such standards are we able to avoid the insidious effects that can accompany any simple, unreflective adherence to conventional guides for action. Many now think wrong, for example, various traditional forms of ritual address or action toward woman or minority groups, in our own and other cultures.

Xunzi faces here, that is, his own version of the general problem of how best to relate "ethos" and "morality," to use the terms Hegel bequeathed to us. Ethos enjoins us to follow out faithfully the inclinations and obligations laid on us by our participation in a specific community. Morality enjoins us to follow out those obligations that arise from reflection on ourselves (and other people) as humans with reasonable needs. The ideal state is a harmonious marriage of the two, a situation where ethos spontaneously produces actions and inclinations that reflect morality. But an ever present problem is "alienation," a state where we think the practices that constitute the ethos are inadequate reflections of the moral norms that reflection produces. Traditional practices about how to address and act toward women and minority groups, for instance, may ill fit my reflective sense of how those people ought to be treated, and that generates alienation in me.[9]

At times, Xunzi appears to think alienation can never exist; he writes as if Confucian rituals represent the perfect marriage of ethos and morality. The sage kings, that is, possessed unique insights and created rituals that will work for any society at any time. Elsewhere, however, he declares that people should select the rituals of certain later kings simply because they know the most about them. Moreover, he also states that a new sage king would reform a community's language, and ritual and language have similar enough functions that reformations in ritual would, therefore, also be expected.[10]

The text presents mixed testimony, then, but most important to us, Xunzi possesses principles that can provide him with criteria for judging and changing rituals. Ritual's adequacy, for example, can be measured by the realization of goals such as the fostering of benevolence (*ren*), or the satisfaction of certain desires, or the maintenance of appropriate social hierarchies. If a ritual fails to develop benevolence or to satisfy desires or to maintain hierarchies then the ritual needs to be changed.[11]

We might think such criteria are too vague to solve the problem, especially as we need clear and specific criteria given the social forces that work to maintain ritual. I think, however, Xunzi's "solution" is neither fatally flawed nor markedly frail. This is especially true if we grant both the inherent difficulty of the problem and Xunzi's surely justifiable emphasis on the need to rely on people rather than rules to solve a problem like this one.

Moreover, other features of the criteria and approach Xunzi might use in judging such rituals appear when we examine his reformulations of religious rituals. In that arena a central concern is the justification of judgments about changing or reinterpreting harmful religious rituals. Let us, then, turn to that arena, the second level of spirituality in Xunzi. We will focus on his belief that certain religious ideas and actions deform our spirituality if improperly understood but develop it if properly understood. That inquiry can best begin by investigating Xunzi's attitudes to conventional religion.

Xunzi's Attitude to Conventional Religion

Xunzi's criticisms of many conventional religious ideas and practices are often stinging, but they do not lead him to reject all religious forms. Rather he rejects some and reinterprets others. His aim in both cases is to make possible a genuine religiosity that he thinks much religiosity impedes. The project is a complex one, then, and I begin our consideration of it with Xunzi's most general criticisms of religion, turn next to his specific evaluation of two types of religion, and end by discussing the principles he uses in his reformulations of what he criticizes. Two notes of caution need, however, to be sounded before we begin our analysis. First, Xunzi never presents his ideas as systematically as I will. Second, in discussing them I will employ the illuminating but perilous procedure of using modern Western notions to elaborate them.[12]

Put most generally, Xunzi thinks that much normal religious activity creates and maintains something like what we mean by false consciousness: the mistaken belief that certain ideas reflect unchangeable reality, even sacred realities, when in fact they are fallible human creations. Religious ideas and practices, that is, often lead people to see necessities in what are, in truth, changeable human products. Xunzi, then, criticizes some aspects of religion because he wants people to recognize they are human creations and therefore can be changed in ways that will improve the human situation.

More specifically, Xunzi attacks two kinds of degraded types of religion. The first is what we will call "technological religion." Much religious activity for him can best be seen as a form of technology or engineering. That is, it is a kind of "making" (or *techne*) that relies on understanding the principles on which things operate. This kind of religion seeks to explain the world, especially its more mysterious parts, and then to utilize those explanations to aid humans.

Xunzi attacks such religion because it fails to employ criteria such as simplicity, efficiency, and predictability. As he says, if people desire a practical good, such as flourishing crops, plowing produces the desired result more simply and efficiently than do attempts to fathom and placate spirits. If people just plow, fewer variables are involved, success is more likely, and complex elaborations to explain failure are unnecessary.[13]

Even more important to us, Xunzi also attacks what I will call "masochistic religion": the kind of submission to another being that arises from seeing one's self as so weak that only the guidance of another being, one perceived as extremely strong, can bring fulfillment. Such submission appeals to people because it seems to cut through the ambiguities and anxieties that arise when people directly face the complex demands of ordinary life. At its weakest the main manifestation is sentimental consolation, at its strongest an intoxicating surrender that fundamentally destroys a person's ability to think and choose.

I understand that special care must be taken with a category like "masochistic religion." Its Freudian overtones do not bother me. (This remains true even if Freud's baroque surrounding theory does bother me, as do those readings of him that see sexuality as primary rather than the maintenance of integrity.) Nor do the overtones of Sartre disturb me. (This remains true even if I would limit severely the range of phenomena Sartre gathers under the dialectic of dominance and submission.)

The deformation Freud and Sartre identify is, to my mind, common and significant. Moreover, it has analogues in traditional Christian ideas about either the semblances of the theological virtues of faith and hope or the relationship between proper pride and false humility.[14] Nevertheless, the phenomena masochistic religion identifies probably appears most clearly in Western theistic religions, violates most evidently Western notions of the individual, and produces some experiences compelling enough to make one wary of always seeing only pathology. Care, then, is necessary when we use the category, especially when we use it outside the West.

At minimum, however, we can say that masochistic and nonmasochistic types of religions define opposed ends of one spectrum. The former seeks the surrender or dissolution of the self, while the latter seeks to protect the self's integral form while also setting it within a religious context. Seen this way, Xunzi's criticisms focus on the former end of the spectrum. They focus on how a religious idea or practice undercuts possible human flourishing by establishing a passive relationship to some force thought to demand the surrender of basic human powers.[15]

Xunzi's criticisms of both technological and masochistic religion are sharply pointed, often dryly witty, and clearly heartfelt. Some practices and ideas of these kinds of religion he surely wants to eliminate. He does not, however, want always just to replace religious ideas and practices with more productive nonreligious ones. Rather he wants to reinterpret many of them. Indeed, Xunzi seeks to produce a religious revolution by redefinition or reinterpretation, to preserve many religious ideas or actions but change their meaning.[16]

Xunzi's reformulations manifest four characteristics. First, the overarching goal of all of them is the protection and encouragement of a view of human flourishing that emphasizes personal balance, the significance of society, and the need to acknowledge human frailty in an appropriately measured fashion. That goal provides the criterion both for dividing necessary from unnecessary religious ideas and actions and for reforming the meaning of the necessary ones. Second, these reformulations critically examine all simple anthropomorphic descriptions of the transhuman realm and replace them with designations that are symbolic or stress the mysterious. Third, the reformulations criticize all depictions that rest on the notion that humans can manipulate their relationships with the transhuman in ways beneficial to them. In fact, they usually redescribe them in terms of how human feelings are rearranged and spiritual attitudes are generated.

Finally, the reformulations display a concern for justifications that manifest the tradition's universal applicability. That is, Xunzi assumes the warrants provided by the notion that something is traditional are inadequate. This means his reformulations are apologetic in the word's full sense. The apology is directed both toward other people and toward the one who reformulates.

This process of reformation, like most such processes, means Xunzi distinguishes between what we can call religion's exoteric and esoteric dimensions. That is, he distinguishes between what most understand, the exoteric dimension, and what a few understand, the esoteric dimensions. This in turn leads him to affirm two notions. One is that religious ideas and practices can be understood at more and less profound levels, a notion that entails the presence of a hierarchy of spiritual achievement. The other, and more controversial, notion is that people can be affected by religious ideas and practices without a clear understanding of why they are so effected. Xunzi's project of reformulation is, then, a complicated one, and we can best consider it further by focusing on the ways in which he treats religious rituals.

Xunzi's Reinterpretation of Religious Rituals: Introduction

The question of the significance of religious rituals was important in pre-Han China. In fact, debates about religious ritual often served to focus debates among competing visions of life, so that describing the age's various views of ritual can help us understand both Xunzi's specific ideas and their general import.

Three kinds of attacks on ritual and three defenses of it were prominent in his time, and Xunzi opposes all of them, even if, like most critics, he also draws from aspects of positions he criticizes. Put telegraphically, the six different positions are as follows. One group attacks rituals as a wasteful, even unjust, use of scarce natural and human resources. Another group attacks them as a social artifice that distorts significant human capacities and reinforces destructive social organizations. A third group sees them as an inadequate form of social control that is best replaced by clear rewards and punishments. One defense of ritual sees in it a process that activates transhuman forces and uses those forces to help humans. Another justifies ritual in terms of the innate human capacities for ritual, or even inertial tendencies toward it; human beings, that is, need ritual if their natures are to be actualized. A last defense believes rituals are sanctified by tradition; they therefore need no real justification and must always be meticulously followed no matter what the apparent price.

Xunzi thinks all of these approaches are flawed, and his examination rests on distinguishing among three kinds of religious rituals. First are rituals that are useless or even harmful; sacrificing a pig to cure an illness falls in this class. Second are rituals that adorn life in important but not critical ways; rituals to produce rain probably fall in this class. Third are rituals that serve a crucial function in human life; death or internment rituals fall in this class.[17]

These distinctions among rituals rest on ideas we have discussed earlier, and those ideas provide criteria that allow Xunzi to do something any sophisticated theorist must be able to do. They allow him, that is, to decide which rituals to change, which rituals to reinterpret, and which rituals to abolish.[18]

His general approach is to specify the human needs or capacities to which a specific ritual responds, decide how crucial they are, and then examine the different ways in which they can be met. Such an analysis leads Xunzi to discard rituals in the first category. The practices of technological religion, such as sacrificing a pig to cure an illness, fail to meet standards noted earlier about simplicity, efficiency, and predictability. Other activities can, that is, produce the desired results in far better ways.

The situation is more complicated, however, with rituals in the last two categories. A death ritual serves a crucial purpose, although the purpose is not what it is often thought to be, the pacification of the ghosts of the dead. A rain ritual, in contrast, is not crucial, but it is important. That is, it does not bring rain, but it does honor something that makes human life possible, and that honoring is an important part of humane culture (文 *wen*). These judgments mean most elements of a death ritual's form must be preserved no matter what the psychic or material cost. But a rain ritual might legitimately be abridged radically, or perhaps even abolished, depending on the circumstances in a community.

Xunzi has, then, criteria to evaluate religious rituals. He is, however, predisposed to maintain many of them, and this predisposition is not simply a matter of temperament. Rather it rests on his idea that defensible religious rituals do something extremely important: They modify emotions, especially those powerful emotions that certain kinds of situations generate. These modifications ensure that such emotions do not disturb the self's equilibrium and proper functioning. Moreover, these modifications allow for the nurture of specific religious emotions by giving them an ordered space in which to develop. Rituals ensure, then, that the emotions of grief caused by a loved one's death, or of reverence aroused by majesty, or of gratitude aroused by benefaction are neither suppressed nor extravagantly expressed.

Xunzi thinks our emotional responses are strongest in "threshold" or "liminal" situations, situations that manifest either the origins or the termination of the self and the community. I conclude by treating rituals dealing with termination, where Xunzi's approach is clearest and perhaps most compelling. But we need also to note his views on rituals dealing with origins.

Those rituals both inform his picture of death rituals and display an important aspect of his spirituality: a consistent focus on the implications of human frailty. The rituals that deal with origins, that is, manifest a crucial but potentially dangerous feature of our human frailty. We are frail not just because we die but also because we arise from sources beyond, or largely beyond, our control. Indeed, as we will see, the death of certain figures who functioned as origins for us has the impact it does just because those origins contributed in such fundamental ways to who we are.

Xunzi's Understanding of Rituals Dealing with Origins

Human life, for Xunzi, has three origins, three sources that make it possible. One is ancestors, the basis of the family, the social organism from which all people move. A second is rulers and teachers, the basis of the cultural order that provides the context that makes possible a fully meaningful life. And a third is Heaven and Earth, the basis that provides the fundamental underpinning for all life.

People respond strongly to these origins because they recognize that with them unpayable debts have been incurred. In most relationships, that is, people receive and give in a fashion that allows for repayment; equity can be restored. In these relationships, however, people receive so much that they cannot ever repay what has been given. When debts are present that cannot be repaid, the only appropriate response is gratitude and reverence.

Our frailty, our fundamental dependence, is expressed, then, when we attend to origins, and we must finds ways to properly express the emotions that result in order to flourish religiously. Moreover, if we do not express them appropriately, we fall prey to one or another human deformation. These rituals protect us, that is, against technological religion's false claims to understand and manipulate origins. But they also protect us against what for many people is an even more dangerous deformation: the subtle and debilitating traps masochistic religion presents.

Ancestors, one of the origins to be ritually honored, functions as a synecdoche for the social, and even biological, unit that generates human beings. Larger and more continuous than any individual, it preserves values, consoles against loss, and provides models for correct relationships. An origin this significant generates reactions that will distort a person's life and even a community's structure unless they are formed by proper ritual expression. (Xunzi, like most Confucian thinkers, believes clarity about proper and improper filial piety is fundamental to human well-being, in part because the shadows cast by masochistic religion can be most dark here.)

Rulers and teachers, another origin, together provide those cultural elements that make possible a fully flourishing life. Human fulfillment rests, that is, on more than just the nourishment that the natural order provides or the nurture that the family provides. It also needs both a just social order and a rich cultural matrix, and those arise from the actions of rulers and teachers. The recognition of this gift, then, also generates a sense of gratitude that demands ritual expression.

The origin presented by Heaven and Earth, which for simplicity's sake I will call the Heavenly origin, is the most complex of the three.[19] The clearest (and most superficial) description of this source is that it generates those basic elements, like the natural biological order, which make possible any kind of life. Much more than just that is involved, however, and we must examine it closely if we are to grasp significant features both of the death rituals and of Xunzi's general views on facing our frailty in the most appropriate religious fashion.

When treating Heaven, Xunzi often argues passionately against notions that religious activity ought to focus on the traffic between humans and Heaven. He believes, so to speak, that the border between Heaven and humans is closed, and no attempts should be made to cross it. One aim, then, of Xunzi's portrait of Heaven is to prevent people from being seduced by the attractive idea that easy answers will appear if only Heaven can be reached and affected.[20]

People should, he thinks, limit most of their intellectual inquiry and practical action to what is of direct use to humanity. That is, they should concern themselves with those characteristics of Heaven that form the situation within which human beings must work and to which they must respond. He even declares that distinguishing between the activities of Heaven and of humans is a mark of true excellence; indeed that sages are noteworthy for how they, unlike others, do not use their great understanding, talent, or perception on Heaven.[21]

Xunzi adopts this position in significant part because he thinks humans can know little with certainty about Heaven and matters related to Heaven. Especially problematic is any easy attribution of human qualities to Heaven, particularly those human qualities that imply Heaven shares our concern to help each other, or at least to help ourselves. That theoretical judgment has significant practical implications because Xunzi believes people have a propensity to look both for consolations and for easy solutions, and a comforting view of what Heaven cares about provides them with both. That propensity, in this case, impedes people's ability to solve specific and pressing practical problems.

Finally, Xunzi's attitude toward Heaven reflects one of his more general principles. He believes that admitting our ignorance about many important matters is religiously significant. He belongs, then, with those Confucians who argue for the spiritual importance of a kind of "religious agnosticism." Indeed, he develops this position considerably beyond the earlier forms seen especially in Kongzi but also in a figure like Mengzi.

Xunzi thinks, that is, that much of religious significance cannot be clearly known, and we must therefore cultivate a kind of intellectual asceticism. That asceticism enables us to surrender one kind of guidance in order to be open to what can better replace it. We must, so to speak, develop in certain areas a powerful incapacity to understand, a nurtured inability to grasp what may seem obvious to many people. Xunzi has grasped well, then, the force of skeptical arguments that appear in Daoist works like the *Zhuangzi* and even accepted some of the religious consequences that flow from them.

One significant result of Xunzi's reinterpretation of Heaven is to picture the world as a place that is neither tailored to human desires nor amenable to human cajoling. Humans operate in a world where many of their deepest aspirations find no easy fulfillment and much of what they value can be pitilessly destroyed. Xunzi focuses, that is, on what Thoreau entitled the inhuman sincerity of nonhuman processes: they act without any consideration of human needs or desires.[22]

Adopting this attitude does not mean, however, that people should simply accept those effects of Heaven that they also attempt to utilize for practical purposes. Rather, people should recognize that Heaven is a mysterious, sacred entity. Its constancy and fecundity display a grandeur that inspires awe and gratitude, and these reactions must be ritually treated.[23]

This view of Heaven, to my mind, fills out rather than contradicts Xunzi's emphasis on the need to separate Heaven and humanity. That is, to fail to differentiate properly between Heaven and human beings is not simply to harm human beings' practical efforts. It is also to stunt human spirituality by deforming appropriate religious attitudes to Heaven. To try to compel or manipulate Heaven is to take time, energy, and money away from their more productive social uses. But it is also to fail to react properly to the numinous entity that is Heaven, to its mysterious, majestic, and fascinating power. It also, thereby, is to fail to worship as one should and to be especially liable to the deformation of masochistic religion.[24]

Heaven is, then, for Xunzi a numinous entity, a power and even "intelligence" that is higher than, and in most ways alien to, human beings. It therefore escapes our usual categories of understanding, and grasping that is extremely important religiously. The numinous, that is, inspires religious awe exactly because it fails to fit into any of the normal categories into which people try to fit it.

Four such normal categories are of special concern to Xunzi: the technological, the trivial, the masochistic, and the moral. Some people, that is, attempt to rationalize Heaven into a force whose qualities can be known and whose actions can be controlled, as do practitioners of technological religion. Many people attempt to trivialize the numinous into, say, the uncanny, as Xunzi thinks the superstitious do. Other people are driven by the distorted reasoning that produces masochistic religion, and they see all that differs from human weakness as numinous. Others still, and this includes notable Confucians, will treat Heaven as a graspable moral being, someone who creates in human beings a nature whose nurture will manifest Heaven's benign character and power.

Xunzi's examination of rituals that honor origins is at its most complex when Heaven is the origin he considers. This occurs because it is the most mysterious, probably the most paradigmatic, and perhaps the most culturally significant of all origins.[25] It therefore focuses the question of how to respond to the forces that shape human life in ways that show appropriate reverence and yet do not fall into one of several religious deformations. The desire to honor origins is a legitimate impulse, but it is also prone to deformations, and therefore rituals must form these impulses in ways that prevent them from poisoning the whole religious life and corrupting people and society. A similar situation obtains with rituals that deal with the end, the death rituals, and to those we now turn.

Xunzi's Reinterpretation of Rituals That Deal with Termination: The Death Rituals

Death rituals deal with the emotions that appear when people face endings. We focus here on the internment rites, the specific rituals that begin just after a person dies. That focus allows us to probe both the death rituals' general rationale and several important facets of Xunzi's overall perspective.

In Xunzi's view, particularly powerful emotions arise when a loved, respected, or honored person dies. They arise for various reasons, only a few of which are uncomplicated. Quite straightforward are the appearance of strong feelings of personal loss and of grief for the deceased. Also clear, if less straightforward, are the perturbing emotions that arise from the recognition of one's own frailty as another's death illimunates it. (Such a recognition may be especially prominent if the deceased is a parent, a protective barrier between people and their own mortality.) These reactions alone do not, however, adequately explain the complexity and strength of the emotions that Xunzi thinks arise when the loss of an origin makes present one's own frailty. To understand that we need to employ an illuminating if also controversial approach, one that uses the idea of the "primordial."[26]

Employing the idea of the primordial reflects a specific understanding (which I share) of how personal religious development occurs. Much genuine contact with religious phenomena, that is, involves connecting with primordial levels of thinking and feeling and therefore also the forces they release. Nevertheless, mature religiosity, indeed mature living, also involves developing ourselves to a level where the primordial no long controls all our responses, even if it may haunt us and at times catch us unawares. The danger in such development, of course, is that we lose our ability to contact the primordial.

This danger is significant because our spiritual health demands that we continue to be animated by what the primordial presents that is of irreducible value. Indeed, we must be able to bring it into our ordinary life, sometimes by integrating it into that life, sometimes by seeing how it challenges the presuppositions of that life. We ought to not, then, simply grow beyond the primordial. We must also be able to return to it, to employ and be employed by it, because only through it can we be open to the numinous.[27]

Xunzi accepts this understanding of the primordial's place, I believe, and in no place is that more evident than in his depiction of death rituals. Xunzi, that is, thinks a loss that makes clear one's own frailty reanimates a set of dangerous, if also possibly productive, primordial reactions. These reactions usually arise from an unalloyed fear of annihilation or its surrogate, a fear of separation from what one loves and honors.

That fear can generate very different, and very dangerous, responses. These responses range from a retreat into a self-enclosed world in which one's impulses define what is true to a manipulative, or even masochistic, submission that is animated by one's fears. In each of them one surrenders what seems valuable in one's self in order to preserve a valued presence.

Primordial reactions like these are constantly present in the sense that they can be animated under the appropriate circumstances. (To use the vocabulary of medieval Christian Scholasticism, they are "passive potentials.") Xunzi thinks they ordinarily, at least for refined people, can be reformed or subdued by proper cultivation. In extraordinary situations, however, primordial reactions will almost surely be reanimated, and rituals like the death rituals are needed to control them. But they must do so in a way that denies neither their power nor the significant religious reactions they potentially contain.

In Xunzi's view, then, the deaths of loved, honored, or respected persons generate a powerful sense of our own frailty, arising either from the simple feelings of loss and grief or the complex reanimation of primordial reactions. These reactions produce a conflict between parts of the self, and that conflict highlights an especially subtle aspect of the distinction between the mind and the emotions that, for Xunzi, defines human beings. The conflict occurs as follows.[28]

The mind declares that the person is dead and gone. Certain of the emotions, however, refuse to accept that judgment. The emotions, that is, act as if the person must still be alive and just has moved to another locale. (The emotions display, then, their "cognitive" or "interpretative" dimension.) These emotional reactions convey, therefore, a view of the situation that opposes the mind's view.

This conflict between the reactions of the mind and of the emotions must be resolved. If no resolution occurs, personal and even social harmony will be damaged. In fact, if these emotions are not both dissipated and respected as they are dissipated they will deform the person or, at the least, reappear later in damaging ways. Moreover, these emotional reactions must be treated lest they block the expression and development of other religious emotions. Most crucial are those emotions that fuel appropriate attitudes to Heaven and therefore correctly place a person before the numinous power that defines all life.

The analysis of what occurs in the case of the respectful dissipation of emotions resembles ideas that appear in contemporary work on the psychology of grief. Grief is portrayed, that is, as an energy that continues to affect the self unless it receives an appropriate release. This portrayal arises from considering examples like the following. A young boy's father dies, no funeral services occurs, and little is ever said directly to him about the death. The son apparently has little reaction to his father's death, but when the mother several years later announces her remarriage, the boy's response is a nervous collapse that includes the hysterical repetition of the phrase "My father is dead." Xunzi pictures grief in a similar if less dramatic way. That is, deep perturbations endure unless the relevant emotions receive an appropriate expression at the time of death.

Xunzi aims, however, to do more than simply bring people back to the kind of emotional equilibrium that allows them to continue their normal lives, the goal of much contemporary work on grief. The appropriate process, for him, also protects and nurtures a set of religious emotions. It both saves them from being blocked by other powerful emotions and gives them a channeled expression that strengthens them. This process allows appropriate reactions to the sacred to replace those found in, say, masochistic religion. It guards against, for example, those reactions that can turn filial piety into a debilitating rather than productive virtue. Moreover, and most generally, the process nurtures the complicated relationship between people's equilibrium and awe before the numinous that is central to Xunzi's religious vision.

This general perspective on the goals of the death rituals leads Xunzi to a delicate, remarkably sensitive interpretation of how the internment rites work.[29] Stretching over three months, these rites harmonize people's mental and emotional sides and nurture appropriate religious emotions through a set of carefully modulated activities. The ritual, he says, trims what is too long, what the emotions demand, and stretches what is too short, what the mind demands. Indeed, the ritual employs in turn what each side of the self desires. Beauty, music, and joy are used to induce an attitude of tranquillity while ugliness, weeping, and sorrow are used to induce an attitude of grief. Neither attitude is allowed to triumph. The mourner moves neither to aesthetic abandon and unrestrained joy nor to frantic activity and injurious sorrow.

The ritual provides people, then, with a strict scenario that specifies what mourners should do and when they should do it. When the person dies, ritual enjoins mourners to delay for a short time the start of the internment procedures. Mourners allow the hope to continue that the deceased will return to life; that is, they treat dead people as if they were alive and would soon awake. Two days pass before the deceased is put in the coffin, three days before the mourning clothes are worn. Mourners then continue to change the dead person's coverings, but they also move the body further and further away from their living area. They both show respect and yet also slowly move the person out of their life. An unadorned body kept too close will become ugly, causing contempt or loathing to arise and allowing grief to pass too soon. A body dispatched too quickly will generate deep-seated perturbations. This process of honoring the body and separating from it both begins the mourner's return to a normal life and makes possible the nurture of specific religious emotions.

The attempt to serve the diverse needs of the mind and the emotions is exemplified by the mourner's placement of certain objects with the dead body. In putting objects with the body, the mourner behaves as if the dead person were merely traveling to another locale where the objects will be used. But the objects lack crucial elements, and that makes clear they will never be employed. For example, one dresses the body in garments, but they lack holding buckles because there is no real need now for clothes. One puts a lute or zither with the body but fills the holes of the lute and leaves untuned the strings of the zither because the instrument will never be played.

Throughout the ritual one acts as if the dead person was merely changing dwelling places and therefore will need the objects. One also makes it clear, however, that the objects will never be used because the person is dead. Placing unusable objects with the body displays well, then, the complex attitude the death rites both manifest and nurture. The rites allow people slowly and painfully to accommodate themselves to the loss of a loved person and the frailty of human life. The mind's perception triumphs, but the emotions' initial responses are not simply rejected and other religious emotions are nurtured.

Xunzi's depiction of the internment rites illustrates clearly his attempt to foment a revolution by redefinition. The rites neither refer to some transhuman realm that can be technologically controlled nor reflect a belief in the dead's continued existence. Rather they overcome a person's initial split between thought and emotion by means of a carefully modulated set of actions that both acknowledges the power of some emotions, while also engineering their dissipation, and allows other emotions to develop. Such activities allow mourners to accept fully, in time, the mind's initial perception but without disregarding the initial feelings they had. Moreover, the activities nurture profound kinds of religious attitudes and emotions that arise from contact with the primordial.

Significant, if speculative, ideas arise if we attempt to specify further the mourner's spiritual state of mind. It seems to resemble the state of "pretending" that underlies important activities like the creation of or participation in imaginative literature. (Indeed, pretending is, I think, crucial to many spiritual activities, a recognition that should lead us to reject emphatically the crude notion that pretending represents an immature state distinguished by its lack of contact with reality.)[30]

Focusing on pretending also enables us to see how, for Xunzi, many religious activities could be called "necessary fictions." That is, pursuit of them demands that a person act as if a fiction is either true—the unsophisticated response—or necessary—the sophisticated response. Xunzi's treatment, from this perspective, might even be seen as an extended meditation on one of the more cryptic and evocative passages in the *Analects* of Kongzi (3.12), the passage that tells us when sacrificing to behave as though the spirit was present.

Critics of Xunzi might declare that even the sophisticated response induces a kind of false consciousness. Such critics fail, however, to realize several things. One is the complex psychic import of the knowledge that the fiction is a fiction. Another is the way in which the proposed attitude also opens a person up to what is not a fiction. Finally, and most important, such critics do not comprehend, or at least fully grapple with, the view of human frailty that underlies Xunzi's perspective.

We are, for Xunzi, frail in ways that usually are difficult for us to accept. Not only do we live between origins and terminations we cannot control, but we also constantly face the numinous. Moreover, we are prone to primordial reactions, and we must treat them in a fashion that both controls their destructive side and nurtures their constructive side.

Stringent limits, then, define what people can do; they cannot immediately form themselves into what simple rational judgments might commend them to be. Roles present themselves, for example, that people have no real choice but to assume, and the role of the mourner is one of them. In recognizing these limits, however, refined people do not take a fictitious necessity for a real necessity as is the case with destructive false consciousness. Rather they recognize they face a real necessity—if a necessity that ought to not exist in the world that the mind alone presents.

The mind, then, may see the mourner's role as a fiction. The whole person ought, however, to see it as a necessary fiction. It must be embraced if those frail divided creatures called human beings, those creatures haunted by the primordial yet also given power and solace by it, are to prosper in both ordinary and religious ways.

Xunzi believes very few people can fathom the spiritual complexity captured by the idea of necessary fictions and thus are able to see the real character of religious rituals.[31] This remains true even if many are effected by rituals in ways they are unable to articulate. As he says, the common people accept them as customs to be followed, officials accept them as socially important, and refined people follow them because they bring comfort. Only the sage fully understands why rituals are necessary.[32] The deep, complex, and subtle ideas underlying religious rituals reflect the depth, complexity, and subtlety of the human situation, and few understand that.

Especially superficial in their view of the human situation are two groups who simply reject ritual, groups Xunzi calls the despisers of custom and the system-makers.[33] The despisers of custom reject ritual because they look only for what is practical, for what makes immediate sense to hard-headed people. They reject ritual as a useless and time-consuming activity.

The system-makers reject ritual because they desire to produce a rigorous and coherent picture of the world that will provide simple, reasonable grounds for their ideas and actions. They reject the internment ritual, for example, because to them the principle of noncontradiction is crucial; a person either is dead or is not dead. They want to face life and death directly, and they put everything into clear-cut categories.

Against both positions, Xunzi argues that when life is seen clearly, and in the death of others we see it clearly, we can neither make it into a coherent understandable whole nor respond adequately to it by focusing on simple practical expedients. Human life is too fragile and delicate, too complex and contradictory, too profound and deep to capture in simple rational systems or sensible practices. We touch life as it actually is only through the complex pathos, the human contradictions, the struggle to find peace, and the openness to the numinous that the death rites exemplify.

Notes

1. For a fuller account of the last level of spirituality, see my treatment of the empty, unified, and still mind in Xunzi: "Xunzi on the Mind: His Attempted Synthesis of Confucianism and Taoism," *Journal of Asian Studies* 39.3 (1980), pp. 465–480. (Especially important treatments of this last level of spirituality appear in *Xunzi* 22–23, K 1.14, 1/4/16–21; 126–137, K 21.5a–21.9, 21/103/16–107/8; and 152–156, K 22.6a–6f, 22/111/20–112/24.) These footnotes either cite specific texts on which my interpretation rests or pursue important but subsidiary theoretical issues or points. I do not, then, enter into the numerous scholarly debates that surround the interpretation of specific issues in the *Xunzi.*

2. Significant parts of Xunzi's understanding of ritual were incorporated into other works, notably an extremely influential book on that topic. That meant his ideas on ritual lived on in the tradition as orphans, cut off from the overall view that informed them. This analysis may, then, help people within and outside the tradition reconsider ideas that often have lived apart from their larger explanatory framework.

I have previously explained my general understanding of this kind of inquiry—which I take to be an inquiry in comparative religious ethics—in "Selves, Virtues, Odd Genres, and Alien Guides: An Approach to Religious Ethics," *Journal of Religious Ethics* 25.3 (1998) 25th Anniversary Supplement, pp. 127–155; and "Taoist Wandering and the Adventure of Religious Ethics," The William James Lecture, *Harvard Divinity Bulletin* 24.2 (1995), pp. 11–15. Also note "Facing Our Frailty: Comparative Religious Ethics and the Confucian Death Rituals," The Gross Memorial Lecture, 1995, Valparaiso University (Valparaiso, IN: Valparaiso University Press, 1995), pp. 1–22 (where earlier versions of parts of this piece first appeared), and *Mencius and Aquinas: Theories of Virtue and Conceptions of Courage* (Albany: State University of New York Press, 1990), pp. 1–17, 95–111, and 175–203.

Finally, my use of the word "spirituality" draws on the work of Pierre Hadot; see especially the collection *Philosophy as a Way of Life: Spiritual Exercises from Socrates to Foucault*, ed. Arnold I. Davidson, trans. Michael Chase (Oxford: Blackwell, 1995). My use does not then, or so I hope, fit with the often vapid, voluntaristic, and antisocial temper found in many contemporary usages. For Xunzi's treatment of "spirit" 神 *shen*, see note 12.

3. *Xunzi* 139–140, K 22.1b, 22/107/22–108/2; 157–163, K 23.1a–1e, 23/113/1–115/8; also note 45–46, K 9.16a, 9/39/9–13; and, more generally, all of chapter 22.

4. Perhaps the most accurate and surely the most delightful rendition of *li* was given by Peter Boodberg, a Sinologist with a love of linguistic roots. He translates *li* as worshipful acconformation to corporate form that creates social coordination based on corpor-ordination.

Whatever may be the best translation, we need briefly to note a significant ethical question about Xunzi's perspective on ritual. It arises when we consider how, for him, ritual manifests and reinforces the pronounced social hierarchy he thinks is necessary. Even if one has no qualms about hierarchical views, his understanding of ritual's importance implies that some basic supports for and features of human flourishing are not available to many people.

That is, if all people need elaborate rituals (e.g., to deal with grief) and if many people have neither the time nor the money to participate in such rituals, then those people are cut off from much they need to flourish fully. (This remains true even if the situation is ameliorated somewhat by Xunzi's claim that everyone, or at least all males, can develop themselves in ways that allow them to inhabit high roles in the hierarchy.) Xunzi's position could, of course, be developed—perhaps in a direction that follows out strands of his thoughts on education—but the changes would be substantial.

5. For a rather theoretical discussion by Xunzi of the general elements in ritual, see *Xunzi* 93–94, K 19.2b, 19/91/7–92/10; 96, K 19.3, 19/92/21–93/4; for comments on its scope and importance, see *Xunzi* 25, K 2.2, 2/5/11–16; 44, K 9.15, 9/39/1–4; 71, K 15.4, 15/72/9–12; 86–87, K 17.9–11, 17/82/10–83/1; for its connection with other important ideas in him, see the relationship to music, *Xunzi* 113, K 20.1, 20/98/21–99/2; 117, K 20.3, 20/100/14–17; to learning *Xunzi* 19–21, K 1.8–11, 1/3/7–4/4; and, most vexing, to "righteousness" *Xunzi* chapter 21.

6. In open religions, fulfillment occurs when people transcend any particular culture and reach a higher realm through, for example, mystical experience or life after death. In locative religions, however, fulfillment occurs when people locate themselves in a proper culture. Neither a differentiated religious community nor a distinct class of religious practitioners will, then, be prominent in locative religions. Rather the religio-cultural system mediates meanings, attitudes, and actions to all people; it contains those ideas, generates those attitudes, and produces those social forms that humans need if they are to live well.

The distinction between locative and open religions is a controversial one, although versions of the distinction have operated in the study of religion for well over a century; in fact parts of current debates (e.g., between the positions of J. Z. Smith and M. Eliade) turn on viability of the distinction. Moreover, the very idea of a religio-cultural system (especially as found in the influential treatment of the early Geertz) is even more controversial, and rightly so in my view.

7. *Xunzi* 118–120, K 20.5, 20/101/6–22.

8. I treat at length the general notion of skillfulness, if in a quite different context, in my "Zhuangzi's Understanding of Skillfulness and the Ultimate Spiritual State," in Paul Kjellberg and Philip J. Ivanhoe, eds., *Essays on Skepticism, Relativism, and Ethics in the "Zhuangzi"* (Albany: State University of New York Press, 1996), pp.

152–182. The similarities and differences between these two accounts of skill illuminate much about the respective positions of the two thinkers.

9. A similar set of issues, and a fuller treatment of Hegel's ideas, appears in my "A Confucian Crisis: Mencius' Two Cosmogonies and Their Ethics," in Robin Lovin and Frank Reynolds, eds., *Cosmogony and Ethical Order: New Studies in Comparative Ethics* (Chicago: University of Chicago Press, 1985), pp. 310–327. Finding standards to judge social rituals (and features of religious rituals) is perhaps the key problem any locative religion faces, because all standards of judgment seem inevitably to be embedded in ordinary activity.

10. For the different notions, see *Xunzi* 27, K 2.5–6, 2/6/12–7/3; 160–165, K 23.2a–4a, 23/114/8–115/27; 41–42, K 9.9–11, 9/37/14–38/3; 141, K 22.2a, 22/108/8–10.

11. *Xunzi* 84, K 17.7, 17/81/16–82/4; 94, K 19.2b, 19/92/3–10; 96, K 19.3, 19/92/21–93/4.

12. A more specific cautionary note concerns difficulties in understanding Xunzi's idea of "spirit" *shen*. The notion never receives a sustained treatment; moreover, comments about it are often cryptic and occasionally appear in places that may not reflect his views. We cannot, that is, even always be sure if *shen* is an entity, a "spirit"; a force, the "spiritual"; or an attribute that someone may possess, the "spirited." (Xunzi seems to draw here on a set of general ideas about which we still know relatively little; see Yearley, "Zhuangzi's Understanding of Skillfulness and the Ultimate Spiritual State," in Paul Kjellberg and Philip J. Ivanhoe, eds., *Essays on Skepticism, Relativism and Ethics in the "Zhuangzi,"* pp. 175–176 and 182.)

We do, however, know some things of importance. Xunzi clearly has doubts about the reality of fearful, disorderly, and possibly vengeful spirits (鬼 *gui*), and he surely expresses sadness, and some contempt, for those who allow their lives to be dominated by ideas about them. *Xunzi* 110, K 19.11, 19/98/7–10; 134–135, K 21.8, 21/106/12–16. In contrast, he treats *shen* with respect. Most generally, he sees it as present if we see the efficacy or beneficial effect of a process but not its actual workings. *Xunzi* 80, K 17.2a–2b, 17/80/1–7. Most important to us, however, he thinks *shen* can transform individuals possessing it and those encountering them, not least because it informs perfected people's freedom from the deleterious effects of external occurrences. See, for example, *Xunzi* 69, K 15.2, 15/71/22–27; and 75, K 15.5, 15/74/1–7. Xunzi's treatment of *shen* manifests, then, an understanding of spiritual fulfillment that goes considerably beyond that found in his normal description of human excellence.

13. *Xunzi* 84–85, K 17.7, 17/81/16–82/3.

14. Versions of the idea of masochistic religion also appear in contemporary thinkers with theological concerns. Especially notable examples are Peter Berger, who draws from Sartre (see *The Sacred Canopy*) and Paul Ricouer, who draws from Freud, especially in his lengthy study of him.

Xunzi's criticisms of positions often center on the masochistic surrender they demand. He focuses, for instance, on the psychic state popular religion's fear of spirits induces; argues that a Daoist obsession with Heaven leads to a forgetting of the importance of human beings; and asserts that the traditionalist focus on past authorities leads to an overlooking of the need to act reflectively.

15. See *Xunzi* 83–84, K 17.7, 17/81/10–14; 125–126, K 21.4, 21/103/8–13; 134–135, K 21.8, 21/106/12–16.

16. Reinterpretations of traditional religious ideas and actions in a thinker like Xunzi have different forms depending on its object (a text or an action); the authority of its object (a statement from Kongzi or from a history); and the possibility of a precise verbal representation of its meaning (a simple declarative statement or a necessarily analogical formulation). Our focus here is on Xunzi's reinterpretation of complex objects with features whose authority is contested that inevitably escape precise representation.

17. *Xunzi* 135, K 21.8, 21/106/15–16; 85, K 17.8, 17/82/6–8; and 96–108, K 19.4a–9c, 19/93/6–97/5.

18. See *Xunzi* 94, K 19.2b, 19/92/3–10; 96, K 19.3, 19/92/21–93/4.

19. We need to recognize that Heaven, for Xunzi, may possess important characteristics of which we know nothing. His discussion of Heaven, that is, reflects the careful distinctions he makes in discussing human actions between possessing a capability and possessing a capability and choosing not to exercise it. That distinction means we can never know Heaven's character fully. See *Xunzi* 167–68, K 23.5b, 23/116/17–23; 79–80, K 17.1, 17/79/16–21; 81–82, K 17.3b, 17/80/17–19. (Xunzi never, however, even entertains the idea—prominent in some forms of Western spirituality and encapsulated in the notions of God's ordained and absolute will—that a real disjunction may be present between what the highest sacred reality really is or desires and what people think it is or desires.) For these and other reasons we need to treat more than just the chapter specifically on Heaven. It concentrates on the need to separate humans and Heaven because of the dangers that arise from failing to do so, and it seems to have (like many other chapters) a very definite audience in mind.

20. *Xunzi* 49, K 9.17, 9/40/8–9; 83–85, K 17.7, 17/81/4–82/8; 110, K 19.11, 19/98/7–10; 134–135, K 21.8, 21/106/12–16.

21. *Xunzi* 79–80, K 17.1, 17/79/16–21; see also 86, K 17.9–10, 17/82/10–18.

22. *Xunzi* 82, K 17.3b, 17/80/17–19; and 17, K 1.5, 1/2/3–7. At one place Xunzi declares that ritual, normally discussed as a human product, is most clearly and grandly evident in Heaven's actions. *Xunzi* 94, K 19.2b, 19/92/3–10. The passage fits uneasily enough with Xunzi's general perspective, unless it is read as a highly charged metaphoric presentation, that some people have doubted whether it either belongs in the text or manifests his mature thought. Whatever the truth here, I believe my characterization represents the central vision of Heaven we find in Xunzi.

23. *Xunzi* 80, K 17.2a–2b, 17/80/1–7; 82, 17.4–5, 17/80/21–81/2.

24. The main source for my idea of the numinous—and further specifications of it like majestic, mysterious, and fascinating—is Rudolf Otto's *Idea of the Holy*. Otto thinks it refers to only one side of the holy, believing that ethical and rational attributes constitute the other side, and that Christianity, and especially Luther, displays best the two sides of the divine. From Otto's perspective, then, Xunzi grasps only one feature, albeit a crucial feature, of the holy, and he errs when he attributes all (or virtually all) ethical and rational attributes to human beings. Otto's claim casts a distinctive light on Xunzi, on Xunzi's relationship to Mengzi, and on comparisons between Christianity and Confucianism when the subject is predicating qualities of the sacred. Moreover, it helps us probe general issues about the relationship of religion and ethics, a subject

on which Otto and classical Confucians manifest related but very different approaches that illuminate each other.

25. Xunzi implies that Heaven's numinous quality makes deformed reactions to it especially likely and potent. Many, perhaps all, such reactions can appear with the other two origins, but they are especially likely to occur if the relationship to Heaven is improper. Masochistic relationships to, for example, parents or teachers occur more frequently and powerfully, then, if one lacks an appropriate relationship to Heaven.

26. A related and far less controversial interpretative approach uses the idea of a horizon: that is, of a general framework that controls the character of our specific perceptions of and reactions to distinct events. Most people's normal horizon fails to highlight their frailty, but the death of significant people can fracture such a horizon. This change, moreover, affects how people react to a multitude of specific occurrences. What formerly was overlooked, seen as neutral, or thought to be easily surmountable can become a troubling, even terrifying event. The persistent cough, the lucky near miss, the conversation about a distant natural disaster now carry a new weight.

27. The notion of the primordial that I use here owes more to Otto and Eliade than it does to Jung or Freud, and Norman O. Brown probably gives the best recent account of it. One might consider using the "archaic" rather than the "primordial," especially because it can mean both beginning and root, but many common uses of the word "archaic" carry very misleading implications. Neither word is, then, adequate, nor are their neighbors in the same semantic field, words like "primeval," "primal," or "pristine," any better. They all imply overly crude views of human development whether the viewpoint prizes the more developed or the less developed. (The fact that we lack exact vocabulary in this area says a great deal about much larger problems in our understanding of the religious life.) Worth underlining, finally, is the relationship of aspects of the ideas of the primordial and of masochistic religion: the improper formation of the inclinations evident in masochistic religion is, for instance, a prominent feature of an inappropriate relationship to the primordial.

28. The question of understanding the emotions, especially as they relate to the mind and to dispositions, is a complex theoretical, historical, and comparative subject. Basic abstract issues are still contested; the West may not display a continuous tradition of thinking about a single set of phenomena, the "emotions"; and the situation outside the West is even more vexing. We are, for example, just beginning to grasp with some subtlety the understanding of 情 *qing* in early China. I do think it clear, however, that Xunzi both has a "cognitive" view of the emotions and often displays a remarkably sophisticated understanding of their various forms.

29. *Xunzi* 98–105, K 19.4c–8, 19/93/19–96/2.

30. Pretending can even resemble the more benign forms of self-deception, those that are a helpful, even necessary, response to certain situations. In these forms, people believe to be true what they also do not believe to be true. This induced duplicity is fueled by the recognition of how the state serves fundamental needs and nurtures basic capacities. In such cases, tempered contact with the primordial is, I think, crucial.

31. The role of belief, what I would call religious belief, in Xunzi's overall views is also relevant here. That is, his belief in the efficacy, and therefore necessity, of the death rituals exceeds any empirical confirmation he has or ever could obtain. Belief's

role in Xunzi differs in major ways from its role in, say, a figure like Luther or Calvin because the respective objects of belief differ. Nevertheless, we can easily overlook the role of religious belief in Xunzi (and other Confucians) if we think about belief only in the terms in which it appears in theistic religions with revealed texts.

A clear example of this is the role of Xunzi's belief in the sages. One can see the sages as highly intelligent social engineers who understood laws about human being that, in theory, most people could grasp. (Xunzi surely presents them in that way at times and, as noted, he even argues that we should follow the later sages because we know more about them.) The sages also, however, can be said to be figures who are what they are because of the mythic stories they inhabit. Seen this way, belief in the sages is part of one's belief in the true story that is a myth.

32. *Xunzi* 110, K 19.11, 19/98/7–10.

33. *Xunzi* 94–95, K 19.2c–2d, 19/92/12–19.

CHAPTER 5

Xunzi's Reinterpretation of Ritual

A Hermeneutic Defense of the Confucian Way

MARK BERKSON

Introduction

By the time of Xunzi's birth at the end of the fourth centuy b.c.e., Confucian ritual had come under attack from a number of directions, most significantly from the Mohists and the Daoists. For the Mohists, ritual was a wasteful, unnecessary activity that took away energy and resources from the valuable pursuits of creating wealth, population, and order in the state. For the Daoists, ritual was a form of artifice that prevented the spontaneous expression of our nature and thus cut us off from the rhythm of the *Dao*. Xunzi, the first systematic Confucian philosopher, took up the task of defending Confucian ritual from these philosophical attacks. At the same time, he faced another challenge. As someone who might be considered both a naturalist and a rationalist, Xunzi was disturbed by the beliefs in ghosts and spirits that motivated many individuals' participation in ritual, believing them to be not only misguided, but potentially harmful.[1]

Xunzi's response to these various challenges was largely an interpretive one. He wanted to defend the Confucian tradition by arguing for a particular understanding of ritual's origin, structure, and efficacy. In doing so, Xunzi provided a new Confucian interpretation that differed from that of his fellow Confucian Mengzi 孟子 (ca. 372–279 b.c.e.), who argued that the Confucian Way (including the specific rituals) is grounded in human nature with its ultimate source in 天 *tian*, Heaven. Thus, Xunzi's new hermeneutic and defense of ritual was a response to challenges from three sources—the Mengzian strand of Confucian thought, the Mohist and Daoist critics who tried to undermine the bases of participation in Confucian ritual, and the many people who participated in the rituals with a supernaturalist understanding. Xunzi had to both argue for the necessity of ritual activity for the individual and society and reinterpret the way rituals were understood, so as to make participation compelling during a period of significant changes in and diversity of worldviews.

In this essay, I will explore Xunzi's understanding of ritual and his hermeneutic achievement. I will show how he tries to address the challenges he sees through a number of related sophisticated philosophical positions that I describe as meta-level awareness and reflexivity, participant-observer consciousness, and symbolic realism. I begin by examining Xunzi's powerful description of death rituals; subsequent sections of the chapter shed light from a variety of perspectives on ritual in general and death rituals in particular.

Throughout the essay, I put Xunzi in conversation with modern Western thinkers. While it is impossible to undertake any sustained, in-depth comparative study here, it is still productive to set particular Xunzian insights against those of Western thinkers, each of whom is able to cast a revealing light on (and, at times, pose a provocative challenge to) an aspect of Xunzi's picture. Xunzi's approach, which is characterized by clarity, theoretical rigor, and systematicity, lends itself well to this type of modest comparative exercise. The challenges to particular aspects of Xunzi's picture will be posed primarily by Sigmund Freud's portrayal of ritual participation. Those thinkers whose projects are, in certain respects, similar to Xunzi, and whose categories of analysis will be applied to Xunzi's thought, are Robert Bellah and Roy Rappaport, whose ritual theory and religious vision resonate with Xunzi's.[2]

Ritual and the Meta-Level Perspective

Whereas every religious tradition has rituals in which participants express reverence for that which is sacred, Confucianism (especially in its Xunzian form), arguably more than most other traditions, at the same time reflects on and reveres ritual itself. A central aspect of Xunzi's vision is a meta-level reflection on ritual. An important chapter of Xunzi's writing "A Discussion of Rites" *Lilun* 禮論 probes deeply into ritual's origin, foundation, benefits, beauty, and significance. Xunzi's theoretical achievements are made possible by his meta-level perspective. This perspective is not that of the removed intellectual; it plays a central religious role and is essential to his "daology." The cultivated person not only participates in and deeply appreciates ritual, but also *reflects* on the formal, expressive, transformative, aesthetic, and symbolic dimensions of ritual.

Xunzi believes that human beings should have reverence not only for that toward which ritual directs us but also toward ritual itself, for ritual both makes possible and makes manifest the goods Confucians value most: the deep and proper connection with other human beings, the community, the sociopolitical order, and the cosmos. Ritual develops, sustains, and expresses human relationship and community. Our relationship is both with others who live among us and with those who lived in the past, for in participating in ritual, we are participating in—in a sense, submitting to—meanings we ourselves did not create. In Roy Rappaport's terms, "the performers of rituals do not specify all the acts and utterances constituting their own performances."[3] They are encoded "by other than the performers."

Much of Xunzi's reflection on ritual deals with the general characteristics of ritual (in addition to his treatment of particular Confucian rituals, such as death rituals) and thus can contribute to any ritual theory. The formal elements of ritual are among those aspects analyzed and venerated. Like Xunzi, Roy Rappaport focuses largely on the formal structure of ritual, arguing that simply from looking at ritual's formal features one can understand why it is the "basic social act." Rappaport lists what he describes as the "logical entailments" of ritual, which include "the establishment of convention . . . the investment of whatever it encodes with morality . . . the sanctification of the conventional order."[4] These very entailments, for Confucians, are worthy of reverence (in addition to the specific object of focus of any particular ritual, e.g., birth or marriage, the bounties of the earth). Beyond the concern for whatever it is that a specific ritual is enacting, expressing, or symbolizing, Xunzi also has a reverential concern for the very logical entailments of the ritual form, ritual *simpliciter*. This is significant because these entailments are independent of the ontological status of the object of any specific ritual and so not dependent on the actual existence of any *particular* object, such as a ghost or spirit or a responsive Heaven. Xunzi, therefore, can preserve the ritual even while dispensing with the putative objects of the ritual (that toward which the ritual is directed, what the ritual is seemingly *about*) because of what the formal structure of the ritual does on numerous levels—aesthetic, expressive, symbolic, and so forth.

Through continued ritual performance and study, one not only cultivates important virtues and emotions, but one also comes to a deeper understanding of, and reverence for, ritual itself—what makes it possible, effective, and valuable, what makes it the *essential humanizing activity*. So when ritual points in the direction of the sacred, it is always pointing, in part, to itself.

An Example: Death Rituals

Grief and Mourning

For Xunzi, the most important Confucian rituals are those surrounding death, for following the death of a loved one there is a great threat of instability and disorder at both the individual and social levels. It is during such times that the power and beauty of ritual can be seen most clearly.[5] In this section, I use the work of modern anthropologists, psychologists, and philosophers to demonstrate the depth, validity, and relevance of Xunzi's explanation of death rituals.

The human response to the death of a loved one involves both strong emotions and changes in behavior. Among the commonly described emotions are sadness, anger, fear, guilt, despair, disbelief, loneliness, and numbness. Behavioral changes often include loss of appetite, disruption of work activities, loss of interest in things ordinarily interesting, a decrease in sociability, disrupted sleep, and disturbing dreams. Paul Rosenblatt writes, "If people who are bereaved are to return to reasonably normal patterns of productivity and social life, they need to 'work through' the loss. Working through processes include acceptance of the loss, extinction of no longer adaptive behavioral dispositions . . . and dissipation of guilt, anger and other disruptive emotions."[6]

Xunzi gives a detailed and moving account of Confucian death rituals in his chapter on rites. Xunzi recognizes that powerful feelings of grief normally accompany the death of a loved one and that these feelings can become harmful or pathological if they are not properly expressed:

> Everyone is at times visited by sudden feelings of depression and melancholy longing. . . . A filial son who has lost a parent, even when he is enjoying himself among congenial company, will be overcome by such feelings. If they come to him and he is greatly moved, but does nothing to give them expression, then his emotions of remembrance and longing will be frustrated and unfulfilled, and he will feel a sense of deficiency in his ritual behavior.[7]

The rituals provide an outlet for that grief, taking the raw emotion and cultivating a beautiful form of spiritual communion with the deceased that brings higher goods to the mourner. "The sacrificial rites originate in the emotions of remembrance and longing, express the highest degree of loyalty, love, and reverence, and embody what is finest in ritual conduct."[8] As we will see, they also provide for a gradual return to normal life, as the transition period is difficult and fraught with danger to the psyche.

While the responses of grief and mourning are parts of human nature for Xunzi, as they are for Mengzi, that does not in any way make them moral—it means that they are only *potentially* moral, but because of their raw power, they are also potentially dangerous to the individual and the larger community.[9] Xunzi focuses on these responses as being the origin of the rites, as they are for Mengzi. But he indicates the damage they can do if they are "frustrated and unfulfilled." For Xunzi, human nature is completely amoral; we are born with no innate moral tendencies, no inner moral guide. We should never simply follow and nurture our natural responses. Rather, the application of conscious activity is required to shape the raw material given to us into something ordered and flourishing, something that will become a beautiful expression rather than a harmful discharge of energy. Ritual, the product of conscious activity, is what does the shaping and molding. Ritual is not an *expression* of human nature, as it is for Mengzi; rather, it is the *transformer* of human nature.

Ambivalence and Emotional Conflict

Death rituals must help mourners deal with conflicting emotions and ambivalent attitudes. For example, mourners face the conflict between the knowledge that the loved one is dead and the inability to face or come to terms with that fact (cognitively, emotionally, or behaviorally). Confucian death rituals provide a moving example of the maintenance of important contradictions for the sake of both stability and meaning. Xunzi recognizes that the mourner is in a state of conflict, because she knows that the loved one is gone, but cannot come to admit that fact. The death ritual allows for this by treating the dead "as though" alive: "In the funeral rites, one adorns the dead as though they were still living, and sends them to the grave with forms symbolic of life. They are treated as though dead, and yet as though still alive, as though gone, and yet as though still present. Beginning and end are thereby unified."[10] There is no naive self-deception here, for the mourner knows the loved one is dead. The mourner is engaging in a sophisticated form of pretending that creates a healthy outlet for the emotions.

The challenges of ambivalence can be addressed effectively in the symbolic and aesthetic realms of ritual; symbols, art, and ritual are able to sustain and often reconcile deep psychological tensions in ways that logic and discursive reason cannot. The richness of human experience requires this ability, and it is accomplished through symbolic objects and actions. In Xunzi's description of death rituals, an object can both be present and absent; an act can be "scripted" yet "spontaneous"; one can be treated "as if alive" and "as if dead." "Beauty and ugliness, music and weeping, joy and sorrow are opposites, and yet rites make use of them all, bringing forth and employing each in its turn."[11]

In observing the process of mourning, Sigmund Freud, like Xunzi, also recognizes the prominent role of such tensions. He cites a number of cases of patients refusing to accept the death of a loved one. He describes the process whereby the ego splits, with one part accepting death and the other denying it. He writes, "This disavowal is always supplemented by an acknowledgment; two contrary and independent attitudes always arise and result in the situation of there being a splitting of the ego."[12] Freud describes a child's reaction to his father's sudden death: "I know father's dead, but what I can't understand is why he doesn't come home to supper." Likewise, Xunzi writes about the filial son who observes his lord or parent no longer breathing: "Weeping and trembling, he still cannot stop hoping that the dead will somehow come back to life; he has not yet ceased to treat the dead man as living."[13]

One of the ways that Confucian ritual allows for the proper expression of these contradictory thoughts and emotions is through the inclusion of altered objects in the coffin. While these will supposedly "accompany" the individual, the mourner acknowledges that they will not actually be employed by rendering them unusable. Xunzi writes:

> Articles that had belonged to the dead when he was living are gathered together and taken to the grave with him, symbolizing that he has not changed his dwelling. But only token articles are taken, not all that he used, and though they have their regular shape, they are rendered unusable. . . . A dead man is treated as though he had merely changed his dwelling, and yet it is made clear that he will never use these things . . . the spirit articles prepared especially for the dead man have the shape of real objects but cannot be used.[14]

This is known in anthropological terms as a "tie-breaking ritual." The strong ties to the deceased make reentry into everyday life and the learning of new behaviors difficult. Thus, ritually marking the end of the relationship (and the beginning of a new one based solely on memory) becomes important. There are many types of tie-breaking customs, including disposal of personal property of the deceased and taboos on the name of the deceased. In modern Taiwan, there are rituals in which each family member "takes hold with one hand of a long, hempen rope, one end of which is attached to the sleeve of the dead person." Each portion of the rope is then cut, "whereupon each person wraps up his portion in a sheet of silver Hades money and burns it. This is called 'cutting off lots.' "[15]

Rappaport states that Arnold Van Gennep "observed that particular kinds of rituals tend to include physical acts that seem to be formally similar to whatever they seek to accomplish. Rites of separation, for instance, often include such acts as cutting something, perhaps the hair."[16] This is making material and observable what is nonmaterial. The materiality of the display, Rappaport suggests, makes it "performatively stronger" than a merely verbal act. One invests more of oneself in physically breaking an object belonging to a loved one than in merely saying words to the effect that he is gone forever. This greater investment makes it more likely that the survivor will accept the death and begin to develop emotions and behaviors better suited to the transformed relationship.

Such rituals are part of the process of coming to accept the death. Rosenblatt writes, "A person at a funeral who voluntarily engages in some effortful acts that indicate acceptance of the death (such as pallbearing or shoveling dirt onto the newly interred coffin) would find it dissonant or inconsistent with self-perceptions to behave in the future as though the death had not occurred and would be inclined to perceive oneself as accepting of the death."[17]

Facilitating Transition

It has been said that the mourner has two powerful conflicting desires to combat at a funeral: the desire to jump into the grave with the deceased (the inability to let go) and the desire to run away (the revulsion at the corpse). The death rituals must account for both, allowing for their proper (and nonpathological) expression and harmonization.[18] Robert Jay Lifton writes of the "universal dilemma around ties to the dead: on the one hand, the survivor's need to embrace them, pay homage to them, and join in various rituals to perpetuate the relationship to them; on the other his tendency to push them away, to consider them tainted and unclean, dangerous and threatening."[19] There is always a combination of impurity and taboo associated with the dead, on the one hand, and the continuing sense of love and connection on the other.[20]

Revulsion at the sight of the corpse is a problem that must be addressed by ritual.[21] The funeral ceremony must account for both the passage of the deceased from taboo corpse to revered ancestor and the passage of the survivor from grieving mourner to nonmourner. Xunzi is doing just this when he writes:

> It is custom in all mourning rites to keep changing and adorning the appearance of the dead person, to keep moving him farther and farther away, and as time passes, to return gradually to one's regular way of life. It is the way with the dead that, if they are not adorned, they become ugly, and if they become ugly, then one will feel no grief for them. Similarly, if they are kept too close by, one becomes contemptuous of their presence. . . . The gentleman is ashamed to have such a thing happen, and therefore he adorns the dead in order to maintain the proper reverence, and in time returns to his regular way of life in order to look after the wants of the living.[22]

The funeral ritual must allow for the transition from the aspect of taint and pollution to connectedness and cherished memory. Lifton writes, "What is involved is the symbolic transformation of a threatening, inert image (of the corpse) into a vital image of eternal continuity (the soul)—or of death as absolute severance to death as an aspect of continuous life."[23] This is because, he goes on, "Survivors' psychological needs include *both* connection and separation." Xunzi allows for a gradual separation and a return to everyday life while carefully maintaining the connection at each step. This way, the necessary severance can occur within what Lifton calls, "a sustaining matrix of connection."

There are a variety of pathologies that might emerge in the aftermath of the death of a loved one. One is known as "morbid grief reaction syndrome," where the mourner might "delay or postpone mourning for weeks, months or even years after the death of a loved one. He may show very little concern or reaction to the death when it occurs."[24] Such a response often leads to disabling or antisocial manifestations of grief in disguised forms, at later times or in unexpected ways. Another is "pathological mourning" or "prolonged grief disorder," related to Freud's description of melancholia. This occurs when the grieving person is unable to let go of the deceased, attempting to preserve as exactly as possible the objects or residence of the deceased and to continue, without alteration, the behavior and activities that the mourner carried out before the death.

For Freud, the crucial "working through" process is described as a labor in which the testing of reality occurs and the "ego succeeds in freeing its libido from the lost object."[25] This process is carried out "bit by bit," having the "nature of a compromise."[26] For Xunzi, this process can only be accomplished by ritual, for it allows for the gradual, step-by-step return to reality that is the balance between a jarring, sudden resumption of normal activity (in which case, grief will be suppressed and the mourner will feel "frustrated and unfulfilled") or the lingering inability to adjust to the new reality.[27] Xunzi observes:

> When a wound is deep, it takes many days to heal; where there is great pain, the recovery is slow. . . . The (mourning period) comes to an end with the twenty-fifth month. At that time, the grief and pain have not yet come to an end, and one still thinks of the dead with longing, but ritual decreed that the mourning shall end at this point. Is it not because the attendance on the dead must sometime come to an end, and the moment has arrived to return to one's daily life?[28]

Ultimately, Xunzi contends, the period of bereavement must be ritually terminated. This does not mean that the pain will be gone. Rather, it means that one must force oneself to reestablish a routine even when one does not want to. This required "return to the everyday" recognizes the danger of an ever-deepening spiral of sadness and pain after the death of a loved one. As we have seen, the rituals allow these feelings, in all of their power, to be given time in which to be expressed. At the same time, the rituals recognize that reentering one's everyday life routine is an essential part of the healing process. It is a way of reconnecting with the world.

We can also imagine cases where someone is emotionally ready to return, or simply wants to reenter the everyday world, but is worried about appearances. For this reason as well, there is a ritually approved moment, often represented in contemporary Chinese culture by the second or final burial, in which one is "allowed" to terminate the formal mourning process. Death rituals involve two kinds of passages—the deceased moves from the realm of the living to that of the dead, a status change that must be culturally marked and accepted (there may be further passages at later times for the deceased, but this first one is fundamental), and at the same time, loved ones move from nonmourners to mourners to nonmourners once again. The second or "final" burial can be seen as a "mechanism that may work to promote the readjustment process" for loved ones.[29] It is this type of ceremony that can mark the official end to the bereavement period and the transition back to nonmourner; it can represent final acceptance of the loss and a "commitment to terminate mourning."[30]

It is on precisely this point that James Harold critiques Xunzi. Harold argues that Xunzian ritual "forces agents to act in ways that alienate her from her feelings," which is a problem for virtue theorists who value the authentic expression of emotions as part of the flourishing life.[31] Harold claims that since Confucian death rituals set a limit on mourning behavior, this forces a mourner to conform to the ritual at the expense of powerful feelings with which he still identifies, resulting in alienation.

As we have seen, emotions—including, and perhaps especially, those with which we strongly identify—can take a pathological turn. If fully expressed, they would run counter to our well-being. In its extreme form, "prolonged grief disorder," grief can produce such extended suffering that, according to Dr. M. Katherine Shear, "it takes a person away from humanity and has no redemptive value."[32]

For this reason, Harold's emphasis on the importance of following our most powerful feelings is problematic. Xunzi, like Freud, reminds us that our natural feelings and desires are fundamentally conflicted. Morality and self-cultivation cannot simply involve being "authentic" to the strongest emotion of the moment, as that may be harmful to ourselves and others. This is a crucial lesson that children must learn, and we all must be reminded of it, particularly at times of crisis when intensely powerful emotions such as anger and grief can cause us harm. This is precisely why ritual is so essential. Harold states, "If I really think of myself in terms of my grief, cannot imagine myself without it, and so on, then the fact that such grief may be objectively unhealthy for me matters not at all."[33] Well, it certainly should matter, as the ultimate goal here is not the unbridled expression of emotion or being true to all of one's emotions (which is impossible, as they are often in tension with each other); the goal is flourishing (or, at the very least, functioning). And to attain some form of well-being, harmful emotions and desires must be shaped and reformed, not clung to in a misguided form of "authenticity."[34]

For Xunzi, the fact that our emotions and desires are so deeply conflicted means that if we were allowed to just follow our natural desires without ritual cultivation, the inevitable result would be not only a diminishment of well-being but also alienation from some portions of ourselves. To follow some desires—such as the desire to be close to the dead—is to become alienated from others—the desire to return to everyday life. In other words, *without* ritual to reconcile conflicting feelings and desires, alienation is inevitable.

The Freudian Challenge

We have seen that there is much in common between Xunzi's and Freud's views of the divided, conflicted self and their understanding of the work that must be done to avoid pathological mourning. However, Xunzi's ritual-based solution to these problems would appear vulnerable to Freudian criticism. Sigmund Freud, as we know, was one of religion's most devastating critics. In the same way that he undermined the foundations of self-understanding, agency, and even love, he also told religious practitioners that their most sublime spiritual moments were nothing more than infantile wish fulfillment. Many who attempt to defend the role of religion in human life begin by rejecting much of the Freudian picture. Xunzi, however, undertook a critique of religion in his own time that was analogous to Freud's in many ways, including arguments against supernaturalism and wish-fulfillment. Thus, in many important ways, Xunzi's religious vision cannot be an easy target for Freudian criticism and possibly poses a compelling alternative that manages to preserve certain forms of religious practice in light of Freud's radical challenge. Examining how Xunzi's vision would stand up to Freudian critique enables us to see why Xunzian Confucianism has such relevance to us in the post-Freudian world.

In his most direct piece on religious ritual, "Obsessive Acts and Religious Practices," Freud argues that rituals can be understood as examples of obsessive acts that undermine proper human functioning and adaptation. He begins by noting "the similarity between obsessive acts in neurotics and those religious observances by means of which the faithful give expression to piety."[35] He portrays those who are "addicted" to obsessive acts as those who suffer from obsessive thoughts and ideas.

For Xunzi, ritual is part of human conscious activity (artifice) based on the ability of the mind to make distinctions, which he believes is essentially human. A possible pathological result of the ability to make distinctions, however, is getting stuck on one thing, becoming obsessed. Xunzi is acutely aware of this problem, and an entire chapter of his book is devoted to "dispelling obsession" *jiebi* 解蔽.

Clearly, there are important differences in the two thinkers' understanding of obsession. But if we bracket the overwhelming focus on sexual desires in Freud (admittedly, with very large brackets), we find that much is shared between the two thinkers' concerns with obsessive behavior. Xunzi observes that the mind can be obsessed by anything that provokes a reaction out of it: "Since each of the myriad things evokes a different reaction, there is none that could not obsess the mind. This is a universal flaw of the operation of the mind."[36]

For Xunzi, the obsession of the ritual participant is a significant problem, but there is also another problem about which he is concerned: the "detached observer," who is reflective and alienated. For him, such an attitude is highly problematic; the ritual is robbed of all of its power, for it is seen as false. Rappaport writes that the conscious minds of those who refuse to partake in ritual expression "become divorced from those deep and hidden portions of themselves to which ritual participation introduced and bound them. . . . The self becomes fragmented and some of the fragments may be lost."[37]

Xunzi tries to cultivate an approach that avoids both obsession and alienation, a form of participant-observer consciousness, bringing together reflectiveness and a sophisticated theoretical awareness, on the one hand, and a full cognitive, affective, and physical commitment on the other. He writes, "He who dwells in ritual and can *ponder* it well may be said to know how to think."[38] Unlike Freud, he believes that these can coexist and that each can strengthen the other; the ability, however, must be cultivated.

A word must be said about the notion of "theoretical awareness" in the ritual context. Robert Campany makes the insightful point that theorizing about ritual is itself a *practice*, a practice done for a reason. In Xunzi's case, one reason it is done is to "alter ritual practice as a social reality."[39] So theorizing and ritual practice are certainly deeply intertwined, each transforming the other. However, Campany argues, they are *not* aspects of the same practice, they are *separate* practices. A person cannot be engaged in both simultaneously; they are different modes. Campany writes, "Quite simply, *theoretical* thinking about ritual practice is thinking from the point of view of a spectator, and this entails giving an account of ritual from a point of view outside ritual, using a language and a framework of understanding that are not derived from the ritual world but in terms of which that world is nevertheless described."[40]

It is probably true that sages did not explicitly theorize when involved in highly formal ritual practice; therefore, Campany has a point when he highlights the difference between the activity of theoretical thinking and the absorption in ritual. By Xunzi's own criteria, if Xunzi had thought through the structure of his "On Rituals" chapter while at a loved one's funeral, it would have been an example of poor ritual practice.

Nevertheless, Xunzi's picture does not completely separate the theoretical from the practical. While a sage might not discursively theorize during ritual practice, his point of view, his orientation in ritual, is *informed* by theoretical awareness and sophisticated interpretive strategies. Furthermore, for Xunzi, the understanding of ritual at this theoretical level is deepened through ritual practice itself, so practice must have some effect on the activity of theorizing. Xunzi's theory emerges from his own participation, which involves a dimension of theoretical awareness; this act of observation and reflection assumes the ability to step back and mentally embrace the ritual as a whole (each act is embedded in the larger context of the ritual, which is itself embedded in a larger system of meaning that extends outward both spatially and temporally). While the body is involved in the moment-to-moment postures and sensory awareness of sights, sounds, smells, textures, and utterances, the mind is directed toward larger contexts of meaning. The postures, sights, sounds, and aromas themselves play a significant role in bringing about expanded awareness, which leads to a deeper appreciation of the ritual act.[41]

In sum, Xunzi worries about the same type of practitioner of ritual that Freud worries about—the one who is unaware of the significance of the event, who submits to it without understanding its meaning, who employs a false consciousness of seeing this created, artificial ritual as having divine origin or supernatural explanation or efficacy. This can lead to a dangerous loss of perspective, and any gains in social order can be losses in terms of individual obsession. Xunzi provides a highly sophisticated answer to this problem by advocating the cultivation of reflectiveness in ritual practitioners. He asks us to be both participant and observer. To accomplish this, the participant must cultivate an "as if" attitude that combines a full investment in ritual with an awareness of its created, symbolic nature.

The "As If" Attitude

Xunzi frequently employs the term 如 *ru*, "as if"—in fact, we might say that it is one of his most important hermeneutic contributions. Here is one representative passage where Xunzi, using the character *ru* (translated "as though," which I have italicized in the passage), shifts the interpretation of a ritual from a literal, supernatural one to one that is symbolic:

> When conducting a sacrifice . . . one speaks to the invocator *as though* the spirit of the dead were really going to partake of the sacrifice. One takes up each of the offerings and presents them *as though* the spirit were really going to taste them. . . . When the guests leave, the sacrificer . . . weeps *as though* the spirit had really departed along with them. How full of grief it is, how reverent! One serves the dead *as though* they were living, the departed *as though* present, giving body to the bodiless and thus fulfilling the proper form of ceremony.[42]

Some therapists argue that it is important for the patient to learn to take on this attitude toward symbols in order for therapy to be successful. Rosemary Gordon writes that if the symbolizing move is never made, then the " 'symbolic' content might very well remain ineffectual in terms of stimulating the growth and development of the person. In fact without the 'as if' attitude a symbolic content may either be acted out in a delusionary manner, or else it may lie around like deadwood, like an *objet d'art* in a collector's glass case."[43]

Xunzi is concerned with both of these problems. He is concerned with those for whom the objects do not resonate, for whom the symbols have lost their power. He is also worried about people reading the objects literally rather than symbolically, which would lead to delusion (e.g., believing in the existence of ghosts, spirits, and an intervening heaven).[44]

Freud argues that the "as-if" attitude must be dismissed if we are to free ourselves from religious illusion. In *The Future of an Illusion*, Freud writes:

> I am reminded of one of my children who was distinguished at an early age by a peculiarly marked matter-of-factness. Whenever the children were being told a fairy-story and were listening to it with rapt attention, he would come up and ask, 'Is that a true story?' When he was told it was not, he would turn away with a look of disdain. We may expect that people will soon behave in the same way towards the fairy tales of religion, in spite of the advocacy of 'As if.'[45]

For Freud, living the "as if" is living in the realm of fantasy and delusion. The motive for seeking refuge in such fairy tales is comfort and protection. But Freud's criticism clearly does not apply to Xunzi, who uses the term "as if" in a fully self-conscious way. Xunzi's sages not only act "as if," they are fully aware that this is what they are doing and of why they are doing it. The Confucian tradition involves nothing like what Freud describes as the essence of *the* religious illusion:

> Over each of us there watches a benevolent Providence which is only seemingly stern and which will not suffer us to become a plaything of the over-mighty and pitiless forces of nature. Death itself is not extinction, is not a return to inorganic lifelessness, but the beginning of a new kind of existence which lies on the path of development to something higher.[46]

Xunzi's vision clearly is not of this sort, as he too rejects these beliefs. Instead of offering a picture of a benevolent deity and immortal soul to provide solace to the mourner, Xunzi elucidates the way the symbolizing attitude, the "as if" (*ru* 如), can reconcile the very tensions that Freud sees operating ("as if alive/as if dead") and thus help the mourner through the difficult transition. Xunzi argues that it is one of the unique benefits of ritual that it can embrace and harmonize opposites. Gordon observes:

> the ability to symbolize, which is the most essential ingredient in all creative endeavor, rests very firmly indeed on the capacity to accept both activity and passivity, the forces of life and the forces of death, tensions and effort as well as surrender; in short, it involves the coming to terms with paradox.[47]

In order for ritual to function in this way without the risk of obsession, the participant must be aware of the symbolic nature of ritual objects and actions. The question this raises is, What happens in a person's consciousness when she participates in a ritual that she knows is scripted and contingent? Does her consciousness impinge on the power of ritual or enrich it? Xunzi argues for the latter.

All this time, the employer of participant-observer consciousness is aware of the paradox but also of the necessity of it.[48] Ritual participation can be seen, perhaps, as a form of sophisticated pretending or play, artificial and invented, yet necessary for conflicted and fragile beings such as ourselves.

The Hierarchy of Understanding

One of the challenges in the Xunzian approach to ritual is that, at the highest level, people must participate fully in ritual while maintaining an awareness of its invented and symbolic nature. However, Xunzi recognizes that not all participants in ritual will have the same understanding. In the following passage, Xunzi describes the various approaches to ritual:

> Only a sage can fully understand (the rites). The sage understands them, the gentleman finds comfort in carrying them out, the officials are careful to maintain them, and the common people accept them as custom. To the gentleman they are a part of the way of man; to the common people, they are something pertaining to spirits.[49]

This passage, which presents a "hierarchy of understanding," suggests that people with a "lower-level" understanding are able to participate in and benefit from the rites alongside those with a "higher-level" understanding. However, Xunzi clearly advocates the fuller, richer understandings of the gentleman and sage:

> If you pray for rain and there is no rain, what of that? I say there is no special relationship—as when you do not pray for rain and there is rain. . . . When Heaven sends drought, we pray for rain; and before we decide any important undertaking, we divine with bone and milfoil. We do these things not because we believe that such ceremonies will produce the results we seek, but because we want to embellish such occasions with ceremony. Thus, the gentleman considers such ceremonies as embellishment (*wen*, "cultural creations"), but the common people consider them supernatural. *To consider them embellishments is fortunate; to consider them supernatural is unfortunate.*[50]

Xunzi is explicit here. While human beings depend on the bounties of Heaven, and should show the proper gratitude for all that it brings, Heaven is not responsive to human prayers, wishes, or desires. There is no personal, reciprocal relationship. Heaven does not possess intentionality, it does not reward or punish. Heaven's way is constant, and its way is one of patterns and regularities with occasional disruptions and irregularities. None of this is in response to anything human beings do; but what human beings do must take into account Heaven's way if we are to harmonize with it.

We see that, for Xunzi, symbolic, reflective understanding does not diminish participation; in fact, it enhances it. It allows the participant to see the power of the ritual to shape and harmonize, to both reflect and create important attitudes and feelings. And importantly, it avoids the risks inherent in the lower rungs of the hierarchy—obsession, the neglect of one's duties and avoidance of responsibility, and abandonment of the reality principle through literalist, supernatural interpretations. In Xunzi's terms, those at the lower end of the hierarchy know only the "model" or "form" of ritual (法 *fa*); they lack, however, the "explanation" or "interpretation" (說 *shuo*).

However, none of this means that the ritual is ineffective for those without such understanding. In fact, it is one of the strengths of Xunzi's picture that it recognizes that many people can participate and come together in the solidarity of shared ritual while their interpretations and understandings differ. This is because common people and sages alike share the same model or form, even though the common people lack the understanding or interpretation. Xunzi writes, "No sage could improve on ritual principles. They are the model for conduct for the common lot of men, although they do not understand them, and are the model for sages, who do understand them."[51] Furthermore, the common people depend on the sages in a number of ways. In order for the rituals to be efficacious for the common people, there must be sages to maintain the proper rituals and guide the participation of the common people. Without such guidance, the common people, according to T. C. Kline III, "will invariably fail to properly fulfill ritual and end up losing much of the efficacy of the ritual order."[52]

Despite the cognitive differences in the way people understand ritual, ritual works powerfully on other levels—for example, the affective and somatic. Catherine Bell argues, "Some level or degree of social consensus does not depend upon shared information or beliefs."[53] Scholars from a variety of disciplines support this. Bell states that the work of James Fernandez shows that ritual is effective in promoting solidarity precisely "*because* it rarely makes an interpretation explicit."[54] The ritual's focus is on common symbols, forms, movements, and sounds—not statements of belief. Bell, summing up James Watson's study of the Taiwanese cult of Mazu, writes: "Watson concludes that the genius of

Chinese policies for national unity lay in their imposition of ritual structures (form), not dogmatic beliefs (content)."[55]

Symbolic Realism

The divergence between Freud's and Xunzi's thought can be illuminated by an examination of the role of symbols in their theories. Freud clearly understood the power of symbols. Both Freud's psychoanalytic method and his analysis of larger cultural forces are grounded in the interpretation of symbols, primarily those that appear in dreams and myths.[56] For Freud, the unconscious makes use of symbols to disguise repressed, forbidden desires; these symbols must then be decoded by the analyst. Symbolization is one of the mechanisms that distort the latent content of a dream into the manifest content, for instance. Freud also notes that the precise nature of physical symptoms might originate in a symbolic event. David Stafford-Clark explains that, for Freud, "physical suffering could occur through symbolization alone."[57] One of Freud's patients, suffering from facial neuralgia, described a "bitter insult" from her husband that was "like a slap in the face," a remark that turned out to be a point of origin for her symptom.[58] Another patient, who experienced sharp pains in her forehead, recalled being observed by her grandmother with a look "so piercing that she felt it had gone right into her brain."[59]

While cases such as these illustrate Freud's focus on the role of symbolization in the particular history of the individual, he was also aware that many symbols have a universal dimension (most famously, phallic symbols), and myths and folklore provide a rich repository of symbols from which to draw. In all cases, the symbols must be unveiled and decoded in order to reveal the sexual and aggressive drives underneath. The Freudian psychoanalytic project is one of uncovering, going underneath the surface. For Freud, symbols function primarily as clever disguises in which our forbidden desires are cloaked. However, he fails to appreciate the way that symbols (particularly religious symbols) and rituals can be transformative because of their power to put people in deeper touch with reality or harmonize them with the social and natural world around them.

On the other hand, Xunzi can be understood as a "symbolic realist," a term borrowed from Robert Bellah.[60] Bellah is a thinker whose task is, in many ways, consonant with that of Xunzi—offering a reinterpretation of religious notions that conveys the powerful truths of human life, is not in contradiction with natural or social science, and can appeal to intellectuals who find themselves faced with the choice between abandoning religion and reinterpreting it. Here is one definition Bellah provides: "Symbolic realism simply holds that religious symbols are not primarily social or psychological projection systems (though they contain some projective elements), but the ways in which persons and societies express their sense of the fundamental nature of reality, the totality of experience."[61] My claim is that those at the higher rungs of Xunzi's "hierarchy of understanding"—the gentleman, the sage—are essentially symbolic realists.

Xunzi frequently speaks explicitly of the symbolic function (象 *xiang*) of ritual and music. For example, one section is entitled "The Symbolism of Music" *Shengyue zhi xiang* 聲樂之象.[62] There Xunzi writes, "The drum symbolizes/represents vastness and grandeur; the bell, fullness and wholeness; the chime stone, restrained control." Examples from his discussion of death rituals include: "Hence the three months of preparation for burial symbolizes that one wishes to provide for the dead as one would for the living."[63] He also discusses the symbolic role of such ritual accoutrements as "the mourning garments and cane, the mourning hut and gruel, the mat of twigs and the pillow of earth."[64] Robert Campany provides a helpful description of Xunzi's use of symbols: "Aspects of the burial—the 'forms' (貌 *mao*) of various constructed objects—likewise 'imitate' or 'symbolize' aspects of the world of the living from which the dead person is now separate: the form of the grave mound imitates (or symbolizes) that of a house, coffins imitate carriages, coffin covers imitate wall hangings in a room."[65]

One problem that we face in modernity is the split that often seems to exist between the "rationalist and the believer," the social scientist and the ritual practitioner. Freud believed that one could not be both. There exists, he argued, a choice between painful truth and seemingly comforting but ultimately harmful delusion. Freud argued that science and religion must inevitably be in conflict, as the former is built upon but the latter rejects the reality principle. This is why Freud argues that religion is a "threat to the advance of the Enlightenment and natural science."[66] An approach to religious ritual grounded in the reality principle is not an option that Freud seems to have entertained. While Freud had a sophisticated appreciation of symbols in the context of dreams and literature, he never acknowledged the therapeutic possibilities of conscious symbolization in religious ritual. Xunzi, on the other hand, believed that we can be both practitioners and scientists, and he was not just a reverent participant in Confucian ritual but also a theorist who explained, analyzed, and interpreted ritual. The explicit recognition of the symbolic dimension of ritual and its psychological efficacy is central to Xunzi's approach.

The reductionistic social scientist searches for truth *behind* the symbols. The symbols are viewed as concealing the truth. For Freud, symbols disguise; they are the cloak that is placed over the contents of the unconscious so as to protect the ego against their threats (this masking function is what allows them past the censors). Freud's goal was to use the symbols to get beyond them, to unearth the unconscious urges underneath them. Symbols, therefore, were useful and important in the process of psychoanalysis, but only for purposes of discovery, not for the process of healing itself.

Xunzi tells us that the truth lies not behind the symbols but *in* them; in fact, it cannot be expressed in any other way. The symbols do not hide or distort reality; they are often the only way to fully express, apprehend, or experience reality. The symbolic realist tells us that those things that are manifested in and shaped through ritual symbols—nonmaterial, vitally important aspects of human experience such as reverence, benevolence, grief, loyalty, connectedness—these are *real* and cannot be reduced to some other language or explained away. For Xunzi, the primary objects of reverence are classified as the 三本 *sanben*, three roots or bases, which are (1) Heaven and earth, (2) Ancestors, and (3) Rulers and Teachers.[67] Xunzi argues that ghosts and spirits have no place here. The rituals are directed at those things that make our natural and social lives possible. Heaven and earth nourish and sustain us, making life possible; ancestors are the roots of the family, which nurtures and supports us; rulers and teachers educate us and bring about order. What we are worshipping, therefore, when we engage in ritual practice, are life, family, and order. Given how important, but often overlooked and taken for granted, these things are, ritual and symbols have a crucial role to play in our lives.[68]

In sum, while Freud and Xunzi both acknowledge the power of human instinctual drives, the presence of conflict and ambivalence in the human mind, the tendency to flee into supernaturalism and wish-fulfillment, and the problem of obsession, they diverge starkly when it comes to their understanding of the function of symbols and thus the possible therapeutic function of rituals. Whereas for Freud symbols serve to mask forbidden desires and disguise reality, for Xunzi symbols can be the most powerful way to represent nonmaterial aspects of reality that are fundamentally important to our humanity and our place in the world. In Confucian thought, symbols are a way to face reality, to come to terms with even those aspects of reality that are threatening or painful (such as death). Thus, the symbolic dimension of ritual in Xunzi's thought can accomplish the very tasks Freud sees as vital to human well-being, such as accepting loss. The drives and appetites that result in neuroses in Freud's model are, in Xunzi's model, reshaped and channeled largely through the power of symbols and ritual.

Ritual as True Fiction

The role of the "as if" attitude and the centrality of creative symbolization in Xunzi's thought mean that, in a way, ritual for Xunzi is like art or literature for Freud. One is employing a similar attitude to that which one has when reading a novel or listening to music: I know that what I am experiencing is not the product of a beautiful, harmonious world that cares for our interests. Nevertheless, what has been *created* is beautiful and harmonious and makes living in the world both possible and meaningful. Fiction, like ritual, can be one of the most powerful avenues directly into reality. It need not be a form of fleeing or separation, although it requires a certain self-conscious "suspension of disbelief." The benefit only comes if the reader "buys into the illusion" or takes on the "as if" attitude.[69] Both fiction and Xunzian ritual (which can be seen as a beautiful, necessary fiction) can act to reveal the truth rather than conceal or flee from it. The participant in ritual who gains a deeper understanding of and connection with reality is analogous to the reader who gains the same benefits through immersion in a work of fiction; neither denies the invented nature of what transforms them.

While Freud valued the role of art and literature, he often dismissed the significance of creativity and imagination in favor of a "realistic" scientific perspective. Freud claims, "As people grow up, they cease to play, and they seem to give up the yield of pleasure which they gain from playing."[70] In addition to being demonstrably false (as any quick reflection on the role of sports, games, and entertainment in the lives of many adults will reveal), this shows Freud's negative valuation of (or at least ambivalence toward) most forms of creativity as a type of infantile escape that adults must grow out of, an attitude seen clearly in his view of religious ritual. Xunzi's point is that it is not the act of invention that is pathological but the fleeing from reality and the embrace of supernaturalism that so often accompany it. For Xunzi, the religious person and the artist can be both honest (about themselves and the world) and well adjusted, both realistic/scientific *and* creative.

Ritual and art can be forms of uncovering reality, not merely evading it. Lionel Trilling's statement about certain works of art can also apply to ritual: "The illusions of art are made to serve the purpose of a closer and truer relation with reality."[71] Freud held that science alone could lead one to a "truer relation" with reality.

Xunzian ritual also shares with the realm of art or fiction the fact that an awareness of the humanly created status of that which deeply engages us produces not disillusionment but admiration or even reverence. We gain a deep sense of satisfaction from our own acts of creation or from appreciating the creations of others. For Xunzi, this is especially true when he contemplates the achievements of the sages who created Confucian ritual, for they were working with a chaotic and unruly human nature that must be ordered and harmonized with an indifferent natural world to create something beautiful. Storr writes about the satisfaction that

> is derived from our appreciation of order and balance. And if we ourselves, in however humble a way, succeed in creating order where none existed, by making sense out of the obscure, wresting a garden from the wilderness, or even arranging a bowl of flowers in a way which we find satisfying, we achieve a fulfillment which can be as gratifying as the satisfaction of our nutritional or sexual requirements.[72]

Xunzi's point is the same—we can achieve a deep satisfaction by appreciating the harmonious order that ritual can create within a human being (a harmonization of emotions, for example), within a community, or between the individual and the larger natural world.[73]

Conclusion

The Xunzian sage, by cultivating a perspective that combines committed practitioner and reflective observer and developing an awareness and appreciation of the symbolic nature of ritual, achieves the deepest understanding and greatest benefits of ritual while avoiding the deformations that plague others in their relation to ritual. Xunzi's rejection of supernaturalism and literalism in favor of the symbolic interpretation, and his notion of participant-observer consciousness as a way to prevent obsession, make him a difficult target for criticism from thinkers like Freud.

Those who are at the highest level of the "hierarchy of understanding" are aware of the fabricated nature of the rites. The notion of fabrication can be quite threatening to many, for it undermines the foundations given to ritual in most traditions, such as divine origin. Rappaport highlights the dilemma for many moderns: "The epistemologies that have been spectacularly successful in illuminating the ways in which physical aspects of the world work, when shone on humanity's conventional foundations, show them to be fabrications and thus, in a world in which objectivity and fact seem to own truth, delusory."[74] In the face of this, one can either deny the methodology that leads to this conclusion (and thus the fact of "fabrication"), which is the tactic of fundamentalists when it comes to the findings of natural or social science, or one can accept the findings of these methodologies and risk alienation from religion and ritual. However, when Xunzi illuminates the fact of fabrication, he does so in a way that elicits not disillusionment or rejection but rather reverence and admiration for the human achievement. One might say that in the case of ritual, the "magic" is even *more* powerful when one knows how the trick works. Xunzi reveres the tradition not *despite* its fabricated nature but precisely *because* of it.

Xunzi's accomplishment is that he does not fall prey to either threatening side—avoiding supernaturalism, irrationalism, wish-fulfillment, and literalism, on the one hand, and reductive rationalism, desanctification, and alienation on the other.[75] He shows us the possibility of a tradition that recognizes the connections that constitute and sustain us (connections to family, ancestors, tradition, and nature) while unflichingly facing the reality of finitude, a human nature that is divisive and disorderly, and a world that is majestic but indifferent.

What is remarkable about Xunzi's Confucianism—and what separates it from the vast majority of other traditions (including Mengzian Confucianism)—is that it does not assume that there is an underlying order (*nomos*), a primordial, divinely sanctioned harmony or goodness to the natural world or cosmos. Thus, ritual does not celebrate or sanctify a preexisting, discovered order; ritual itself creates this order even as it sacralizes it.[76] One celebrates not only the order itself but also the ongoing creating and sustaining of it in ritual activity.[77]

Because rituals are a human creation, historical through and through, Xunzi is aware of the fragility of the ritually constructed order. He recognizes the crucial role that each generation plays in learning, upholding, and transmitting this order through education and ritual participation. The tradition provides the thread that connects the present with the past and ensures a future for humanity (while biological reproduction ensures a future for the species, cultural transmission ensures the continuing *humanity* of the species). Xunzi emphasizes the remembrance of the dead and education of the young, two vitally important activities that ultimately amount to the same thing.

Xunzi's hermeneutic innovation can make an important contribution to contemporary ritual theory. His reinterpretation of ritual can speak to many who find themselves alienated from the rituals of their traditions. He is a pragmatic naturalist, a social scientist who is the "enlightenment critic of supernatural religion" of his time, and a "symbolic realist" *avant la lettre*. He shows us the beauty, power, and truth in the symbolic and tells us that the sacrality of religious symbols is not lost but is rather reinforced, when they are stripped of literalism and supernaturalism. For that reason, Xunzi's reinterpretation of religion in the third century b.c.e. can still speak powerfully to us today.

Notes

Parts of this chapter were presented at the International Conference on Freud and Chinese Religions at Rutgers University on October 4, 2008.

1. Belief in the existence of ghosts and spirits was not only held by the "unsophisticated" but was also given philosophical justifications by sophisticated thinkers like Mozi.

2. All citations from the work of Roy Rappaport come from his remarkable final work, *Ritual and Religion in the Making of Humanity* (Cambridge: Cambridge University Press, 1999). Rappaport opens his book with a statement that illustrates the way in which his view is grounded in a picture of humanity that he shares with Xunzi. He writes that humanity is "a species that lives, and can only live, in terms of meanings it must construct in a world devoid of intrinsic meaning but subject to physical law." Rappaport, *Ritual and Religion in the Making of Humanity*, p. 1.

3. Ibid., p. 32.

4. Ibid., p. 27.

5. For a sensitive treatment of death rituals in the *Xunzi*, see Lee H. Yearley, "Facing Our Frailty: Comparative Religious Ethics and the Confucian Death Rituals," The Gross Memorial Lecture, 1995, Valparaiso University (Valparaiso, IN: Valparaiso University Press, 1995), pp. 14–18.

6. Paul R. Rosenblatt, Patricia Walsh, and Douglas Jackson, *Grief and Mourning in Cross-Cultural Perspective* (New Haven, CT: Human Relations Area Files Press, 1976), p. 6. Numerous studies are cited to support these general claims. For another discussion of the range of emotional and behavioral reactions following the death of a loved one, see Dale V. Hardt, *Death: The Final Frontier* (Englewood Cliffs, NJ: Prentice Hall, 1979), p. 128ff.

7. *Xunzi* 109, K 19.11, 19/97/20–22.

8. *Xunzi* 110, K 19.11, 19/98/1–2.

9. This is true of all feelings, including the love for others. If uncultivated, even love for a child can lead to unethical action (e.g., undermining the career of another so as to help your child advance). This is why ritual cultivation of all feelings is necessary. See Eric L. Hutton, "Does Xunzi Have a Consistent Theory of Human Nature?" in T. C. Kline III and Philip J. Ivanhoe, eds., *Virtue, Nature, and Moral Agency in the "Xunzi"* (Indianapolis, IN: Hackett, 2000), pp. 220–236.

10. *Xunzi* 103, K 19.7a, 19/95/6–7.

11. *Xunzi* 100, K 19.5b, 19/94/8–9.

12. See Sigmund Freud, *An Outline of Psychoanalysis*, trans. James Strachey (New York: W.W. Norton, 1989), p. 92.

13. *Xunzi* 99, K 19.4c, 19/93/20.

14. *Xunzi* 104, K 19.7a, 19/95/12–13.

15. This practice is described by He Liankui in "Sangcang," in *Taiwan fengtu zhi* (Taipei, 1956), pp. 80–84. It is reprinted in Jordan Paper and Lawrence Thompson, eds., *The Chinese Way in Religion* (New York: Wadsworth Publishing, 1998), p. 48. There are a number of contemporary cultures in which the practice of breaking accompaniment objects is observed. Such a custom is found among the Ainu of northern Japan and the people of the Nicobar Islands in the Bay of Bengal. See Rosenblatt et al., *Grief and Mourning in Cross-Cultural Perspective*, p. 72.

16. Rappaport, *Ritual and Religion in the Making of Humanity*, p. 141.

17. Rosenblatt et al., *Grief and Mourning in Cross-Cultural Perspective*, p. 88.

18. For a discussion of these tensions in Melanesian funeral rites, see Bronislaw Malinowski, *Magic, Science, and Religion and Other Essays* (New York: Free Press, 1948), p. 30.

19. Robert J. Lifton, *The Broken Connection: On Death and the Continuity of Life* (New York: Basic Books, 1983), p. 92.

20. This notion of ambivalence can be seen in the common Chinese belief in the two-part nature of the soul. One part, the 魄 *po*, represents the aspect of death as threatening, disintegrating, and earthbound (it is the 陰 *yin* component, associated with 鬼 *gui* "ghost"), while the other, 魂 *hun*, represents the ongoing connection with the family, the surviving "spirit" of the deceased (it is the 陽 *yang* component, associated with 神 *shen* "spirit"). It makes sense, then, that the former resides in the earthly grave and must be propitiated and the latter, associated with the heavenly realm, is thanked and honored. See Lawrence Thompson, *Chinese Religion* (New York: Wadsworth Publishing, 1979), pp. 11, 19, and 47. See also Kristofer Schipper, *The Taoist Body* (Berkeley: University of California Press, 1993), p. 36.

21. Rosemary Gordon examines the human response to the sight of an inert body where there was once an animated, loved human being, making the dead an "absent

presence." See Rosemary Gordon, *Dying and Creating: A Search for Meaning* (London: Society of Analytical Psychology, 1978), p. 21.

22. *Xunzi* 99–100, K 19.5a, 19/94/3–6.

23. Lifton, *The Broken Connection: On Death and the Continuity of Life*, p. 95.

24. Hardt, *Death: The Final Frontier*, p. 130.

25. Sigmund Freud, "Mourning and Melancholia," in *General Psychological Theory: Papers on Metapsychology* (New York: Touchstone/Simon and Schuster, 2008), p. 171.

26. Ibid., p. 163.

27. Channing Lipson explains this "return to daily life" from a Freudian perspective: "Acknowledgment of this reality threatens to flood the ego with the totality of libidinal and aggressive cathexes formerly invested in the object. Mourning is the ego's method of retarding the flood by loosening the attachment in small quantities . . . (there is a) series of partial detachments. . . . This is suggested by the gradual diminution of sadness and the slow renewal of energy that take place during mourning." Channing Lipson, "Denial and Mourning," in Hendrik Ruitenbeek, ed., *The Interpretation of Death* (New York: Jason Aronson, 1983), p. 274.

28. *Xunzi* 106, K 19.9a, 19/96/5–8.

29. Rosenblatt, *Grief and Mourning in Cross-Cultural Perspective*, p. 8.

30. One of the most thoughtful early anthropological studies of secondary burials is Robert Hertz's "A Contribution to the Study of the Collective Representation of Death," in *Death and the Right Hand*, trans. Rodney Needham and Claudia Needham (Glencoe, IL: Free Press, 1960). Hertz demonstrates that one way in which death is represented is through certain ways of handling and manipulating the remains of the dead.

31. James Harold, "Is Xunzi's Virtue Ethics Susceptible to the Problem of Alienation?" in *Dao* 10.1 (Spring 2011), p. 79.

32. Fran Schumer, "After a Death, the Pain That Doesn't Go Away," *New York Times*, 9/29/09, D1.

33. Harold, "Is Xunzi's Virtue Ethics Susceptible to the Problem of Alienation?" p. 80.

34. Psychiatrists who study prolonged grief disorder say that, for the sufferer, "life has no meaning; joy is out of bounds." The disorder is linked with higher incidences of drinking, cancer, and suicide attempts. Dr. Shear concludes, "Simply put, complicated grief can wreck a person's life." One patient who suffered from prolonged grief disorder and successfully sought help said of the treatment, "It really gave me my life back." Schumer, "After a Death, the Pain That Doesn't Go Away." Harold's emphasis on the essential importance of grief, rather than on the healthy functioning of the whole person, would deprive an individual of the chance to "get her life back."

35. Sigmund Freud, "Obsessive Acts and Religious Practices," trans. R. C. McWatters, in Philip Rieff, ed., *Character and Culture* (New York: Collier Books, 1963), p. 25.

36. *Xunzi* 122, K 21.2, 21/102/13.

37. Rappaport, *Ritual and Religion in the Making of Humanity*, p. 447.

38. *Xunzi* 95, K 19.2d, 19/92/17; emphasis mine.

39. Robert F. Campany, "Xunzi and Durkheim as Theorists of Ritual Practice," in Frank Reynolds and David Tracy, eds., *Discourse and Practice* (Albany: State University of New York Press, 1992), p. 214.

40. Ibid.

41. This is related to the problem of the role of theoretically informed thought in other sensory experiences, such as listening to music. It seems as if someone who sits through a Beethoven symphony continuously thinking about the structure of the symphony or its position in Beethoven's larger *oeuvre* misses a lot in the performance. In a sense, they are not fully present, are not focused on the music as it is being played. On the other hand, a listener who simply experiences the notes in a moment-to-moment, ongoing succession, decontextualized from the larger structure, has an impoverished experience as well. Appreciation of things that are complex takes time, repeated experience, and expanded awareness. This involves (but is not limited to) a perspective informed by theoretical knowledge. So I would hold that at the highest levels, listening to great music, like participating in ritual activity, involves not simply a deep moment-to-moment sensuous absorption but also a theoretical awareness (though not necessarily the activity of discursive thinking itself).

42. *Xunzi* 110–111, K 19.11, 19/98/7–10; emphasis mine.

43. Gordon, *Dying and Creating: A Search for Meaning*, p. 111.

44. The literalist-supernaturalist delusion can, in extreme cases, lead to inhuman acts, a notable example being that of "accompaniment burials." Xunzi thoroughly condemns the practice, whereby a powerful figure, normally a ruler of great stature, would be buried alongside an accompanying subterranean retinue (e.g., soldiers, loyal servants, concubines), members of which were "sacrificed" (in theory willingly) for this purpose. The practice was based on a belief that the spirit of the deceased entered the next world bearing with him the objects and people put with him in the grave. This is why great wealth, horses, and clothing were buried alongside rulers—they would need them. Xunzi, who emphasizes in his discussion of altered objects that these items are to be taken symbolically, not literally, addresses the practice by writing, "To execute the living so that they can escort the dead is termed 'predation'" (*Xunzi* 105, K 19.8, 19/96/1). The inexcusable practice is based on a misguided supernaturalism.

45. Sigmund Freud, *The Future of an Illusion*, trans. W. D. Robson-Scott (New York: Anchor Books, 1964), p. 14.

46. Freud, *The Future of an Illusion*, pp. 14ff.

47. Gordon, *Dying and Creating: A Search for Meaning*, p. 24.

48. Yearley writes that "for Xunzi, many religious activities are 'necessary fictions.'" Yearley, "Facing Our Frailty: Comparative Religious Ethics and the Confucian Death Rituals," p. 18.

49. *Xunzi* 110, K 19.11, 19/98/2–3. See Campany's discussion of this passage in Campany, "Xunzi and Durkheim as Theorists of Ritual Practice," pp. 211ff.

50. *Xunzi* 85, K 17.8, 17/82/6–8; emphasis mine.

51. *Xunzi* K 30.1, 30/143/20–21.

52. From a private communication. I am indebted to T. C. Kline III for this point.

53. Catherine Bell, *Ritual Theory, Ritual Practice* (New York: Oxford University Press, 1992), p. 183.

54. Ibid.

55. Ibid., p. 184.

56. As Emil Benveniste observes, the entire process of psychoanalysis operates through language, which "is nothing but symbolism." Emile Benveniste, *Problems in*

General Linguistics, trans. Mary Elizabeth Meek (Coral Gables: University of Miami Press, 1971), p. 73.

57. David Stafford-Clark, *What Freud Really Said* (New York: Schocken Books, 1997), p. 38.

58. Ibid., p. 37.

59. Ibid., p. 38.

60. I thank Chris Jochim for directing me to the Bellah article.

61. Robert Bellah, "Christianity and Symbolic Realism," *Journal for the Scientific Study of Religion* 9.2 (1970), p. 113. Bellah argues that while scientific symbols are those that express the nature of objects, religious symbols are those that "express the feelings, values and hopes of subjects, or which organize and regulate the flow of interaction between subjects and objects, or which attempt to sum up the whole subject-object complex, or even point to the context or ground of that whole. These symbols too express reality . . ." Bellah, "Christianity and Symbolic Realism," p. 93.

62. *Xunzi* 117–118, K 20.4, 20/100/19–101/4.

63. *Xunzi* 99, K 19.4c, 19/93/24–94/1.

64. *Xunzi* 99, K 19.4c, 19/93/24–94/1.

65. Campany, "Xunzi and Durkheim as Theorists of Ritual Practice," p. 205.

66. Alister McGrath, *The Twilight of Atheism* (New York: Doubleday, 2006), p. 70.

67. *Xunzi* 91, K 19.2a, 19/90/20–22.

68. Actually, as Bellah points out, Freud really *did* understand the power of symbols—after all, in order to explain one of his most important discoveries, he uses a *myth*—that of Oedipus. He employs the mythic language of struggle between *eros* and *thanatos*; and his therapy emphasizes the exploration of dreams—an implicit recognition that symbols are important in the process of healing. Yet he aimed to go behind the symbols to unmask the psychic forces that produce them, never seeing, as Jung did, the therapeutic power of the symbols themselves. Xunzi sees how ritual symbols can shape disordered, potentially destructive impulses into something harmonious and beautiful, to create ordered individuals and communities out of potential chaos.

69. I am indebted to Laura Medin for this point.

70. Sigmund Freud, "Creative Writers and Day-Dreaming" (London: The Hogarth Press and the Institute of Psychoanalysis, 1959), Standard Edition, Vol. XI, p. 145.

71. Lionel Trilling, "Freud and Literature," in *The Liberal Imagination* (London: Secker and Warburg, 1951), p. 45. Quoted in Anthony Storr, *The Dynamics of Creation* (New York: Ballantine Books, 1993), p. 191.

72. Storr, *The Dynamics of Creation*, p. 210. Freud questions the very notion of "higher-order" goods, stating that "we can only say figuratively that such satisfactions seem 'finer and higher.' But their intensity is mild as compared with that derived from the sating of crude and primary instinctual impulses; it does not convulse our physical being." For Freud then, the beauty of a religious ritual or a work of art is a pale substitute for what we really want: satisfaction of our sexual or aggressive desires. Might it be, however, that these are distinct orders of human satisfaction, that the aesthetic or religious is not merely a culturally acceptable substitute for the sexual? We need not downplay the importance of sexual gratification to recognize that, however much of it a person gets, his or her life would still lack something vital if it were not for ritual and art.

73. Xunzi frequently employs words with a strong aesthetic dimension: "beauty" (*mei*, 美), "elegance" (*ya*, 雅), "cultural ornamentation" (*wen*, 文), "model" (*fa*, 法), etc. For example, Xunzi writes, "If there were no conscious activity, then human nature would have no way to beautify itself" (*Xunzi* 102, K 19.6, 19/1–2).

74. Rappaport, *Ritual and Religion in the Making of Humanity*, p. 451.

75. Edward Slingerland has rightly argued against John Knoblock's claim that at Xunzi's hands, "ritual became a secular matter detached from the religious system that produced it." Edward G. Slingerland, *Effortless Action: Wu-Wei as a Spiritual Ideal in Early China*, PhD dissertation, Stanford University, 1998, p. 385. As Slingerland emphasizes, demythologization (demystification) is *not* the same as secularization. In fact, what makes Xunzi so appealing for our time is that he showed how to reinterpret the tradition (away from supernaturalism and literalism) while retaining its deeply "religious" nature. (On the use of the term "religious" to describe Confucians, see Mark Berkson, "Chapter Three: Death in the Xunzi," in *Death and the Self in Ancient Chinese Thought: A Comparative Perspective*, PhD dissertation, Stanford University, 1999, pp. 357–70).

76. This creation was the act of the sage kings; but a *re-creation* occurs with each performance of the *li*.

77. For these reasons, Xunzi is a better resource on which to draw for the task of fitting the classical Confucian vision into twenty-first-century American society than either Kongzi or Mengzi. Kongzi did not provide the theoretical foundation needed to justify the Confucian vision; Mengzi grounded his defense of Confucianism in foundational, metaphysical claims, a kind of essentialism that may not hold up in our contemporary multicultural society (i.e., the argument that the particular Confucian rituals are derived from our very nature, which is grounded in Heaven).

Xunzi's approach works better, because in addition to highlighting the beauty and efficacy of Confucian ritual, he also recognizes that they are human constructions and provides criteria by which any good (effective, beautiful) ritual can be judged, opening up the possibilities that modified Confucian rituals, and even non-Confucian rituals, would meet these criteria. For Xunzi, rituals must (a) satisfy human psychological, physical, and social needs; (b) cultivate the proper attitudes, emotions, and character so that one can become a good person; and (c) harmonize people with each other in communities and with other beings in the larger natural world. Since rituals, for Xunzi, are grounded not in Heaven/*tian* (although we must take the ways of Heaven into account if we are to harmonize with it) nor in human nature but are rather the creation of sages who used their minds to create rituals that work, then it becomes possible that with the radical transformation of the world since Xunzi's time, new rituals could be created to harmonize human beings with different social and natural environments. Xunzi is not an essentialist, but he is certainly no relativist. Rather, he shows us the possibility of a bounded plurality of effective ritual expressions.

Comparative Approaches

CHAPTER 6

Ritual and Tradition in Xunzi and Dōgen

JAMES ROBSON

Introduction

Seeing the names Xunzi 荀子 (310–219 b.c.e.) and Dōgen 道元 (1200–53 c.e.) brought together as a pair for possible comparative consideration will no doubt strike some readers as curious. Not only are these two figures separated by more than thirteen hundred years, but they are also representative of two different cultural milieus: China and Japan. While in recent years we have become accustomed to seeing comparative studies of two Chinese religious thinkers (Xunzi and Mencius, for example), or comparative work done on either Chinese or Japanese religious thinkers and later Western thinkers (Mencius and Aquinas, Zhuangzi and Kierkegaard, and Dōgen and Heidegger, for example), it has not been so common to juxtapose two thinkers found within different Asian traditions.[1] Moreover, Xunzi and Dōgen may seem like odd bedfellows since we are also quite unaccustomed to seeing a Confucian thinker compared to, rather than explicitly contrasted with, a Buddhist figure.

In the pages that follow, however, the focus of my study will not be to argue that I can trace distinct historical connections between Xunzi and Dōgen or argue that Dōgen read and was influenced by Xunzi's works but will rather look at these two thinkers in terms of structural, and at times substantive, affinities in their approaches to ritual and tradition.[2] I will not, that is to say, conclude that Dōgen was in any way a kind of latter-day Xunzian, but rather I will have succeeded in my task if the reader of this chapter comes away with the impression that these two thinkers were both, in sometimes surprisingly similar ways, exploring and grappling with key issues about the predicament of what it is to be human, about how to live together harmoniously with others, and about the role of ritual in relation to both of those concerns. At the same time, I hope to show that, despite their spatial and temporal separation from Western ritual theorists, these two thinkers are worthy of participating in conversations with those theorists and that both of these thinkers have theories of ritual that are nonetheless today intelligible and philosophically significant.

Both Xunzi and Dōgen are immensely complex thinkers, and this essay is merely a brief and selective treatment of their work, which makes our task a difficult one. I will, therefore, be limiting my discussion to two aspects of their thought: ritual and tradition. In establishing these parameters, many of their more famous doctrines and ideas will remain undiscussed.[3] Throughout this discussion, I will also have to remain cognizant of their many differences and to the difficulties involved with how technical terms are used by each thinker, but due to limitations of space I will be unable here to provide the depth of analysis that a more comprehensive comparative project would entail.[4]

After first providing a brief introduction to the historical context of each thinker, I will move to a consideration of different aspects of ritual found in Xunzi and Dōgen. Our treatment of Xunzi and ritual will force us to call into question, or at the very least modify, some of the assumptions and conclusions drawn by those scholars who have compared Xunzi as a ritual theorist to Emile Durkheim.[5] By bringing Dōgen and his elaborate ritual theory into discussion with Xunzi, I contend that certain key aspects of Xunzi's ritual theory, precisely those where he differs most from Durkheim, may also help us elucidate certain heretofore unconsidered aspects of Dōgen's ritual theory and practice. Closely related to our discussion of ritual will be two further sections that deal with issues of how ritual is intimately connected with self-cultivation, "tradition," and the role of the teacher/master.

Considering the relatively recent interest in both Xunzi and Dōgen, it is significant to recall that in the centuries following their deaths the writings of each of these thinkers came perilously close to falling out of history. While some would now argue that Xunzi has been more influential to the Confucian tradition than he has heretofore been given credit, it is nonetheless true that for much of Confucian history, particularly that influenced by Neo-Confucian writers, Xunzi was considered to be somewhat of an apostate due to his rejection of Mencius's view that human nature is good. Yet, it is clear from the number of new books on Xunzi that his rehabilitation has begun.[6] In some cases, however, the character of this "rehabilitation" seems to still be colored by Neo-Confucian readings of Xunzi and involves an attempt by modern scholars to make Xunzi more palatable to their own ideas of what Xunzi "really" thought.

Likewise, Dōgen's writings sat veritably untouched inside Sōtō Zen monasteries until he was rediscovered during the Tokugawa period (seventeenth century). When his work finally started to reemerge, it was "marked" by initial interpretations of Tokugawa sectarian scholars like Manzan Dōhaku 卍山道白 (1634–1714) and Menzan Zuihō 面山瑞芳 (1683–1769).[7] Dōgen's later reception by foreign scholars and Zen practitioners was further colored by the works of D. T. Suzuki, a Rinzai Zen layman and promoter of Zen in America, who all but ignored Dōgen in his influential introductions of Zen. When Suzuki did mention Dōgen in his *Studies in the History of Zen Thought*, however, it was merely to critique his doctrine and practice.[8] A vexing problem for interpreters of Dōgen in Japan and the West has been his last writings, often referred to as the twelve-fascicle *Shōbōgenzō*, where Dōgen's writings become more polemical (in terms of the rejection of other lineages), exclusive (in terms of the need to join the monastic community), traditional (in the sense that he began to frequently cite "classical" Indian Buddhist texts, like the Lotus Sūtra, and write more on traditional Buddhist doctrine, like karma theory), and concerned with minute details of correct ritual performance. Two aspects of Dōgen's thought have been particularly difficult for his modern interpreters to acknowledge. Perhaps due to certain Protestant-inspired assumptions commonly held about Buddhism, Dōgen's focus on ritual and ritualization has not received the kind of attention that it deserves. Likewise, modern attitudes toward individualism, and the fear of its loss, have kept scholars from seriously considering the importance of the social/group aspect of Dōgen's creation of Eiheiji as a well-regulated monastic community.[9]

Historical Contexts

Before moving on to a consideration of Xunzi and Dōgen's ideas, it is pertinent to pause for a moment to consider the historical contexts within which each lived, and were a product of, since the contingencies of those times forced certain questions to the forefront of their thought. While there is no doubt that "Warring States Period" (481–221 b.c.e.) China is a long way from Kamakura Period (1185–1333) Japan, I draw attention to some historical similarities between the two epochs and propose that by understanding the historical challenges that Xunzi and Dōgen were faced with, it is possible to understand more clearly the ways that history impinged on their philosophical thought.

The fourth to third century b.c.e. in China is predominantly characterized as a time of dissolution and decay following the breakup of the great central power that was attained under the Zhou dynasty. Heiner Roetz, in his attempt to account for the flowering of Chinese philosophical thought in what he calls (following Karl Jaspers) the "axial age" (ca. 600–200 b.c.e.), proposed that

> Chinese philosophy was the answer to the political and social changes which had their roots in the Western Zhou and Chunqiu eras. . . . By the middle of the millennium, China had split into a number of

> principalities led by former vassals. Their territories developed into de facto independent states. This political polycentrism laid the seeds of war, but at the same time it was culturally extraordinarily fertile.[10]

Thus, as many have noted, at the time of Xunzi's writing there were already in the air a plethora of competing philosophical theories (Confucius, Mencius, Mozi, the Legalists) and rival interpretations about how to confront the particular problems of the age. Xunzi, it might be said, no longer looked out onto a secure, ordered country and social world with what J. Z. Smith has called "cosmological conviction."[11] Rather, to further extend Smith's insights back to Xunzi's time, he looked out on a world "perceived to be chaotic, reversed, liminal, filled with anomie," and he was compelled to help discern patterns and propose new, or better yet revive older, forms of orientation.[12]

Dōgen's historical context in thirteenth-century Japan suggests some striking parallels with Xunzi's Chinese context. Zen arose in the aftermath of the end of the Heian period (794–1185), which had been a time of relative peace and security, and during the rise of the Kamakura period, one of the most volatile and dramatic times in Japanese history. "The transition from Heian to Kamakura," Carl Bielefeldt has suggested,

> was a time of radical historical change, and Dōgen's contemporaries were aware of their historical situation in a way and to a degree that probably no generation before them had been. For many Buddhists it was the long-predicted age of the end of the dharma (*mappō*), in which the human condition had sunk to a state no longer equal to the successful negotiation of the bodhisattva path.[13]

Coterminus with the dissolution of Heian social and political order was the rise of many new Buddhist schools. During the Kamakura period we see, for example, the rise of Jōdo 淨土, Jōdo Shinshū 淨土真宗, Zen 禪, and Nichiren 日蓮, forms of "new" Buddhism. While it would be overstating the case to say that Dōgen was trying to cure all the ills of his day, it does not stretch credulity too far to see his religious career as an attempt to reform not only the Buddhism of his day but also the society and individuals around him. Rather than reject the present world and put faith in the possibility of escape to the Pure Land, Dōgen sought to engage directly with the reality of the present world. What in particular gave Dōgen the motivation to persevere in the face of such a bleak situation was his confidence in the efficacy of the "one vehicle" or "supreme vehicle" (最上乘 *saijō jō*; *ekayāna*), which was none other than the practice instituted by the Buddha and carried down to the present by a lineage of patriarchs. For Dōgen, as well as for Xunzi, a key aspect of the "reformation" of the individual and society was ritual, which we now turn to, though for both of these figures the appeal to the past and tradition is the fire that gives ritual much of its power and efficacy and is the subject of the second half of the chapter.

Ritual and Ritual Self-Cultivation

In the following discussion of ritual in Xunzi and Dōgen, I will take as my starting point the foundational essay by A. R. Radcliffe-Brown that sought to lay out the characteristics of the social-functionalist approach to ritual, which he proposed is found in nascent form in the *Xunzi*, and how that theory of ritual has certain affinities with ideas proposed by Emile Durkheim. I will also be making reference to the more recent essay by Robert Campany that makes basically the same point.[14] While much of what has been proposed regarding the affinities of Xunzi and Durkheim remains unproblematic, by highlighting what seem to me as two main disanalogies in Radcliffe-Brown and Campany's comparisons of Xunzi and Durkheim, we will then be in a better position to explore how two primary aspects of Xunzi's ritual theory (left undeveloped in the previous studies) have significant parallels with Dōgen's ideas about ritual.

Radcliffe-Brown took an important step in being one of the first scholars to take Xunzi's ritual theory seriously. Much of his essay "Religion and Society" is filled with perceptive insights about the social function, expression, and description of Xunzi's ritual theory, and he purports to find some surprising similarities with the ritual theory of Emile Durkheim and others.[15] Yet, while there may be significant similarities between Durkheim and Xunzi on certain points, there are nonetheless some key aspects and fundamental points that are significantly different. For the purposes of this chapter, I will limit my discussion to what I see as the major disagreement between the theories of Durkheim and Xunzi and then propose that it was Radcliffe-Brown and Campany's over-optimistic attempt to put Xunzi in a Durkheimian box that led them to misrepresent certain aspects of Xunzi's ritual theory.

Durkheim's emphasis on the importance of the social or communal aspect of ritual is undoubtedly the hallmark of his ritual theory and certainly provides a plausible starting point for a consideration of both Xunzi and Dōgen's ideas about ritual practice. Indeed, it is precisely this aspect of Durkheim's theory that is the focus of Radcliffe-Brown's essay and the basis for the comparison with Xunzi. Yet, anyone who has read through Durkheim's descriptions of what happens at those times of ritual social integration could not fail to be struck by their ecstatic and wild collective effervescence. For example, describing the changes that a practitioner undergoes in a ritual, Durkheim writes that "changes are not merely of shades and degrees; men become different. The passions moving them are of such an intensity that they cannot be satisfied except by violent and unrestrained actions, actions of superhuman heroism or of bloody barbarism."[16] During ritual gatherings, a kind of delirium infects the group such that Durkheim proposed that it is precisely "in the midst of these effervescent social environments and out of this effervescence itself that the religious idea seems to be born."[17] One of Durkheim's recent interpreters has also commented on what happens at these times of social integration:

> [It] happens on those awe-inspiring ceremonial occasions when the whole community assembles for its general rites of the clan or tribe. In these great and unforgettable ceremonies, the worshippers seal their commitment to the clan. In their moments of great excitement, in the wild emotional ecstasies of chanting and dancing, individuals manage to lose themselves in the heaving mass of the crowd; they allow their private—that is, profane—selves to sink into the single self of the clan.[18]

There is no denying that in the end there is a heightened sense of social cohesion that is fostered through ritual, but there seems to be a qualitative difference between the nature of ritual that is depicted in Durkheim and what one finds in Xunzi. In short, the centrality of collective effervescence in Durkheimian ritual theory is exceedingly difficult to reconcile with Xunzi's picture of ritual and is an important silence in the essays by Radcliffe-Brown and Campany.

Furthermore, by limiting one's theoretical tools to Durkheimian theory, one is faced with a problem first articulated by Mary Douglas, namely, "granted that societies or groups exhibit creativity and renewal during periods of effervescence, the question remains what binds people together in periods of calm, when routine behavior is the order of the day."[19] I later propose, as Maurice Halbwachs did in his addendum to Durkheim's theory, that rituals and ritualization do not necessarily always entail ecstatic rites and may be extended to the quotidian aspects of ordinary or everyday life. First, however, we will ask: What for Xunzi is the role of ritual if it is not to produce collective effervescence?

For Xunzi, ritual is precisely that activity that makes distinctions and establishes order. In the beginning of the "A Discussion of Rites" *Lilun* 禮論 chapter of the *Xunzi*, it is clear how important the ordering function of ritual is:

> The gentleman, having provided a means for the satisfaction of desires, is also careful about distinctions to be observed. What do I mean by distinctions? Eminent and humble have their respective stations, elder and younger their degrees, and rich and poor, important and unimportant, their different places in society.[20]

Rather than providing an arena where society comes together in a collective effervescence that everyone gets swept up into equally, as in the Durkheimian case, Xunzi's rituals are refined moments where the desires are controlled and distinctions and hierarchies are set or reconfirmed.[21] Indeed, rather than promote the excessive display of emotion and desire, Xunzi's worst-case scenario for a ritual sounds much like what a successful ritual would be like when viewed from the perspective of Durkheimian ritual theory. "All rites begin in simplicity," Xunzi writes,

> are brought to fulfillment in elegant form, and end in joy. When rites are performed in the highest manner, then both the emotions and the forms embodying them are fully realized; in the next best manner, the emotional content and the forms prevail by turns; *in the poorest manner, everything reverts to emotion and finds unity in that alone.*[22]

Xunzi emphasized the correct form of ritual expression as much as he emphasized its content. The most debased form of ritual in Xunzi's scheme is precisely the type of ritual that Durkheim praises and even tries to reinstitute. Xunzi's notion of how ritual makes distinctions and establishes hierarchy is another key area where Durkheimian ritual theory is particularly inapplicable. As other critics of Durkheim have pointed out, most notably Anthony Giddens, Durkheim only spoke of social solidarity and not about social divisions.[23] The obvious difference between modern critics of Durkheim's silence on social class and hierarchy, who take him to task from a Marxist perspective for ignoring issues regarding the role of religion and ritual in establishing and maintaining the legitimation of one class over another, and Xunzi, whose ritual theory includes much on the distinctions and hierarchies set in rituals, is that for Xunzi these distinctions were a good and necessary thing for a well-ordered society and worthy of praise rather than critique.[24]

While certain of Durkheim's notions of social integration and communal experience no doubt also help to illuminate some of the heretofore unemphasized aspects of Dōgen's ideas of monastic rituals, it is also equally difficult to reconcile Dōgen's picture of ritual with Durkheim's descriptions of collective effervescence. In fact, it is precisely on the issue of how ritual provides necessary distinctions that Xunzi's theory of ritual can help us see the importance of hierarchy in Dōgen's writings on ritual.

As we will see shortly, Dōgen was emphatic about the importance of the correct performance of monastic rituals, and much of Dōgen's later writings were dedicated to different facets of ritualized monastic practices. Two later ritual texts, for example, dealt with hierarchical distinctions and how to behave to fellow monks based on seniority in the monastery. The first text, *Tai taiko goge jari hō* 對大己五夏闍利法 (1244), established sixty-two rules for how junior monks should behave in relation to senior monks, and the second text, *Nipponkoku Echizen Eiheiji chiji shingi* 日本國越前永平寺知事清規 (1246), instructed the senior monks how to behave to the junior monks.[25] It is not surprising, then, that the sociologist Robert N. Bellah emphasized, contrary to popular opinions about "democratic" Zen, that Dōgen's monastic system was filled with distinction-making and hierarchy-establishing rituals, and that these were necessary and good. "[If] nothing is higher than anything else," Bellah writes, "if nothing is better than anything else, if there is no reason to choose one thing rather than another, then sociologically that is chaos. Of course in the context of monastic life, there is plenty of effective hierarchy."[26] Despite popular images of wild Zen monks and their crazy antics, with Dōgen and Xunzi, it is very difficult to imagine solemn monastic rituals breaking out into collective rituals of ecstasy and effervescence.

Deemphasizing the collective effervescence aspect of ritual for Xunzi and Dōgen, however, is not to say that one should completely throw out the importance of the social/communal aspect of ritual; it is merely one facet of a variety of dynamics inherent to ritual processes. As was alluded to earlier, we "moderns" tend to have a certain disdain for any intimations of loss of individuality. Yet, for Xunzi and Dōgen there is a sense that other important goods come out of collective social rituals, precisely because of their apportioning and guiding of desires and emotions. For Xunzi, in addition to their "function" (as A. R. Radcliffe-Brown has said) in providing social order or even cosmic order, rituals serve to allow for the best and most satisfying expression of a full range of human emotions.[27] Indeed, as P. J. Ivanhoe has clarified, Xunzi is making the very strong claim that:

> a proper sense of right and wrong and the ability unwaveringly to pursue the former and turn away from the latter can arise only out of the reflective practice of a particular set of rituals: those of Confucianism. Only this particular set of rituals can satisfy human needs and desires and expand the horizon of our meaningful activities, thereby bringing order to society and harmoniously situating the human realm within the larger natural world.[28]

For Dōgen, however, while many commentators have interpreted his move from Kyoto to Echizen Province as a turning in (ascetic move), or turning away from society (isolationist move), I suggest that this phase of his life might be read as rather the attempt to create a model social/communal setting regulated by ritual and appropriate hierarchies that might serve as a model to a world increasingly full of social disorder.[29] One might ask then if Dōgen eventually arrived at a perspective similar to Xunzi's, namely, that without effective controls there will be social turmoil.[30] Interestingly, Alasdair MacIntyre has proposed a similar scenario for the rise of Benedictine monastic communities during the sixth century in Europe. As interest and support of the Roman imperium waned, St. Benedict organized a local community that was bound by specific regulations in order to create an ideal community, set off from the chaos of normal society, where civility and the intellectual and moral life could be sustained.[31]

For both Xunzi and Dōgen there also seems to be something more that arises out of communal participation in rites. In other words, in the process of being "saved from" something (social chaos), we are also "saved toward" something else. While it is difficult to formulate precisely what it is that arises out of collective experience, and the parameters of this chapter do not allow for a full exploration of these ideas, I think that the anthropologist Paul Rabinow moved in an interesting direction with his bold (bold, that is, for anthropologists who are usually reluctant to broach the issue of ethics) attempt to extend Aristotle's concept of "friendship" (*philia*), and the language of virtues, to "practices."[32] To define "practice" Rabinow adopts Alasdair MacIntyre's definition from *After Virtue*:

> any coherent and complex form of socially established cooperative human activity through which goods internal to that form of activity are realized in the course of trying to achieve those standards of excellence which are appropriate to, and partially definitive of, that form of activity, with the result that human powers to achieve excellence, and human conceptions of the ends and goods involved, are systematically extended.[33]

While some scholars have tried to understand Xunzi's view of ritual and moral cultivation in similar terms, I also think it might be a fruitful way (without over-romanticizing monastic harmony) to understand at least in part what is going on in a communal monastic setting and in societal or interpersonal ritual "practices." Yet, in order to understand how rituals can have a wider scope and be extended to ordinary activity such that they can be considered as "practices" in MacIntyre's sense, we must first liberate ritual from the confines of its narrow definition as something set off in time and space as exemplified in Campany's discussion of Xunzi's *li*.

As is well known, Durkheim's theory of ritual is undergirded by the dichotomy of "sacred" and "profane." Simply put, the "profane" for Durkheim is the quotidian or everyday activities of life. The "sacred" on the other hand is always set off either physically, temporally, or both. In my reading, it is precisely this dichotomy that Campany picks up from Durkheim and misleadingly reads back into Xunzi's theory of ritual. Campany, in introducing the term *li* as Xunzi uses it, says that "from the total spectrum of human action, Xunzi isolates a particular sphere with its own distinctive form and coherence."[34] Campany further remarks that "in assigning that sphere a name—*li*, a term translatable both as a specific body of rites ('the' rites) familiar to Xunzi and his audience and as something like 'ritual' in the generic sense—he already marks it off as somehow distinct from other sorts of activity."[35] Campany's interpretation of ritual, or "the rites," as something set off from our everyday lives not only distorts Xunzi's picture of ritual but also fails to see how ritual and ritualization can (indeed must), when properly done, become an integral part of a self-cultivation practice that is actualized at each and every moment of one's life.

At many points in the *Xunzi*, we are given the sense that ritual or ritual behavior is not as set off from the quotidian as Campany has proffered. In the "Discussion of Rites" *Lilun* 禮論, for example, we read: "Therefore the gentleman understands how to make rites florid and how to make them lean, but he chooses to abide in the middle state, and no matter whether he walks or runs, hurries or hastens, he never abandons it. It is his constant world and dwelling."[36] Another eloquent statement of how what is learned or acquired in ritual self-cultivation can be extended to ordinary experiences is found in the chapter "Encouraging Learning" *Quanxue* 勸學. Here Xunzi says: "The learning of the gentleman enters his ears, clings to his mind, spreads through his four limbs, and manifests itself in his actions."[37] The type of "learning" Xunzi is concerned with here is defined in the preceding section of "Encouraging Learning" as "[beginning] with the recitation of the Classics and [ending] with the reading of the ritual texts."[38] At this point in his definition, Xunzi makes an interesting qualification to his conception of the learning process when he says that "we may speak of an end to the program of learning, but the objective of learning must never for an instant be given up."[39] Therefore, for Xunzi ritual mastery in all aspects of one's life is the distinguishing characteristic of a sage, yet the sage's work is never done—it must be actualized in each instant in every action.

> If all matters pertaining to temperament, will, and understanding proceed according to ritual, they will be ordered and successful; if not they will be perverse and violent or slovenly and rude. If matters pertaining to food and drink, dress, domicile, and living habits proceed according to ritual, they will be harmonious and well regulated; if not they will end in missteps, excesses, and sickness. If matters pertaining to deportment, attitude, manner of movement, and walk proceed according to ritual, they will be refined; if not they will be arrogant and uncouth, common, countrified. Therefore, a man without ritual cannot live.[40]

Reading this quotation in conjunction with the previous points on the ongoing actualization of sagely behavior, it is clear that for Xunzi ritual was something that was to be enacted in our every movement or activity and was not something merely confined to auspicious times in the Imperial Temple. Dōgen, as we will see shortly, has a strikingly similar understanding of ritual and the ritualization of everyday activities.

As previously mentioned, in Dōgen's later years he became increasingly obsessed with ritual behavior that involved all aspects of monastic life, but earlier texts like the "Instructions to the Chief Cook" *Tenzo-kyōkun* 典座教訓 suggest that a nascent form of this interest was held by Dōgen from early in his career. Other exemplary texts written by Dōgen later in life concerning the ritualization of everyday activities include: "Table Manners" *Fu shukuhanpō* 赴粥飯法, which has minute instructions for the taking of food and of table manners; and the "Rules for the Practice of the Way" *Bendōhō* 辨道法, which includes instructions on washing the face, wearing the robe, and so forth.

Rather than merely interpret these new practices as a means to bring a recalcitrant monastic community under control (i.e., some kind of Buddhist Legalism), it is possible to emphasize instead the moral self-cultivation aspect of those rites. Hee-Jin Kim proposes that

> a prime characteristic of Dōgen's thought lies in his passionate search for the translation of moral visions—hence spiritual vision—into the daily activities of monastic life . . . moral visions made concrete and routine in the daily behavior and activities of the monastics. Scrupulous instructions, exhortations, and admonitions with respect to rules, manners, virtues, and behavior, are not codes that bind the monastic's outward movements, but are ritualized expressions and activities of Buddha-nature and absolute emptiness.[41]

Kim's comments about Dōgen's use of ritual practice are worth lingering on for a moment.

Dōgen's emphasis on the ritualization of everyday activities extended from how to prepare food and eat to how to use the bathroom and brush one's teeth. For Dōgen, as with Xunzi, there is a specific set program of rituals that must be adhered to since they alone allow for the expression of our Buddha-nature. Put in other words, Dōgen writes that "ritual conduct (作法 *sahō*) is the supreme principle; the realization of the Way is ritual conduct."[42] For Dōgen, again like Xunzi, ritual self-cultivation is something more than mere forced habituation or training. That the ritualization of everyday activities is not just a mere "show" in order to give the monastics a sense of decorum is clear from a passage in the *Shōbōgenzō Zuimonki* 正法眼藏隨聞記:

> Dōgen said: "Even by the standards of ordinary society, lack of propriety—such as changing your clothing improperly, even when you are where people cannot see you or are in a darkened room; or sitting or lying indecently so that parts that should be hidden are exposed—is an insult to heaven and to ghosts. Hide what should be hidden, and be ashamed of what is shameful, just as if you were always in the presence of others. This reflects the intent of the precepts. Those versed in the Way must not make distinctions about whether they are inside a room or outside it, or whether it is light or dark, and do bad things

> just because they are out of sight of people who know the Buddhist regulations."[43]

The implication of these passages, as well as many others in Dōgen's corpus, is that ritual practices, particularly *zazen*, when done in the proper way and with the right motivations are nothing less than the manifestation of one's Buddha-nature. Ritual conduct is the realization of the Way, and this should be realized at all times and in all places, whether one is alone or in the presence of others. Dōgen's emphasis here on maintaining diligence in practice while alone or in public no doubt calls to mind the Confucian notion of "acting with care when alone" 慎其獨 *shenqidu*. The sense of always acting "as if" in the presence of others is echoed in the "Discussion of Rites" chapter of the *Xunzi*, where there is repeated emphasis to act "as if" the departed are present.[44]

We might propose that for Dōgen correct ritual practice itself becomes something like an all-encompassing "virtue" in Alasdair MacIntyre's definition:

> A virtue is an acquired human quality the possession and exercise of which tends to enable us to achieve those goods which are internal to practices and the lack of which effectively prevents us from achieving any such goods. . . . The exercise of the virtues is not a means to the end of good for man. For what constitutes the good for man is a complete human life lived at its best, and the exercise of the virtues is a necessary and central part of such a life, not a preparatory exercise to secure such a life . . .[45]

In order to solidify this speculative comment, a full exposition of Dōgen's complex thoughts on Buddha-nature would be necessary, but for the purposes of this chapter I refer to the insights in Masao Abe's essay "The Oneness of Practice and Attainment: Implications for the Relation between Means and Ends," which contains an in-depth presentation of some of the main issues involved.[46] Simply put, Abe focuses on a central question that was posed by a young Dōgen who brooded over the possible reconciliation of the Tendai doctrine of "original awakening" 本覺 *hongaku*, which posits that everyone is originally awakened, with the injunction to undertake Buddhist practice. Dōgen formulated his doubt in the following way: "Both exoteric and esoteric Buddhism teach the primal Buddha-nature and original self-awakening of all sentient beings. If this is the case, why then in the Buddhas of all ages did the longing for awakening arise and they engage in ascetic practice?"[47] After traveling to China to study under a Chan master, Dōgen ultimately came to a resolution of this conundrum by understanding the relationship between inherent Buddha-nature and Buddhist practice as not mutually exclusive. "This Dharma is amply present in every person," Dōgen wrote, "but unless one practices, it is not manifested; unless there is realization, it is not attained."[48] In acknowledging the potential for realizing one's inherent Buddha-nature, it would appear more appropriate to invoke Mencius and his notion of "incipient sprouts" and leave Xunzi out of the discussion, but Dōgen's complex formulation of his idea of the relationship of that inherent quality in all humans and the expressed need to realize it through practice does not fall clearly into the polarities that have been traditionally proposed to exist between Mencius and Xunzi. While it might prove useful to explore those issues further, suffice it to say for now, however, that Dōgen's view does not fall neatly into either a Mencius/"discovery" or Xunzi/"development" model but is something more like what I would tentatively call a "performative realization" model. That is to say, we have a certain capacity for reformation, but this capacity has not been filled in or realized.[49] Indeed, Dōgen proposes what might be termed a "middle way" between the polarities of "discovery" and "development," by suggesting that "as for the truth of the Buddha-nature: the Buddha-nature is not incorporated prior to attaining Buddhahood; it is incorporated upon the attainment of Buddhahood. The Buddha-nature is always manifested simultaneously with the attainment of Buddhahood. This truth should be deeply, deeply penetrated in concentrated practice."[50] Dōgen concluded, in other words, that "in the Buddha Dharma, practice and realization are identical."[51] Carl Bielefeldt, in his description of Dōgen's ideas of practice and realization, has written that,

> for Dōgen, it lay in the Buddhahood built into the very structure of consciousness. However it was defined, the practices derived from the principle did not, ultimately speaking, lead to anything: they were supposed rather to be the expression in the act of the practitioner of his acceptance of, and commitment to, the principle. . . . As Dōgen would say, practice and its verification are not different.[52]

In this understanding, therefore, I would propose that we are not so distant from MacIntyre's definition of virtue quoted earlier. Correct practice as the manifestation or verification of one's Buddhahood might be understood as the one virtue that subsumes all virtues, as someone interested in the "supreme vehicle" (最上乘 *saijō jō*; *ekayāna*), like Dōgen, might say.

It is still unclear, however, what kind of "practice" is suitable for the expression or verification of one's Buddha-nature. For Dōgen and Xunzi, there are precise ways to do things that are better or more efficacious than other ways, and one of the most important rationales given by each of them has to do with their grounding in "tradition," "the Way of the sages," or "the Way of the Buddhas and bodhisattvas."

Teacher/Master and Tradition

As is often suggested, since Xunzi did not hold that we possess innate moral "sprouts," as Mencius said we did, he deemphasized our ability to look within ourselves as a means for guidance on the Way and instead focused on the importance of learning from a teacher and the participation in and reflection on a tradition of Confucian rituals. In the "Improving Yourself" *Xiushen* 修身 chapter, Xunzi is clear about the dual importance of having a teacher as one's guide in the correct learning of the rites. "Ritual," Xunzi insists, "is the means by which to rectify yourself; the teacher is the means by which ritual is rectified. If you are without ritual, how can you rectify yourself? If you have no teacher, how can you understand the fitness of ritual? . . . Hence to reject ritual is to be without law and to reject your teacher is to be without a guide."[53] Teachers, serving as guides, are able to teach, because they have already rectified, or reformed, themselves and they are able to interpret the rites for others since those ritual actions do not come with explanations of what is to be learned from them. "In learning," Xunzi says, "nothing is more profitable than to associate with those who are learned . . . if you make use of the erudition of others and the explanations of gentlemen, then you will become honored and make your way anywhere in the world."[54] Thus, even without innate "sprouts" we all can, with enough effort and guidance, become like Yao or Shun, since they, like us, also had to reform themselves. Yet, we do not need to reinvent the wheel and can benefit from the accumulation of the sages' wisdom ("erudition of others") and the important transforming power of the rituals they created that are maintained within the tradition.

While submission to the guidance of a teacher is integral to Xunzi's theory, it is also important to stress the adherence to a traditional ritual program that was instituted by the sages. "In order to reform our bad nature," P. J. Ivanhoe explains,

> we must sign up for and successfully pursue a thorough, prolonged and difficult course of learning. We must re-form our nature—as a warped board is re-formed by steam and pressure—so that it assumes a proper shape and can fit into the grand Confucian design. This grand scheme is a kind of master plan, worked out over long periods of time by a series of gifted sages through a process of trial and error.[55]

It is significant to note here that, in addition to stressing the importance of perseverance on a long and arduous project, Xunzi does not see the sages as having invented everything in a flash. Rather, the sages are distinguished for having systematized the rites, like a potter fashioning bowls, that were developed over a long period of time.[56]

At the end of the "Human Nature Is Bad" Xing'e 性惡 chapter, Xunzi further emphasizes the importance of tradition and the teachings that are handed down within a succession of teachers, stretching back to the hazy mythical sage kings. After having cited a litany of historical exemplars who reformed their natures, Xunzi concludes:

> In the same way a man, no matter how fine his nature or how keen his mind, must seek a worthy teacher to study under and good companions to associate with. If he studies under a worthy teacher, he will be able to hear about the ways of Yao, Shun, Yü, and Tang, and if he associates with good companions, he will be able to observe conduct that is loyal and respectful.[57]

Thus, for Xunzi, the combination of the fruits of tradition with the guidance of a good teacher are the key facets in the successful negotiation of the path of self-cultivation.

While Dōgen may be even more emphatic than Xunzi about the role of tradition, he also tends to be more exclusive in his conception of what constitutes a valid teacher. Dōgen clearly puts more emphasis on a single exclusive lineage of "true" teachers, culminating (of course) in himself. Yet, much of Dōgen's more general comments about ritual, tradition, and the role of the master/teacher bear a resemblance to Xunzi's, particularly regarding the efficacy of an accumulated tradition.

After becoming dissatisfied with the Buddhism taught by the Tendai prelates on Mt. Hiei, Dōgen set out in 1223 on a pilgrimage to China in search of the true dharma. After some time of initial frustration with the teachers in China—usually those followers of Dahui Zonggao 大慧宗杲 (1089–1163)—Dōgen finally met Tiantong Rujing 天童如淨 (1163–1228), whom he considered an "Old Buddha" and the only master in China who preserved and was presently teaching the way of the Patriarchs. What is emphasized most by Dōgen in his writings about Rujing is his position in a line of Buddhist Patriarchs that reach all the way back to the historical Buddha śākyamuni. Therefore, Rujing was significant to Dōgen for two main reasons. First, he was the living master in a lineage of Patriarchs who transmitted the "true" dharma of the Buddha and the Patriarchs and the only master alive from whom he could receive a "face-to-face transmission" (面授 *menju*). Second, from other sources it is clear how shocking it was for Dōgen to go to China and to see firsthand the completely different form of practices, rituals, and architecture that were embodied in Song dynasty Chan monasteries. For Dōgen, then, Rujing was transmitting practices and rituals that he considered to be representative of the "true" Way of the ancient Buddhas and Patriarchs that had not as yet been transmitted to Japan.

The importance of studying with a good master for Dōgen was twofold. On the one hand, of course, there was much to be learned that could only be taught in the interaction with a good teacher. On the other hand, the contact with an enlightened patriarch connected one to a lineage of enlightened masters reaching back to śākyamuni. In teaching the importance of a good teacher, Dōgen instructed:

> An old Master said: "Developing a close relationship with a good person is like walking in the fog or dew. Although your clothing does not actually get wet, it gradually becomes damp." What he is saying is that if you are close to a good person, you unconsciously become good yourself. This was the case some time ago of the boy who attended Master Chü-chih. There was no way of distinguishing when he studied and when he practiced, and he himself was also unaware of it, but because of the long association with the Master, he gained enlightenment.[58]

In this passage we can see many striking similarities with Xunzi's views on the role of the master. The master is depicted as a guide who is capable of teaching and transforming you, yet the process entails a long period of association. The main difference between the two seems to reside in the fact that for Xunzi the reformation process was a more active one of "bending and shaping," while for Dōgen the reformation process was less invasive.

At one point in the *Shōbōgenzō Zuimonki* Dōgen shows familiarity with an indigenous Chinese teaching about the importance of submitting to the Way of a teacher. Dōgen said, "Someone once asked a Daoist sage: 'How does one become a sage?' He answered: 'If you want to become a sage, just like the Way of the sages.' Therefore, if students want to attain the Way of the Buddhas and the Patriarchs, they must like the Way of the Buddhas and the Patriarchs."[59] One of the reasons that is given for why the master's teaching is effective and transformative is because he is a representative of a long tradition of direct transmission of the Buddha's enlightened teachings. "Thus, for Dōgen," Bielefeldt emphasizes, "no text or set of texts determined the orthodox understanding; this was done only by the enlightenment of the Buddha and the historical continuity of the tradition with that enlightenment."[60] There are many places in Dōgen's corpus where he emphasizes this aspect of the teaching, but I will merely cite one example here. In the "Face-to-Face Transmission" *Menju* 面授 chapter of the *Shōbōgenzō*, Dōgen is explicit about the importance of the teaching being connected back to the Buddhas of the past. In the beginning of that chapter he writes:

> This is the meaning of transmitting the treasury of the true dharma eye face to face from Buddha to Buddha, ancestor to ancestor. It was correctly transmitted by the Seven Buddhas to venerable Mahākāshyapa. From Mahākāshyapa there were twenty-eight transmissions up to and including venerable Bodhidharma. Venerable Bodhidharma himself

> went to China and gave face-to-face transmission to Huike, Great Master Zheng-zong Pujue. There were five transmissions through to Great Master Dajian Huineng of Mt. Caoxi. Then there were seventeen transmissions through to my late master, old Buddha Tiantong of the renowned Mt. Taibo, Qingxuan Prefecture, Great Song.[61]

The importance of the actual transmission from master to disciple within the Chan/Zen tradition is given substantial form in lineage transmission documents (詞書 *shisho*). By the time of Dōgen's visit to China these documents were considered treasures. Within the Sōtō tradition, the lineage was literally considered a bloodline, like a family, and to symbolize this, the transmission documents were written with a mixture of the master's and disciple's blood. Upon seeing one of these documents Dōgen was moved to write, "Upon seeing this I was convinced that there is indeed a transmission of the dharma between correct heirs. This was a teaching I had heretofore not encountered. The Buddha and ancestors had taken the opportunity to respond to help a descendant of theirs. I was extremely moved by this."[62] Therefore, rather than merely serving as documents that recorded the correct lineage transmission from master to disciples, these transmission documents had a special status that symbolized a connection all the way back through a lineage of Patriarchs to the Buddha himself.

While it is important to note that for Dōgen the true dharma was passed down from master to disciple, he also held a view akin to Xunzi's about the accumulation of the correct teaching, and did not see śākyamuni as the sole inventor of the tradition; he was just the key systematizer—like Xunzi's sages. Indeed, throughout the *Shōbōgenzō*, Dōgen traces the teachings back beyond the historical Buddha to the Seven Buddhas of the past. One might speculate that this historical perspective was one reason why Dōgen rejected the commonly accepted notion that the age of the end of the dharma (*mappō*) had arrived. By taking seriously the notion of lineage and tradition, Dōgen was able to confidently believe that he had access to the same experience that the Buddha himself had, thus he referred to his teacher Rujing as an "old Buddha." Bielefeldt, in his treatment of Dōgen's rejection of *mappō* ideology and the question of whether the teaching of the true vehicle was accessible in his day, concludes that

> the one vehicle was nothing but the enlightened practice of the Buddha himself that validated the entire tradition: where that practice was present, there was true religion. And the practice was present in the present age, since "the eye of the true *dharma*" had been handed down by the Buddha through the lineage of the Patriarchs of India and China to Dōgen himself. To accede (承當 *jōtō*) to this lineage was itself to participate in the one vehicle.[63]

In relating ritual to tradition, it is also clear from Dōgen's writings that it is the proper performance of those rituals that not only manifests one's Buddha-nature, as we saw earlier, but it is precisely those rituals that also link one to the Buddhas and Patriarchs of the past who performed the same rites. Of course for Dōgen, one of the most important things to do ritually was the practice of 坐禪 *zazen* or 只管打坐 *shikan taza*. The rationale for Dōgen's emphasis on these types of practice can be found in the "Bendōwa" in answer to a question about why one should only do *zazen*:

> The great teacher śākyamuni Buddha, beyond doubt, rightly transmitted [*zazen* as] the wonderful means for attaining the Way. Also, the *tathågatas* of the three periods all attain the Way through *zazen*. That is the reason they have transmitted it from one to another as the right entrance. That is not all. Patriarchs from the western skies of India to the eastern earth of China all have gained the Way through *zazen*. Therefore, I now point it out to men and devas as the right entrance.[64]

Zazen for Dōgen, then, is clearly more than an exercise in mindfulness and meditation, as it is advertised by some of his modern interpreters. By situating Zen meditation back into a ritual context, we are in a better position to realize the further meaning than accrues to the act of *zazen* for Dōgen. While the focus of much Zen scholarship prioritizes the intellectual, or mental, aspects of Zen meditation, Dōgen does not limit his discussion of *zazen* to the exclusively cerebral rewards. Dōgen situates his treatment of meditation in the context of his ideas about the ways that particular ritual actions link the practitioner to a lineage of Patriarchs and past Buddhas. This linkage is not only actualized in the practice of *zazen*. Indeed, one finds in Dōgen's writings that even the seemingly mundane way one washes one's face can also (if done properly) link one to the ritual tradition of the Buddhas. In the "Washing the Face" *Semmen* 洗面 fascicle of the *Shōbōgenzō* he writes,

> The way of washing our face has spread from India to China. This is clearly told in various precept-*sūtras*. But the true way is transmitted by the Buddhas and Patriarchs. It has been practiced by them not only for hundreds of years but also from time immemorial. It means not only the way of washing away dirt or grease, but also the life of the Buddhas and Patriarchs.[65]

Although some interpreters of Zen's focus on the ritualization of quotidian actions have stressed that this attention to detail and precision is meant to make each action as "mindful" as possible, there is clearly another dimension of meaning in the correct performance of those actions for Dōgen, whereby the practitioner is putting into action the "true way transmitted by the Buddhas and Patriarchs."[66] Lineage and tradition for Dōgen were paramount for the realization of enlightenment, and without the guidance of a master it would be impossible to link oneself up with the teachings of the Buddhas and Patriarchs of the past.

Conclusion

By focusing our purview exclusively on Xunzi's and Dōgen's views of ritual and tradition we have been forced to pass over significant aspects of their thought and practice and to ignore some of the more famous works in their extensive writings. Undoubtedly one of the most challenging aspects of writing a study involving comparative issues is what evidence is garnered to support one's ideas and what other material is left aside. These choices are crucial, and I suspect that someone else could write a different essay about these two thinkers that emphasizes their differences, perhaps even their incommensurability, more than I have done here.

In any case, the main point of bringing Xunzi and Dōgen together in this chapter has not been to show how one's thought is just like the other. Rather, I have tried to engage each thinker with certain issues to show that the insights about ritual and tradition in each of their works can be, indeed deserve to be, brought into dialogue with other established theorists of ritual. In recent years Emile Durkheim has been proposed as the ritual theorist closest to being a Western analogue to Xunzi. Indeed, Xunzi's ideas have been depicted as a kind of precursor to Durkheimian ritual theory. Without denying the value of bringing those figures together, I have warned that a certain amount of caution is needed in extending that comparison too far. The social-functionalist interpretation of ritual is just one dimension of Durkheim's theory that has been extracted by those who have been struck by similarities in Xunzi's writings. Were we to consider other facets of Durkheimian ritual theory, such as the emphasis on the ecstatic nature of ritual or the notion that ritual as a sacred activity is something that is demarcated and set off from our profane quotidian lives, we might find Xunzi being somewhat uncomfortable with the company he was being asked to keep. Yet, by analyzing other dimensions of Xunzi's ritual theory, indeed precisely those where he differs most from Durkheim, we have been able to draw this complex thinker into a somewhat different dialogue with Dōgen, a Buddhist thinker who shares many issues and concerns about the nature and function of ritual with Xunzi. By focusing on the theories of ritual and tradition in these two East Asian thinkers, I have sought to demonstrate that they are both significant theorists of ritual whose ideas are intelligible, challenging, and relevant to contemporary discussions taking place in a variety of disciplines.[67]

Notes

1. On these comparative approaches see, for example, Bryan W. Van Norden, "Mengzi and Xunzi: Two Views of Human Agency," in T. C. Kline III and Philip J. Ivanhoe, eds., *Virtue, Nature, and Moral Agency in the "Xunzi"* (Indianapolis, IN: Hackett, 2000), pp. 103–134; Lee H. Yearley, *Mencius and Aquinas: Theories and Conceptions of Courage* (Albany: State University of New York Press, 1990); Philip J. Ivanhoe and Karen L. Carr, *The Sense of Anti-Rationalism: Zhuangzi and Kierkegaard's Religious Thought*, revised second ed. (Createspace.com, 2010); and Joan Stambaugh, *Impermanence Is Buddha-Nature: Dogen's Understanding of Temporality* (Honolulu: University of Hawaii Press, 1990), which considers Dōgen's philosophy in relation to Heidegger. These citations are not, of course, meant to be exhaustive of what is available. For further references to studies that bring Xunzi's philosophical perspective into comparison with Western philosophy, see Paul Rakita Goldin, *Rituals of the Way: The Philosophy of Xunzi* (Chicago: Open Court, 1999). There are others who have also attempted to bring Dōgen's philosophical perspective in conversation with other philosophers or have warned against the possibilities of that kind of project; see John Maraldo, "The Practice of Body-Mind: Dōgen's *Shinjingakudō* and Comparative Philosophy," and Thomas P. Kasulis, "The Incomparable Philosopher: Dōgen on How to Read the *Shōbōgenzō*," in William R. LaFleur, ed., *Dōgen Studies* (Honolulu: University of Hawaii Press, 1985), pp. 112–130.

2. There may, however, be good reason to establish more substantive connections between Dōgen and the Confucian tradition, particularly considering the familiarity that Dōgen seems to have had with Chinese Confucian texts as manifest in the record of Dōgen's teachings by his desciple Ejō, in the *Shōbōgenzō Zuimonki* 正法眼藏隨聞記, in Ōkubo Dōsh 大久保道舟, ed., *Dōgen zenji zenshū* 道元禪師全集, 2 vols. (Tokyo: 1969–1970), 2:419–495. For a modern Japanese edition of this text, see Watsuji Tetsurō 和辻鉄郎, ed., *Shōbōgenzō Zuimonki* (Tokyo: Iwanami shoten, 1929; reprint 2000). This text may, however, reflect more of Ejō's thought than Dōgen's; see William M. Bodiford, *Sōtō Zen in Medieval Japan* (Honolulu: University of Hawaii Press, 1993), pp. 24–25. Hereafter works found in the *Dōgen zenji zenshū* will be referred to as *DZZ*. Texts in the *Taishō shinshū daizōkyō* 大正新修大藏經 will be abbreviated as *T.#* (followed by the number in that collection).

3. For a more extensive treatment of Xunzi, see John Knoblock, *Xunzi: A Translation and Study of the Complete Works*, 3 vols. (Stanford, CA: Stanford University Press, 1988–1994), and the recent work by Paul Rakita Goldin, *Rituals of the Way: The Philosophy of Xunzi*. For a more extensive treatment of Dōgen, see Carl Bielefeldt, *Dōgen's Manuals of Zen Meditation* (Berkeley: University of California Press, 1988) and the essays collected in William R. LaFleur, ed., *Dōgen Studies*.

4. It is appropriate to mention here that I have resisted establishing a precise definition of the term "ritual" in this chapter. For now I retain a broad and multidimensional interpretation of "ritual." For a sense of the diversity and complexity of what is considered "ritual" and the diversity of approaches to the study and theorizing of ritual, see Catherine Bell, *Ritual: Perspectives and Dimension* (Oxford: Oxford University Press, 1997) and *Ritual Theory, Ritual Practice* (New York: Oxford University Press, 1992).

5. A. R. Radcliffe-Brown, "Religion and Society," in *Structure and Function in Primitive Society* (New York: Free Press, 1965), pp. 153–177; and Robert F. Campany,

"Xunzi and Durkheim as Theorists of Ritual Practice," in Ronald L. Grimes, ed., *Readings in Ritual Studies* (Upper Saddle River, NJ: Prentice Hall, 1996), pp. 86–103 and also in Frank Reynolds and David Tracy, eds., *Discourse and Practice* (Albany: State University of New York Press, 1992), pp. 197–231.

6. See the introduction in T. C. Kline III and Philip J. Ivanhoe, eds., *Virtue, Nature, and Moral Agency in the "Xunzi"* (Indianapolis, IN: Hackett, 2000) and Philip J. Ivanhoe, *Confucian Moral Self Cultivation*, second ed. (Indianapolis, IN: Hackett, 2001), p. 38.

7. Carl Bielefeldt, "Recarving the Dragon: History and Dogma in the Study of Dōgen," in William R. LaFleur, ed., *Dōgen Studies*, p. 23.

8. On the reception of Dōgen's thought in modern times and the slant given to it by D. T. Suzuki, see Carl Bielefeldt, *Dōgen's Manuals of Zen Meditation*, pp. 3–4.

9. The first (and only) scholar to mention the social aspect of Dōgen's thought and practice was Robert N. Bellah, "The Meaning of Dōgen Today," in William R. LaFleur, *Dōgen Studies*, p. 154.

10. Heiner Roetz, *Confucian Ethics of the Axial Age* (Albany: State University of New York Press, 1993), p. 33.

11. Jonathan Z. Smith, "The Influence of Symbols on Social Change: A Place on Which to Stand," in *Map Is Not Territory: Studies in the History of Religions* (Leiden: E. J. Brill, 1978), p. 462.

12. Ibid., p. 474.

13. Bielefeldt, *Dōgen's Manuals of Zen Meditation*, p. 166. On the fall of the Heian period and the rise of the Kamakura period in relation to Japanese Buddhism, see also Yoshiro Tamura, *Japanese Buddhism: A Cultural History* (Tokyo: Kosei Publishing, 2000), pp. 85ff.

14. Radcliffe-Brown, "Religion and Society," pp. 157ff; and Robert F. Campany, "Xunzi and Durkheim as Theorists of Ritual Practice," in Ronald L. Grimes, ed., *Readings in Ritual Studies.*

15. Radcliffe-Brown, "Religion and Society," pp. 157ff.

16. Emile Durkheim, *The Elementary Forms of the Religious Life* (New York: The Free Press, 1915), p. 241; see also the passages on p. 258.

17. Emile Durkheim, *The Elementary Forms of the Religious Life*, p. 218. This passage is cited in Brian Morris, *Anthropological Studies of Religion: An Introductory Text* (New York: Cambridge University Press, 1987), p. 120, in his discussion of the psychological aspects of rituals and the critiques of Durkheim's theory by Evans-Pritchard.

18. Daniel L. Pals, *Seven Theories of Religion* (Oxford: Oxford University Press, 1996), p. 104. For further explication of this interpretation of Durkheimian ritual theory, see Catherine Bell, *Ritual: Perspectives and Dimension*, p. 24.

19. Cited in Lewis A. Coser, introduction to Maurice Halbwachs, *On Collective Memory* (Chicago: University of Chicago Press, 1992), p. 25.

20. *Xunzi* 89–90, K 19.1c, 19/90/10–11.

21. On issues of power and hierarchy in ritual, see the review of different theories in Catherine Bell, *Ritual Theory, Ritual Practice.*

22. *Xunzi* 94, K 19.2c, 19/92/3–4 (emphasis added).

23. Anthony Giddens, *Durkheim* (London: Fontana/Collins, 1978).

24. For more on Xunzi's theories regarding ritual and the setting of hierarchies, see Paul Rakita Goldin, *Rituals of the Way*, pp. 75ff.

25. *Tai taiko goge jari hō* 對大己五夏闍利法, *DDZ*, 2:308–312; *Nipponkoku Echizen Eiheiji chiji shingi* 日本國越前永平寺知事清規, *T.*#2584.

26. Bellah, "The Meaning of Dōgen Today," p. 156.

27. See Radcliffe-Brown, "Religion and Society," pp. 157ff. On the latter point see Philip J. Ivanhoe, "A Happy Symmetry: Xunzi's Ecological Ethic," chapter 2 in this volume.

28. Philip J. Ivanhoe, "Human Nature and Moral Understanding in Xunzi," in T. C. Kline III and Philip J. Ivanhoe, eds., *Virtue, Nature, and Moral Agency in the "Xunzi,"* pp. 237–249.

29. Many of these issues are already found in nascent form in Dōgen's establishment of an independent Zen community at the Kōshōji in Fukakusa. On this period of Dōgen's life, see William M. Bodiford, *Sōtō Zen in Medieval Japan*, pp. 24ff.

30. On this issue, see Francis H. Cook, "Dōgen's View of Authentic Selfhood and Its Socio-ethical Implications," in William R. LaFleur, ed., *Dōgen Studies*, p. 133.

31. Alasdair MacIntyre, *After Virtue*, second ed. (Notre Dame, IN: University of Notre Dame Press, 1984), p. 263. I would like to thank T. C. Kline III for bringing this passage to my attention.

32. Paul Rabinow, *Essays on the Anthropology of Reason* (Princeton, NJ: Princeton University Press, 1996), p. 6.

33. MacIntyre, *After Virtue*, p. 187.

34. Campany, "Xunzi and Durkheim as Theorists of Ritual Practice," p. 88.

35. Ibid.

36. *Xunzi* 96, K 19.3, 19/93/1–2.

37. *Xunzi* 20, K 1.9, 1/3/14.

38. *Xunzi* 19, K 1.8, 1/3/7.

39. *Xunzi* 19, K 1.8, 1/3/8.

40. *Xunzi* 25, K 2.2, 2/5/12–15.

41. Hee-Jin Kim, *Dōgen Kigen: Mystical Realist* (Scholars Press, 1975), pp. 172–173.

42. Ibid., p. 175.

43. Reihō Masunaga, *A Primer of Sōtō Zen: A Translation of Dōgen's "Shōbōgenzō Zuimonki"* (Honolulu: University of Hawaii Press, 1971), pp. 37–38. For the Japanese text, see Watsuji Tetsurō, ed., *Shōbōgenzō Zuimonki*, p. 57. An interesting comparison might be made here to the example of the child playing chess discussed in MacIntyre, *After Virtue*, p. 188.

44. See, for example, the concluding line of the "Discussion of Rites" *Lilun* chapter, *Xunzi* 111, K 19.11, 19/98/9–10.

45. Cited in Rabinow, *Essays on the Anthropology of Reason*, p. 7.

46. Masao Abe, "The Oneness of Practice and Attainment: Implications for the Relation between Means and Ends," in William R. LaFleur, ed., *Dōgen Studies*.

47. Ibid., p. 99.

48. Ibid., p. 102.

49. On the tricky issue of "discovery" vs. "recognition" vs. "enactment" models in Chan/Zen buddhology, see Carl Bielefeldt, *Dōgen's Manuals of Zen Meditation*, p. 163.

50. This passage is from the fascicle titled "Buddha Nature" *Busshō* 佛性, *DZZ* 1:14–35. For a modern Japanese edition, see Mizuno Yaoko 水野弥穂子, *Shōbōgenzō*

正法眼藏 (Tokyo: Iwanami, original 1990; reprint 1999), p. 1:87. Translation is from Norman A. Waddell and Abe Masao, "Buddha-nature," *Eastern Buddhist* 9.1 (1976), p. 88, which is cited in Abe, "The Oneness of Practice and Attainment: Implications for the Relation between Means and Ends," p. 103.

51. Abe, "The Oneness of Practice and Attainment: Implications for the Relation between Means and Ends," p. 107.

52. Bielefeldt, *Dōgen's Manuals of Zen Meditation*, p. 166.

53. *Xunzi* 30, K 2.11, 2/8/1–3.

54. *Xunzi* 20, K 1.10, 1/3/20–21.

55. Ivanhoe, *Confucian Moral Self Cultivation*, pp. 40–41.

56. This notion of "accumulation" was first formulated by Edmund Burke and carried forward by Edward Shils, among others. For the application of the notion of "accumulation" to Xunzi, see the essay by T. C. Kline III, "Moral Agency and Motivation in the *Xunzi*," and Philip J. Ivanhoe, "Human Nature and Moral Understanding in Xunzi," p. 238, see especially n. 8, both in T. C. Kline III and Philip J. Ivanhoe, eds., *Virtue, Nature, and Moral Agency in the "Xunzi."*

57. *Xunzi* 170, K 23.8, 23/117/16–17.

58. For the Japanese text, see Watsuji Tetsurō, ed., *Shōbōgenzō Zuimonki*, p. 89. My translation here is based on that in Masunaga, *A Primer of Sōtō Zen: A Translation of Dōgen's "Shōbōgenzō Zuimonki,"* with some modifications.

59. Masunaga, *A Primer of Sōtō Zen: A Translation of Dōgen's "Shōbōgenzō Zuimonki,"* p. 80.

60. Bielefeldt, *Dōgen's Manuals of Zen Meditation*, p. 168 and see pp. 157ff. for further comments on the importance of the patriarchal tradition.

61. This passage is from the fascicle titled "Face-to-Face Transmission" *Menju* 面授, *DZZ* 1:446–53. For a modern Japanese edition, see Mizuno Yaoko, *Shōbōgenzō*, p. 3:143. The translation cited here is by Kazuaki Tanahashi, ed., *Moon in a Dew Drop: Writings of Zen Master Dōgen* (New York: North Point Press, 1985), p. 175.

62. This passage is from the fascicle titled "Lineage Transmission Document" *Shisho* 詞書, *DDZ* 1:337–47. For a modern Japanese edition, see Mizuno Yaoko, *Shōbōgenzō*, p. 2:377.

63. Bielefeldt, *Dōgen's Manuals of Zen Meditation*, p. 167.

64. Norman A. Waddell and Abe Masao, "Bendōwa," *The Eastern Buddhist* 4.1 (1971), pp. 137–138.

65. "Washing the Face" *Semmen* 洗面, see Mizuno Yaoko, *Shōbōgenzō*, p. 3:120.

66. On the interpretation of Zen ritual as inculcating a kind of "mindfulness," see Ronald Grimes, *Beginnings in Ritual Studies* (Columbia: University of South Carolina Press, 1995), pp. 158–178. For a discussion of Grimes's theory and those who criticize it as an idealized picture of Zen monastic practice, see Catherine Bell, *Ritual: Perspectives and Dimension*, p. 151.

67. Indeed, a quote from Xunzi is used as an epigraph for Catherine Bell's recent book on ritual in which she cites his approach to ritual as a guiding principle in her own considerations; see Catherine Bell, *Ritual: Perspectives and Dimension*, p. xii.

CHAPTER 7

Sheltering Under the Sacred Canopy

Peter Berger and Xunzi

T. C. Kline III

Jonathan Z. Smith has argued that understanding a given tradition's conception of the ideal relationship between the individual and her social environment is fundamental to understanding that tradition's ethical worldview. More specifically, he identifies two basic forms that this ideal relationship can take.[1] Within the first model—the "locative" or "closed" religious worldview—individuals must strive to place themselves in the proper relationship to the rest of the cosmos through fully inhabiting social roles and institutions. Under the second model—the "dynamic" or "open" religious worldview—individuals occasionally strive to break out of or go beyond the social roles and institutions of their culture. The importance of the relationship between individuals and their social environment is recognized in different ways by a broad range of philosophers. For example, existential philosophers such as Søren Kierkegaard and Martin Heidegger argue that we must come to a full and accurate understanding of our relationship to our social environment in order to live authentically. On the other side of the philosophical spectrum, philosophers like Alasdair MacIntyre also argue for the need to fully recognize and embrace the relationship between individuals and the community in which they live.

Interest in this question and recognition of its importance is not restricted to the European philosophical tradition. Early Chinese philosophers recognized and addressed it as well. One of the most sophisticated and interesting attempts to deal with this issue can be found in the writings of Xunzi 荀子, a third-century-b.c.e. Confucian. In this essay, I will examine Xunzi's understanding of the relationship between individuals and their social environment in terms of Xunzi's conception of the relationship of individuals to the Confucian ritual order, an order that embodied the social norms and institutions of the Confucian tradition. Specifically, I will focus on how Xunzi thought Confucians ought to understand their participation in this ritual order, exploring in the process what we can learn from Xunzi about how we should conceive of and pursue religious practice.

The method employed in examining Xunzi's conception of religious practice will be comparative. I examine Xunzi's theory of ritual practice in comparison with Peter Berger's discussion of religious worldviews in *The Sacred Canopy: Elements of a Sociological Theory of Religion*.[2] Since a comparative project of this type, involving thinkers distant from each other in both history and culture, is still the exception and not the rule, let me begin by discussing the advantages of such an approach.

Comparative Inquiry

Xunzi develops a sophisticated and coherent conception of religious practice. His conception of religious ritual is similar enough to contemporary Western theories to allow comparison yet different enough to make such a comparison worthwhile. By bringing Xunzi's understanding of religion into the present academic conversation about religious practice, we can deepen our understanding not only of Xunzi's theory but also of those with which we compare it.[3] As Lee Yearley argues in his own comparative study, *Mencius and Aquinas*, through the comparative process we are able to discern the "similarities within differences and the differences within similarities."[4] Comparison enables us to recognize with greater subtlety and precision the features of what we compare. Through comparison, we can sometimes reveal aspects of an account that are difficult to see in isolation; comparison thereby gives us a more thorough, complex, and nuanced understanding of the constituent elements of any theoretical account than could be achieved by a study of that account alone.

Of course, if the comparison is to be fruitful, there must be some *prima facie* similarity between the thinkers whose works are compared—some commonality of interests, beliefs, perspectives, methods, or capabilities. Unlike Xunzi, we live in an age of disciplinary segregation; few, if any, modern scholars have attempted to develop and defend as broad a theory of ethics and society as Xunzi proposed. To cover the same ground as Xunzi, one would have to be philosopher, anthropologist, sociologist, and theologian. There are only a few modern scholars who meet or at least come close to fitting this description, and Berger belongs in this group. Moreover, Berger and Xunzi both take for granted that religious practices and moral codes are socially constructed and that some understanding of this fact is fundamental to exemplary human life. I will therefore bring Xunzi's views on religious practice into conversation with Berger's sociological understanding of religion in an effort to deepen our understanding of both.

The value of the comparative approach, however, is not limited to revealing what might otherwise remain hidden—the author's assumptions, internal logic, or blind spots. It offers more than an enhanced power of noticing the otherwise unnoticeable. With the presentation of an alternative, we gain a norm against which an account can be judged; indeed, the very fact that there *is* an alternative constitutes an implicit critical judgment, obliging us to evaluate the (comparative) adequacy of each. The juxtaposition of ancient and contemporary sources enables us to raise questions about contemporary theories that would not arise within the modern framework of the theories themselves. Xunzi's philosophy arose in early China, in a historical and cultural context significantly different from that of modern Europe and America. However, he addresses many problems that are still being confronted by contemporary theorists. By comparing his work with Berger's, I hope to show that his treatment of those problems is neither entirely alien to our way of thinking nor surpassed by it. Indeed, I will argue that, with regard to several important issues, Xunzi provides a better account of religious practice than can be found among our contemporaries.

Xunzi's work offers a means of addressing what I see as a flaw endemic to much contemporary writing on religious practice. Like most modern theorists of religion, Berger leaves inchoate or implicit the conception of human nature that animates important aspects of his theory. While Xunzi's understanding of religious practice shares deep similarities with Berger's theory, it is explicitly and systematically tied to a substantial theory of human nature. For this reason, Xunzi's theory provides particularly rich and powerful resources for thinking critically about Berger's model. By bringing the theories of Xunzi and Berger into conversation with each other and exploring the ways in which the former can enrich the latter, we can not only significantly strengthen Berger's theory but also contribute to the development of a sound theory of religious practice. A not incidental benefit of this process is the opportunity to give close attention to Xunzi's theory of ritual practice, which, though it holds great promise, has as yet received little attention in Western literature.[5]

Peter Berger

Like Xunzi, Berger develops a theoretical framework for understanding how human beings create societies; how they build institutions, ritual, and other mechanisms for maintaining the social order; and how they then come to interact with their own creations. He, too, attempts to explain individual development within the context of social institutions. For Berger, all of these elements constitute his sociological theory of religion, a theory that he fully develops in *The Sacred Canopy*.[6] Given the goals of this chapter, it will not be necessary to provide a complete account of Berger's theory. Rather, the focus will be on understanding how he conceives of the interaction between the individual and her social environment. With this aim in mind, I will briefly sketch the outlines of his theory and then consider several areas where bringing Xunzi and Berger into conversation with each other reveals important aspects of both their theories.[7]

Berger begins his study of religion with an observation that Xunzi would have wholeheartedly supported. Society, according to Berger, is completely a product of human activity—what Xunzi calls "deliberate activity" 偽 *wei*—yet human beings are also products of their society. On the one hand, without human beings there would be no such thing as society or social organization. As Xunzi argues, many higher animals may have the instinct to form collectives, but only humans have the capacity and need to organize their own collectives into social structures that are able to utilize the resources around them.[8] According to Berger, this organization of human collectives into societies is purely the result of human activity. Yet, on the other hand, human beings are born into social organizations. These societies inevitably shape their identities and provide them with the symbols, meanings, and social practices through which they inhabit their world. Moreover, society is prior to any particular individual and will most likely last beyond her death. In this sense, society produces the individual. Berger's main project, then, is to explain the role of religion in this process of world construction and individual socialization.

The fundamental premise of Berger's theory is that human beings are continuously interacting with society in three different ways, or, as Berger describes it, they are engaged in a dialectical process consisting of three moments—externalization, objectification, and internalization. *Externalization* represents the unceasing mental and physical activity of human beings that creates and sustains the society and culture within which they live. *Objectification* refers to the process by which these created products of human activity take on a reality outside and separate from the activity of their producers; products of human activity become objects in the social world. *Internalization*, then, reverses the process of externalization. Human beings reappropriate the objects of their creative activity, internalizing them as structures within their subjective consciousness. This internalization can take place within a single human lifetime, or it can take place across generations. Parents may help in the process of externalization and objectification, and then it is their children who engage in the internalization. It is this cross-generational process that makes tradition and the maintenance of the worldview possible despite the deaths of members of the community.[9]

According to Berger, these three types of interaction with the social world are entailed by the inherent biological structure of human beings because human beings are born "unfinished" (Berger 4). In other words, human beings are unlike lower animals in that we are not born with a fully formed set of instincts that define our individual and social activity. Wolves, for instance, are born with a set of instincts that make it possible for them to coordinate with the pack and hunt for their own food without having to undergo an extensive period of learning. Because their drives are so specialized and firmly ingrained from birth, animals live securely, but only within "a world that is more or less completely determined by . . . instinctual structure. This world is closed in terms of the possibilities, programmed, as it were, by the animals' own constitution" (Berger 5). In contrast, human beings live within a world of limitless possibilities. The newborn human animal seems to be almost infinitely malleable. Our instinctual structure is "underspecialized and undirected towards a species-specific environment" (Berger 5). Denied the instinctually structured world of other animals, we must create a world for ourselves to inhabit, a way of ordering our experience. "The world building activity of man, therefore, is not a biologically extraneous phenomenon, but the direct consequence of man's biological constitution" (Berger 5). By creating the world we inhabit, humans, through our own activity, develop the specialized drives and dispositions that allow us to find stability in the originally chaotic world. "[M]an not only produces a world, but he also produces himself" (Berger 6). Usually this development of drives and dispositions takes place through a process of socialization by which we internalize habitual structures and disposition, thus ordering our experience and making it possible for us to function in the world. This socialization, then, constitutes the fundamental influence of society on human beings.

Berger refers to the socially constructed world that orders human experience as the *nomos* of society, more commonly called a worldview. The worldview of a society permeates all levels of experience. At its most basic and pervasive level, a worldview begins, as did Adam's in the Garden of Eden, with a naming of the things and meanings that constitute the world. It begins with ontology. At a more complex level, it includes pretheoretical interpretive schema, moral maxims, and traditional wisdom. Finally, at the highest level, are ritual, institutions, and theoretical frameworks for explaining and maintaining the worldview. In Berger's theory, all of these elements of the worldview, taken together, constitute the "knowledge" of a given society. "Whatever the variations, every society provides for its members an objectively available body of 'knowledge.' To participate in the society is to share its 'knowledge,' that is, to co-inhabit its nomos" (Berger 21).

Berger maintains that worldviews are inherently precarious because they are a constructed product of human activity and not truly an element of the prehuman world. Essentially, society consists in the collective activity of all those who participate in the society. Because humans have no existence outside of this activity, any elements of human experience that produce deviations in normal activity become a threat to the continued existence of the worldview. According to Berger, forgetfulness, self-interest, stupidity, and catastrophe all constitute threats. If a worldview is to successfully provide the stable structures enabling people to order their experience for any extended period of time, mechanisms to overcome these obstacles must exist. As a first line of defense, rituals and institutions are created to uphold and to remind us of the particular ontology and interpretive schema of the worldview. Society is coercive in that it must continually demand adherence to the basic elements of the social worldview or risk fading out of existence. Rituals and institutions must be passed down from generation to generation in order for the society to survive. Invariably, in the course of this process of transmission, individuals or events will disrupt the usual social order and call into question society's specific rituals and institutions. In order to respond to these events and maintain the social order, something further is needed. For Berger, this necessary element is legitimation, "socially objectified 'knowledge' that serves to explain and justify the social order" (Berger 29).[10] Historically, according to Berger, the most effective and prevalent form of legitimation has been religion.

The central role of religious legitimation is to explain the anomic, disruptive events of human life so that they can be reintegrated into the worldview as a whole. Even death, the ultimate disruptive event for the continuation of the social order, can be given a place in the proper explanation and development of a human life. Berger calls these religious reintegrative explanations theodicies. Although he uses this term more broadly than is common in religious studies, his use still conforms to the basic problem of explaining those elements of human experience that threaten the social order. All theodicies, Berger believes, rest on a fundamental, irrational attitude of the self submitting to the ordering power of society (Berger 54). "Every society entails a certain denial of the individual self and its needs, anxieties, and problems. One of the key functions of nomoi is the facilitation of this denial in individual consciousness" (Berger 55). Theodicies, or some other form of legitimation, are thus a necessary component of any society; a worldview unable to explain and integrate the disruptive events of human experience could not exist for long.

Despite their vital role in explaining and reintegrating anomic events into the worldview, theodicies also pose a danger. To integrate the anomalies of suffering, injustice, and death into a human meaning system, theodicies embody patterns of meaning that have no reality apart from human activity. They thus represent the most powerful patterns of objectification—and that is the source of their power as legitimations. When confronted with the necessity to submit to the ordering power of society's *nomos*, an individual may react in one of two ways. On the one hand, she can reappropriate the social order and the socialized self by "recollecting" that the social order is originally a human construction made partially out of her own activity. On the other hand, she may refuse any reappropriation of the social order and self and, instead, treat these phenomena as objects confronting her in the same way as laws of nature. Seen in this way, the social order appears external to her, and she fails to recognize any element of its constructed nature. This latter reaction constitutes what Berger refers to as "alienation" (Berger 85). Alienation, then, becomes the dark underside of religious legitimation. In fact, within Berger's understanding of religion, all religions, insofar as they attempt to explain and integrate chaotic phenomena, intrinsically involve some degree of alienation. Extreme forms of alienation, such as masochistic religiosity, can be avoided by repeated recollection of the human origin of the social order. However, complete elimination of alienation occurs only in moments when the individual steps outside of the social order and directly confronts the chaotic world for what it is. Berger believes that the individual lives authentically only in these moments when she is without the comforting shelter of any form of legitimation or ordering of experience. If, instead, she submerges herself in the social order and its legitimations, reifying these social constructions as external and immutable, she practices bad faith. She reduces herself to the level of an animal who lives within a world bounded by its habitual drives, failing, or perhaps refusing, to recognize that she helped to build her own cage.

It is important to notice that Berger does not claim that we are born unalienated and become alienated through contact with the legitimations of our society's worldview. Rather, he believes that any form of social awareness of ourselves as persons and of the worldview into which we are born requires a certain amount of alienation (Berger 83–84). We start out as children with an alienated vision of the world, in which the elements of the worldview are understood as necessary, fixed, and immutable (Berger 84). Living authentically is an accomplishment and is not the original position from which we have fallen. Like Xunzi, he does not believe in an original, untainted human condition that was somehow lost or corrupted in the process of socialization. On the contrary, our task as human beings involves overcoming our initial alienation by realizing the constructed nature of the social order and the worldview within which it functions.

The central components of Berger's sociological theory of religion can thus be summarized: Religious worldviews are constructions by which societies legitimate the social order and maintain their constellation of things, meanings, rituals, and institutions. Religious legitimations, or theodicies, function to explain and integrate those aspects of human experience that threaten the continuance of the existing social order. They are constructed and maintained by human activity, yet when this aspect of their existence is forgotten, they also inherently carry with them the danger of alienation.

Xunzi

> When we sacrifice for rain, it rains. Why? I say, there is nothing to ask "why?" about. It rains even though we don't sacrifice. The sun and moon undergo an eclipse and you try to save them. In a drought

> you pray for rain. You consult the tortoise shell and yarrow stalks before deciding an important matter. These rites aren't to be regarded as attempts to obtain something we seek but as elements of culture. Although the gentleman looks on them as a matter of humane culture, the lower gentry see them as a matter of dealing with spirits. Regard them as a matter of humane culture and good fortune follows; regard them as a matter of dealings with spirits and misfortune follows.[11]

Given that Xunzi is often described as an unmasker and debunker of religion, some may be surprised by the claim that he can be seen as arguing for a positive conception of religion, yet consider the passage above.[12] More specifically, consider what Xunzi does *not* advocate in this passage. He does not argue that the people should stop performing the rain sacrifice. He does not claim that the sacrifice, in itself, is worthless or harmful to the people, nor does he deny that it contributes to their well-being. Quite to the contrary, he strongly implies that these religious rituals play a critical role in human flourishing. What Xunzi clearly *does* condemn are misinterpretations of the true sense and function of sacrifices. He insists that at least the elite members of society must perform religious rituals with a proper understanding of their nature and purpose.

Imagine a village full of discouraged, drought-weary, and hungry people. The rain sacrifice is performed. All of the villagers gather as the leaders of the village present offerings at the altar and ask the spirits to send down rain and relieve their suffering. The ritual expresses the community's hopes and fears. It brings them together in a forum that allows such feelings to be publicly expressed and shared. This shared expression helps alleviate the individual despair and fear of the present dire situation and focuses the community's attention and energy on their shared future prospects. The ritual sustains order and "humane culture" in an otherwise chaotic, disruptive, and debilitating situation.

In passages like the one above, Xunzi reveals his deep concern with religious practice. Rather than advocating an antagonistic or agnostic attitude toward ritual, Xunzi's philosophy of ritual and religion has much in common with Berger's. Both philosophers understand society as a collective, human construction and seek to understand and explain how this construction came to be, how it is maintained, and how it enables or discourages human flourishing. They describe human beings as essentially social creatures, meaning, first, that all human beings must undergo a process of socialization in order to become fully human. At birth we lack the dispositions and interpretive schema that enable us to function as humans in the world. The second implication of being essentially social creatures is that we can become fully human and flourish only in society. In addition, both Berger and Xunzi believe that the successful process of socialization inherently requires some amount of denial and transformation of individual drives.[13] Accordingly, both give a prominent role to ritual as the social mechanism that functions to "remind" people of their society's worldview and its boundaries. Both recognize that there will be different levels of understanding regarding the constructed nature of the social order. Whereas Berger discusses this point in terms of different levels of legitimation, Xunzi describes different levels of ritual understanding. "He who dwells in ritual and can ponder it well may be said to know how to think; he who dwells in ritual and does not change his ways may be said to be steadfast. He who knows how to think and to be steadfast, and in addition has a true love for ritual—he is a sage."[14] For both thinkers, what is at issue is the degree to which a person realizes that she lives in a society in which the boundaries and contours of the social world are products of human activity.

Berger and Xunzi also agree about the pervasive nature of the worldview and its legitimations. Legitimation (in Berger) or ritual order (in Xunzi) begins at the lowest level with the naming of what exists in the world. At its highest level, the worldview is legitimated and explained by the types of theory and explanation exhibited in the theoretical writings of Berger and Xunzi. In general, few people will achieve these higher forms of understanding. However, to be a participating member in the social order, a person must have nearly complete knowledge of the lower levels. To lack understanding of the lowest levels is to be an outsider to the given society.

Each of these similarities between Berger's and Xunzi's understandings of ritual and religion leads to a host of worthwhile and productive questions. Rather than pursuing these similarities further, I focus on a significant set of differences that these similarities might obscure. First, Berger's and Xunzi's conceptions of human nature differ. Consistent with his understanding of other aspects of the social world, Berger claims that "human nature" is also a constructed human product, or at least a result of such "world-building activity" (Berger 7). Since Berger conceives human nature to be constructed in this way, no conception of human nature can claim to explain human nature prior to the creation of society. As I noted earlier, Berger holds that human beings are not only *unfinished* at birth, they are barely begun (Berger 6). Berger argues not only that human dispositions and drives are not fully formed at birth but, further, that without socialization there are no original dispositions and drives from which a human being can even begin to take shape. At birth, human beings lack even the rudimentary drives and dispositions that would enable them to survive. Given this understanding of human nature, it would appear that without socialization we would not last long on the planet. In Berger's view, the gulf between human beings and other animals looms implausibly large.[15]

Xunzi also believes in a significant distinction between human beings and other animals, yet the divide is not nearly so pronounced as Berger would have it. Xunzi believes human nature is substantial, rather than socially constructed. We are born with a well-defined set of drives. Among these are such basic drives as our familiar desires for sexual gratification, food, safety, and comfort. Equal in importance are drives oriented toward sensory satisfactions—for example, our eyes prefer beautiful sights, our ears favor melodious sounds, our mouths relish certain flavors, and so forth.[16] We are also born with more general, yet no less important, dispositions, such as an inherent fondness for our own profit or benefit (好利 *haoli*)—that is, we are prudential creatures.[17] In addition, we possess a range of natural capacities, among them the potential to fulfill role-specific duties and to transform ourselves through ritual.[18] Such drives, dispositions, and capacities are all inherent parts of human nature and exist prior to any type of social order. Thus, according to Xunzi, humans, like other animals, come into the world with a complex cognitive and sensory apparatus capable of interpreting and functioning in the world. Humans have natural drives, dispositions, and capacities that distinguish us from any other animal. Nevertheless, because humans and animals are both born with substantial natures, biologically they are much closer together than Berger's theory allows.

The specific content Xunzi ascribes to human nature has implications for his theory that further distinguish it from Berger's.[19] To begin with, Berger argues that society does not grow out of any substantial content of human nature. "Its [society's] patterns, always relative in time and space, are not given in nature, nor can they be deduced in any specific manner from the 'nature of man' " (Berger 7). Berger believes that the "nature of man" is itself a product of the social order. In contrast, Xunzi insists that human nature is bad. It has substantial content that directly contributes to the structure of the social order. When left to follow our own original natures, human beings tend to disrupt the social order and live in conflict and chaos. Most of the drives and dispositions of human nature that lead to this chaotic situation are not themselves inherently bad or chaotic. They simply lack the proper order and restraint that would allow their expression and fulfillment in ways that would not result in the violation of the interests of others or of the natural world. Thus, for Xunzi, as for Berger, socialization or ritual cultivation is absolutely necessary; the social order and its worldview provide this socialization. Nevertheless, Xunzi's understanding of this process of socialization is profoundly different from Berger's. For Berger, socialization *makes* one into a human being, and he sees this "making" as creation *ex nihilo* (Berger 33). The human infant is the *tabula rasa* upon which is stamped the imprint of its society. For Xunzi, socialization makes someone human in that it harnesses and transforms the drives and dispositions he already possesses; these natural drives and dispositions take on a pattern that conforms with the social order, with the human "Way" 道 *Dao*. The difference between the two thinkers' understanding of this process of socialization, or, we might say, cultivation, cannot be overstated.[20] In order to emphasize the importance this difference has for appreciating the differences folded within the similarities discussed above, we will examine the description and evaluation of individuals who have attained the highest stages of cultivation according to their respective theories. Both thinkers provide explicit and detailed descriptions of such exemplars: for Xunzi, there is the Confucian sage; for Berger, there is the person living authentically.[21]

Sagehood and Authenticity

Xunzi's and Berger's conceptions of paradigmatic individuals have much in common. Both the sage and the authentic person exhibit a deep understanding of the constructed nature of the social order. They realize that human activity, and human activity alone, constitutes and maintains the social order, and they have a reasonably sophisticated theoretical understanding of their respective worldviews and the role of religious practice.[22] Both paragons self-consciously participate in and perpetuate the ritual cultivation and socialization that maintain the social order. They see the social order as necessary and good, although for Berger's authentic person it may have its inherent dangers as well. Differences arise, however, in the attitude each paragon takes toward the phenomenon Berger refers to as alienation.

For Xunzi, the sage has transformed his natural drives, dispositions, and capacities so that they accord with the human *Dao*. Because his cultivated dispositions are in perfect harmony with society and the natural world, he is able to fulfill his desires and express his emotions without transgressing the boundaries of the harmonious social order.[23] When faced with a given situation, his dispositions and perceptions move him to act in the appropriate way, at the appropriate time, and to the appropriate degree. He effortlessly perceives and follows the patterns of the *Dao* in both the human and the natural worlds.[24] Xunzi regards this type of effortless harmony as the highest level of ritual cultivation. Although the sage recognizes the constructed nature of the human *Dao*, he has transformed himself into a creature that never transgresses, nor desires to transgress, the boundaries set by the constructed worldview. He now lives always and completely within the worldview of the Confucian Way. There are no moments of disruption, and all phenomena are integrated into comprehensible patterns.[25]

However, considered from Berger's perspective, the Confucian sage appears to have turned himself back into an animal. He appears to have become fully alienated from the worldview that he perpetuates and follows. He lives within a world defined by his now instinctual drives and dispositions, a form of behavior that Berger attributes to the lower animals. The explanations and patterns of the social order have become immutable and fixed for him, at least in the sense that they are the one *Dao* that leads to the greatest harmony among humans, Heaven, and Earth. From the point of view of Berger, the Confucian sage represents not so much an achievement to be praised and idealized as a degenerate form of human activity to be condemned.

We reach a similar sort of conclusion when we evaluate Berger's conception of the authentic person from the standpoint of Xunzi. Berger's authentic person is the counterpart to the inauthentic. Whereas the inauthentic person fails to recognize the constructed nature of the social order and treats the worldview as objective and "other," the authentic person fully recognizes her creative activity as supporting and maintaining a social order that is being projected onto an essentially chaotic cosmos. Only in moments of ecstasy, when she steps out from under the worldview that constitutes the sacred canopy of the social order and faces the chaotic and terrifying cosmos, is she most truly authentic.[26] Although such moments will be brief and will be followed by a return to living within in the social order, if she keeps such experiences, and the recognition of the frailty of the human order that they reveal, ever present in her consciousness, then she lives as authentically as is humanly possible.

For Xunzi, such moments of ecstasy, in which chaos peeks through the patterns of the *Dao*, indicate a failure of individual cultivation. Only the uncultivated see and feel the world as chaotic and disordered. This is not to say that the sage cannot perceive chaos in the world. He can, of course, recognize the chaos of the original nature of human beings, as well as the political and social chaos apparent in eras of bad rulership. However, he interprets these chaotic phenomena to be the result of the failure of people properly to cultivate their capacity to follow the *Dao* and harmonize their activity with the patterns of the social and natural order. He understands chaos as a contingent failure to adhere to the patterns of society and the cosmos that are objectively part of the world. Only in the view of the uncultivated masses, who are unable to see these patterns and understand how to follow them, will action appear to lead to chaos and appear to be played out in a chaotic world—a world without any guiding patterns. In fact, the more uncultivated the individual, the more chaotic the world within which he lives. From Xunzi's point of view, these moments of ecstasy, as Berger describes them, should motivate the individual, possibly out of fear, to cultivate himself more strenuously. The goal of cultivation, after all, is to bring one's emotions and dispositions into harmony with the social and natural orders. As this task is accomplished, one becomes more able to recognize and understand patterns of behavior that lead to conflict and chaos and to see them as failures to follow the *Dao*.

These differences in Xunzi's and Berger's characterizations of the fully cultivated person stem not only from their different conceptions of human nature but also from their different metaphysical views. Berger considers the natural world to be an inherently chaotic place. Although humans order the cosmos by projecting their worldviews onto it, ultimately this order is illusory, a creation of human activity. Any worldview, such as religious theodicies, that attempts to transform this humanly created order into the unchanging order of the cosmos alienates human beings by obscuring the true nature of the cosmos and the relation of human activity to the cosmos. In reality, the cosmos and the anomie of the "real" world always linger behind the social constructions. Occasionally they break through in the experience of ecstasy, moments of authenticity. Yet these moments of disruption must be the exception rather than the rule; otherwise, they threaten the social order. Humans must always shelter under the sacred canopy of their social order. Like Berger, Xunzi holds that, before the sages created the rites, human beings and the world were in a state of chaos. Natural resources—animals, plants, building materials, metals, waterways—were not properly developed and ordered until the sages developed methods and regulations for ordering and cultivating them. Nevertheless, Xunzi does not believe that the fundamental nature of the cosmos is chaotic. There are patterns to the seasons, cycles of waxing and waning, growth, maturity and decay, and regularities such as the rising and setting of the sun. The human *Dao* constructed by the sages is not merely a projection onto a chaotic world but the effective ordering of humans and the natural world in terms of the patterns of behavior and cycles of movement that preceded the arrival of the sages. The *Dao*, if properly followed, brings the various elements of the cosmos into concrete and lasting harmony.[27] No human illusions are involved.[28] From Berger's perspective, a worldview such as Xunzi's, which posits patterns and order to the cosmos, would be considered an alienating theodicy. As Van Harvey remarks in his examination of Berger, "[A]ny philosophical or religious view that rejects the notion of a primeval chaos and that regards a symbolic structure as true because it corresponds to the objective structures of being is, by definition, alienating. It embodies a false consciousness."[29] This position would seem to leave Berger with no way to distinguish a social organization that is based upon beliefs wholly consistent with the best that psychology and natural science can offer from one based upon mere hallucinations. These differences in metaphysical assumptions further support and explain the different evaluations of the sage and the authentic person considered above.

Reconsidering Berger

Berger's assumptions leave him with a visible tension in his theory, a tension that could be avoided were he to explicitly adopt a more substantial theory of human nature.[30] In fact, something like Xunzi's conception of human nature may be lurking in the background of Berger's model.

One of the central assumptions of Berger's theory, an assumption that he continually emphasizes, is that any social order is always precariously balanced on the edge of chaos. Any serious disruption of the human activity that constitutes the worldview threatens society. It would seem that worldviews and the societies they engender are rather frail and ephemeral things. As I have already noted, Berger mentions four factors that contribute to the precarious nature of society. The first three factors relate to human behavior: forgetfulness, self-interest, and stupidity (Berger 29). Catastrophes, an inevitable feature of any human life, constitute the fourth. The most obvious of these catastrophes is death. Along with the chaotic nature of the cosmos, these four factors motivate Berger's assumption that "all socially constructed worlds are inherently precarious" (Berger 29).

At the same time, there are also factors in Berger's theory that point toward the conclusion that socially constructed worlds are, in fact, quite stable. The process of socialization that Berger describes produces humans with alienated consciousness. They begin by viewing the social order and its ontology as fixed elements of the external world. Recognizing the constructed nature of society and overcoming alienation happen only with great effort. Human beings are creatures who tend to objectify their own creations. So, it would seem that the vast majority of people will normally remain alienated and continue to hold their worldview as immutable and authoritative. Constant interaction with other members of their society, who share in perpetuating the common worldview, also would seem to contribute to the tendency among people to remain firmly entrenched in the social order. Even the fear associated with ecstatic moments would be expected to push people back under the canopy of socially constructed meanings and away from confrontation with the chaotic cosmos. All of these elements of Berger's theory, considered together, support the claim that worldviews are more stable than Berger suggests. They will rarely give way to chaos.

In fact, one could argue that the tendencies of human behavior that Berger lists as supporting his claim about the precarious nature of the constructed worldview—stupidity, self-interest, and forgetfulness—can equally well be understood as forces tending to contribute to alienation and, thereby, the continuation of the social order. The disruptive factor of stupidity is easily turned to support an opposite conclusion. According to Berger, authenticity requires at least some theoretical understanding of the creative nature of human activity and the essential nature of the cosmos. However, stupidity would seem to prevent an individual from achieving precisely this kind of understanding, thus cutting off the possibility of authenticity and driving people back to unreflective belief in their worldview. A similar case can be made for the force of self-interest. It appears much more likely that a person's interests will be better served by general adherence to the social order and its ontology than by trying to go against it. In general, self-interest is best served by pursuing the most effective means for acting within the social order. It is through social institutions, in accordance with the social order, that most effective human action is accomplished. Acting contrary to the social order, especially the social institutions that constitute part of this order, makes it more difficult to get things done and thus thwarts the pursuit of self-interest. Here again, the force purported to disrupt the social order seems actually to support it. And finally, while it is true that a social order is endangered if people forget the practices and activities that constitute it, forgetfulness can only be a serious threat if a great many people forget *en masse*. It is more reasonable to suppose that any individuals who begin to forget these practices and activities would quickly be reminded by others. Thus, the phenomenon of forgetfulness actually offers an occasion for emphasizing and strengthening general support for the worldview.

Within Berger's theory, then, there seem to be factors that motivate opposing judgments about the stability of any social order. His metaphysical assumptions about the nature of the cosmos seem to support the claim of instability, yet his lack of any substantial conception of human nature prior to socialization and his account of psychological development seem to support the claim for stability. It is not clear that Berger's theory has the resources to resolve this tension.

If Berger were to accept the view that there is a substantial human nature prior to socialization and that this nature, when not transformed through the process of socialization, tends to lead people toward chaos and conflict, then from the beginning he would have strong support for the claim that the social world is a rather thin defense against the chaotic nature of the unordered cosmos. Furthermore, if he were to include in his conception of human nature a strong sense of self-interest and a healthy dose of fear of chaos (both of which he willingly admits are true or human psychology in general), he might be able to argue for stability as well. Once such a conception of human nature is in place, it can readily be argued that even the least sophisticated human beings can understand that it is in their best interest to adhere at least minimally to the requirements of the given social order, since nonadherence leads to chaos and conflict, a situation to which human beings have a built-in aversion. Drives arising within human nature as originally given would support the perpetuation of society and its order. Berger could then explain the existence of these two forces and how they relate to each other. Moreover, a substantial conception of human nature modeled on that of Xunzi is highly plausible. Berger himself already admits that people have a strong fear of death and are self-interested. When he advances these claims about human psychology, they do not appear to be claims about the society-specific imprinting of a worldview; rather, they appear to be claims about the general nature of all human beings. Explicitly admitting that these features of human psychology constitute part of a human nature that exists prior to socialization does not seem to be an illegitimate step, nor one that Berger should avoid. As I have argued, there are reasons for believing that such an addition would actually strengthen Berger's claims.

Conclusion

In the midst of a drought, the rain sacrifice is performed. By participating in the communal rite, the villagers shelter under the sacred canopy of the social order, the religious worldview of early China. The rite provides shelter from the encroaching fear and chaos of the situation. It reconstitutes and maintains the social order. Xunzi, like Berger, recognizes and understands the religious significance of the rite in terms of its ability to provide shelter from the anomic events of life that threaten to disrupt the social order. According to Xunzi, the Confucian sages created the rites, the *Dao*, for the purpose of providing this shelter and bringing human culture into existence. The sage, in turn, exemplifies the person who embodies the *Dao*, who lives life completely under the shelter of the sacred canopy.

Berger shares Xunzi's understanding of the role of the social order and religious legitimations. Both agree that human activity creates and maintains the social order, yet they have different conceptions of the exemplary human life. Both agree that the exemplary human life requires that the person be fully aware of the constructed nature of the sacred canopy, but Berger, unlike Xunzi, holds that the authentic person must occasionally step out from under the sacred canopy and stand naked before the chaotic cosmos. It is, in Berger's opinion, the recollection of these moments of authentic awareness that allows a person to live authentically, with full understanding of the constructed and fragile nature of the social order.

As we have discovered, they conceive of the exemplary life differently because they conceive of human nature and the nature of the cosmos differently. In turn, the comparison of Xunzi and Berger allows us to suggest one way in which Xunzi may have a better understanding of human nature than Berger. If Berger were to adopt a conception of human nature similar to Xunzi's (a conception that seems to be already implicit in his work), he would be able to justify and explain not only the fragility but also the stability of the social order. Conversely, there may be ways in which Xunzi's views could benefit from the insights of Berger's theory. Through comparative examination of their respective theories, our understanding of each theory deepens. Such study also allows us to critically evaluate the virtues and plausibility of each view. This type of mutual conversation can only strengthen our understanding of the issues that Xunzi and Berger address in their work. We learn more about the sacred canopy as we live beneath its shelter.

Notes

This essay first appeared in the *Journal of Religious Ethics* 29.2 (2001), pp. 261–282. I would like to acknowledge the help of Diane Yeager, the anonymous reviews for the journal, as well as Eric Hutton and P. J. Ivanhoe. This essay was greatly improved because of their kind and generous advice.

1. Jonathan Z. Smith, "The Influence of Symbols on Social Change: A Place on Which to Stand," *Worship* 44 (1970), pp. 457–474.

2. Peter L. Berger, *The Sacred Canopy: Elements of a Sociological Theory of Religion* (New York: Doubleday, 1967). Further references to *The Sacred Canopy* will be in the text in parentheses as "Berger" followed by the page number.

3. Xunzi's conception of religion and ritual already has been fruitfully compared to the work of Emile Durkheim by Robert Campany, "Xunzi and Durkheim as Theorists of Ritual Practice," in Frank Reynolds and David Tracy, eds., *Discourse and Practice* (Albany: State University of New York Press, 1992), pp. 197–231; and A. R. Radcliffe-Brown, "Religion and Society," in *Structure and Function in Primitive Society* (New York: The Free Press, 1965), pp. 153–177. However, I would argue that comparing Xunzi's overall approach to religious practice to Berger's sociological theory of religion yields better conceptual results.

4. Lee H. Yearley, *Mencius and Aquinas: Theories of Virtue and Conceptions of Courage* (Albany: State University of New York Press, 1990), pp. 1, 203. For a full discussion of Yearley's understanding of comparative religious philosophy, see especially his concluding chapter. For similar comparative projects examining an early Chinese and a European philosopher, see Karen L. Carr and Philip J. Ivanhoe, *The Sense of Anti-Rationalism: Zhuangzi and Kierkegaard's Religious Thought*, revised second ed. (Createspace.com, 2010) and Aaron Stalnaker, *Overcoming Our Evil: Human Nature and Spiritual Exercises in Xunzi and Augustine* (Washington, DC: Georgetown University Press, 2006). Another useful comparative study, one that spans premodern and modern Europe, is Van Harvey, *Feuerbach and the Interpretation of Religion* (Cambridge: Cambridge University Press, 1997); chapters 7 and 8 will be particularly relevant to any discussion of comparative analysis. For an excellent collection of essays addressing the theoretical issues involved in comparative study of religion, see Kimberly C. Patton and Benjamin C. Ray, eds., *A Magic Still Dwells: Comparative Religion in the Postmodern Age* (Berkeley: University of California Press, 2000).

5. It should be noted that I am purposely leaving open the possibility that Berger's theory might conversely be used as a critical resource for thinking about and suggesting changes in Xunzi's theory. As will become apparent, I am focusing narrowly on an important point at which I believe Berger's theory needs critical revision, and Xunzi's theory provides resources for both appreciating the deficiencies and pointing the way to a remedy. Any comparison of the sort I am conducting here has more dimensions than can be pursued in any single article, and I hope the exploration I have begun here will continue.

6. Berger is a prolific author and editor whose published work now spans four decades. I have confined my consideration to *The Sacred Canopy* because it is the one work in which he directly addresses the question at issue. Much of the groundwork for the discussion in *The Sacred Canopy* was laid out in Peter L. Berger and Thomas Luckmann, *The Social Construction of Reality: A Treatise in the Sociology of Knowledge* (New York: Doubleday, 1966).

7. This synopsis of Berger's theory of the sociology of religion is indebted to Van Harvey's two thorough and insightful studies of Berger's work. See Van Harvey, "Some Problematical Aspects of Peter Berger's Theory of Religion," *Journal of the American Academy of Religion* 41.1 (1973), pp. 75–93; and *Feuerbach and the Interpretation of Religion* (Cambridge, England: Cambridge University Press, 1997), pp. 229–280.

8. 故義以分則和，和則一，一則多力，多力則彊，彊則勝物，故宮室可得而居也。故序四時，裁萬物，兼利天下，無它故焉，得之分義也。 *Xunzi* 45–46, K 9.16a, 9/39/9–13.

9. For further discussion of the issue of internalization across generations, see Berger and Luckmann, *The Social Construction of Reality*, pp. 67–72.

10. Here Berger's usage approximates Max Weber's understanding of the concept of legitimacy as applied to political authority. However, political legitimacy, for Weber, is more theoretically oriented than Berger's views concerning the legitimation of worldviews.

11. 「雩而雨，何也」曰「無何也，猶不雩而雨也。日月食而求之，天旱而雩，卜筮然後決大事，非以為得求也，以文之也。故君子以為文，而百性以為神。以為文則吉，以為神則凶也。 *Xunzi* 85, K 17.8, 17/82/6–8. Translation adapted from Edward J. Machle, "Xunzi as a Religious Philosopher," chapter 1 in this volume, p. 25–26.

12. Machle, "Xunzi as a Religious Philosopher," pp. 21–23.

13. I have deliberately used the term "drives" rather than "desires." My purpose in doing so is not to make reference to Sigmund Freud but to avoid the overly broad philosophical use of the term "desires." Within this conception of drives are to be included our sensory preferences, as listed below, as well as our tendency to form bonds with others and the psychological capacities that make self-cultivation possible. For a full discussion of the drives that Xunzi associates with human nature, see Eric L. Hutton, "Does Xunzi Have a Consistent Theory of Human Nature?" and T. C. Kline III, "Moral Agency and Motivation in the *Xunzi*," both in T. C. Kline III and Philip J. Ivanhoe, eds., *Virtue, Nature, and Moral Agency in the "Xunzi"* (Indianapolis, IN: Hackett, 2000).

14. 然而不法禮、不是禮，謂之無方之民；法禮、是禮，謂之有方之士。禮之中焉能思索，謂之能慮；禮之中焉能勿易，謂之能固。能慮能固，加好者焉，斯聖人矣。 *Xunzi* 95, K 19.2d, 19/92/14.

15. Berger argues for a radical separation of humans from other animals. However, those philosophers who are familiar with contemporary biology and write on the subject tend to have a more moderate view. For a well-argued and informed discussion of the relationship between humans and other animals, see Mary Midgley, *Beast and Man: The Roots of Human Nature* (New York: Routledge, 1995).

16. 若夫目好色，耳好聲，口好味，心好利，骨體膚理好愉佚，是皆生於人之情性者也；感而自然，不待事而後生之者也。 *Xunzi* 160–161, K 23.2a, 23/114/11–13. See also K 11.7b, 11/53/12–20.

17. 今人之性，生而有好利焉。 *Xunzi* 157, K 23.1a, 23/113/3. See also K 4.8, 4/14/17 and 4/15/7–8, as well as K 5.4, 5/18/13–14.

18. 義與利者，人之所兩有也。雖堯，舜不能去民之欲利，然而能使其欲利不克其好義也。 *Xunzi* K 27.63, 27/132/1–2. For a discussion of the transformative efficacy of ritual, see also the entire "A Discussion of Rites" *Lilun* 禮論 chapter.

19. Scholars who have studied Xunzi's philosophy have, from the very first, focused a great deal of attention on his conception of human nature. Much of this attention has been due to Xunzi's advocating the slogan that "human nature is bad" in opposition to Mengzi's claim that "human nature is good." Often, the study of Xunzi's understanding of human nature has occurred in the framework of this dispute, since the slogans themselves tell us nothing substantial about the philosophy underlying them. For some recent work on Xunzi's theory of human nature, see Donald Munro, "A Villain in the *Xunzi*," in Philip J. Ivanhoe, ed., *Chinese Language, Thought, and Culture: Nivison and His Critics* (Chicago: Open Court, 1996), pp. 202–223; as well as Bryan W. Van Norden, "Mengzi and Xunzi: Two Views of Human Agency," and Philip J. Ivanhoe, "Human Nature and Moral Understanding in the *Xunzi*," both in Kline and Ivanhoe,

eds., *Virtue, Nature, and Moral Agency in the "Xunzi,"* and most recently, Aaron Stalnaker, "Chapter Three: Ugly Impulses and a Muddy Heart," in *Overcoming Our Evil: Human Nature and Spiritual Exercises in Xunzi and Augustine* (Washington, DC: Georgetown University Press, 2006), pp. 56–84.

20. For a full discussion of Xunzi's theory of moral cultivation, see Jonathan W. Schofer, "Virtues in Xunzi's Thought," in Kline and Ivanhoe, eds., *Virtue, Nature, and Moral Agency in the "Xunzi,"* pp. 69–88.

21. As Pierre Hadot has argued in his study of Greek and Hellenistic philosophers, each philosophical school depicts its ideal for human life through the portrayal of the sage, the wise human being. Pierre Hadot, "Forms of Life and Forms of Discourse in Ancient Philosophy," French original 1983, trans. Arnold I. Davidson and Paula Wissing, in Arnold. I Davidson, ed., *Philosophy as a Way of Life* (New York: Blackwell Publishers, 1995), pp. 57–59. Although it is admitted that few, if any, humans achieve sagehood, the ideal embodies the school's conception of the perfected human life that we all ought to strive to achieve. Given this understanding of the sage as the embodiment of the human ideal, it is a particularly fruitful place to begin to appreciate the ethical significance of similarities and differences between Berger's and Xunzi's theories.

22. It is unclear whether or not Berger holds that the person living authentically needs to be theoretically sophisticated. Berger never states outright that this would be a necessary condition for being able to recognize the constructed nature of society and reappropriate it in a proper, unalienated fashion. However, his discussion of the strong, alienating factors of the social order seems to imply that to live authentically one would have to have a reasonably clear and complex grasp of the theoretical framework Berger advocates. Otherwise, it seems difficult to understand how one would come to recognize the objectified and internalized elements of the worldview as constructed and constituted by nothing more than human activity.

23. Compare this ideal with the final stages of cultivation described in Kongzi's thumbnail biography in *Analects* 2.4.

24. In *Confucius: The Secular as Sacred* (New York: Harper and Row, 1972), Herbert Fingarette interpreted this effortless action to suggest that the sage makes no choices. Joel Kupperman has argued that this understanding of the sage is inaccurate. For an insightful discussion of the Confucian sage and his relationship to choice and responsibility, see Joel J. Kupperman, "Confucius, Mencius, Hume and Kant on Reason and Choice," in *Learning from Asian Philosophy* (New York: Oxford University Press, 1999), pp. 102–118.

25. This description of the Confucian sage suggests that Xunzi and Berger might also be understood as representing two different types of religious worldview, or "human stance," described by Smith. Xunzi could be seen to represent the closed, or locative, vision of the cosmos, and Berger, the open, or dynamic, vision. Smith argues that the difference has profound consequences. "The question of the character of the place on which one stands is *the* fundamental symbolic and social question. Once an individual or culture has expressed its vision of its place, a whole language of symbols and structures will follow." Smith, "The Influence of Symbols on Social Change: A Place on Which to Stand," p. 469.

26. This connection of authenticity with the experience of standing naked and alone in the face of the reality of existence comes most directly from Heidegger. Berger

at one point talks of society as "in the last resort, men banded together in the face of death" (Berger 51).

27. For a description of this harmonious relationship among humans, Heaven, and Earth, see Philip J. Ivanhoe, "A Happy Symmetry: Xunzi's Ecological Ethic," chapter 2 in this volume.

28. Although no fantasy or wishful thinking is involved in the harmony produced by humans following the *Dao*, one could argue that illusion does find its way into the picture. The aesthetic sense of the *Dao* that is revealed in Xunzi's paeans to the ritual order could be seen as human illusion. However, this illusion does not hide a misunderstanding of the human situation. Xunzi believes not only that the *Dao* is consistent with the way things are but also that it most perfectly and completely sets human beings in relation to the way things are. The *Dao* brings harmony to the human social order as well as to the cosmos.

29. Harvey, "Some Problematical Aspects of Peter Berger's Theory of Religion," p. 91.

30. Harvey, in his review article on *The Sacred Canopy*, points to a slightly different tension in Berger's work. See Harvey, "Some Problematical Aspects of Peter Berger's Theory of Religion." He believes that Berger cannot criticize submission to the social order as bad faith and at the same time hold that human nature is completely constructed by society. If human nature is constructed as Berger claims, it would seem that there would be nothing left of identity or self that would be inherently denied expression within the social order. If, outside of the society, one has no nature to speak of, how could society be somehow denying expression of this nature? Harvey does not suggest a solution to this problem. However, as is the case with the tension I examine in detail in this section, an adoption of a substantial conception of human nature that is prior to social organization would go a long way to resolving this dilemma.

Selected Bibliography

This bibliography of scholarship on Xunzi in English is divided into two parts. The first part contains articles, essays, books, and dissertations that focus on Xunzi's writings. The second part includes general studies of Chinese philosophy that have a substantial section on Xunzi. When feasible, the specific chapter or section of these general studies is cited. For references to secondary literature in East Asian languages, see the bibliographies in either John Knoblock, *Xunzi: A Translation and Study of the Complete Works*, or Paul R. Goldin, *Rituals of the Way: The Philosophy of Xunzi*.

Works on Xunzi

Dissertations

Goldin, Paul R. *The Philosophy of Xunzi*. PhD dissertation, Harvard University, 1996.
Hagen, Kurtis. *Confucian Constructivism: A Reconstruction and Application of the Philosophy of Xunzi*. PhD dissertation, University of Hawaii, 2002.
Hutton, Eric L. *Virtue and Reason in Xunzi*. PhD dissertation, Stanford University, 2001.
Kuller, Janet A. H. *Early Confucian Resistance to Taoist Thought: A Study of Anti-Taoism in the "Hsün Tzu."* PhD dissertation, University of Chicago, 1974.
Kline, T. C., III. *Ethics and Tradition in the "Xunzi."* PhD dissertation, Stanford University, 1998.
Lee, Janghee. *The Autonomy of Xin and Ethical Theory in Xunzi*. PhD dissertation, University of Hawaii, 2001.
Lundberg, Brian. *Musical and Ritual Therapeutics in the "Xunzi": The Psychophysical Dynamics of Crafting One's Person*. PhD dissertation, University of Hawaii, 2000.

Sato, Masayuki. *Confucian State and Society of Li: A Study on the Political Thought of Xun Zi.* PhD dissertation, Leiden University, 2001.

Stalnaker, Aaron. *Overcoming Our Evil: Spiritual Exercises and Personhood in Xunzi and Augustine.* PhD dissertation, Brown, 2001.

Tsui, Chee Yee, *A Study of the* Hsün Tzu, Ph.D. dissertation, University of Toronto, 1981.

BOOKS AND ARTICLES

Adshead, Samad A. M. "The Rectification of Names from Confucius to Hsün Tzu." *Milla wa-milla* 8 (1968), pp. 56–61.

Allinson, Robert E. "The Debate Between Mencius and Hsün Tzu: Contemporary Applications." *Journal of Chinese Philosophy* 25.1 (1998), pp. 31–49.

Behuniak, James. "Nivison and the 'Problem' in Xunzi's Ethics." *Philosophy East and West* 50.1 (2000), pp. 97–110.

———. "Reply to David Nivison." *Philosophy East and West* 50.1 (2000), pp. 116–118.

Campany, Robert F. "Xunzi and Durkheim as Theorists of Ritual Practice." In Frank Reynolds and David Tracy, eds., *Discourse and Practice.* Albany: State University of New York Press, 1992, pp. 197–231.

Chen, Bo. "Xunzi's Politicized and Moralized Philosophy of Language." *Journal of Chinese Philosophy* 36.1 (2009), pp. 107–139.

Cheng, Andrew Chih-yi. *Hsün Tzu's Theory of Human Nature and Its Influence on Chinese Thought.* Beijing: 1928.

Cheng, Chung-ying. "Xunzi as a Systematic Philosopher: Toward an Organic Unity of Nature, Mind, and Reason." *Journal of Chinese Philosophy* 35.1 (2008), pp. 9–31.

Cheung, Leo K. C. "The Way of the *Xunzi*." *Journal of Chinese Philosophy* 28.3 (2001), pp. 301–320.

Chong, Kim-chong. "Xunzi and the Essentialist Mode of Thinking on Human Nature." *Journal of Chinese Philosophy* 35.1 (2008), pp. 63–78.

———. "Xunzi's Systematic Critique of Mencius," *Philosophy East and West* 53.2 (2003), pp. 215–233.

Cook, Scott. "Xun Zi on Ritual and Music." *Monumenta Serica* 45 (1997), pp. 1–38.

Creel, Herrlee G. "Confucius and Hsün-tzu." *Journal of the American Oriental Society* 51 (1931), pp. 23–32.

Cua, Antonio S. "The Conceptual Aspect of Hsün Tzu's Philosophy of Human Nature." *Philosophy East and West* 27.4 (1977), pp. 373–389.

———. "Dimensions of *Li* (Propriety): Reflections on Hsün Tzu's Ethics." *Philosophy East and West* 29.4 (1979), pp. 373–394.

———. *Ethical Argumentation: A Study in Hsün Tzu's Moral Epistemology.* Honolulu: University of Hawaii Press, 1985.

———. "The Ethical Significance of Shame: Insights of Aristotle and Xunzi." *Philosophy East and West* 53.2 (2003), 147–202.

———. "Ethical Uses of the Past in Early Confucianism: The Case of Xunzi." In T. C. Kline III and Philip J. Ivanhoe, eds., *Virtue, Nature, and Moral Agency in the "Xunzi."* Indianapolis, IN: Hackett, 2000, pp. 39–68.

———. "Hsün Tzu and the Unity of Virtues." *Journal of Chinese Philosophy* 14.4 (1987), pp. 381–400.

———. "Hsün Tzu's Theory of Argumentation: A Reconstruction." *Review of Metaphysics* 36.4 (1983), pp. 867–894.

———. *Human Nature, Ritual, and History: Studies in Xunzi and Chinese Philosophy* (Washington, DC: Catholic University Press, 2005).

———. "The Possibility of Ethical Knowledge: Reflections on a Theme in the *Hsün Tzu*." In Hans Lenk and Gregor Paul, ed., *Epistemological Issues in Classical Chinese Philosophy*. Albany: State University of New York Press, 1993, pp. 159–184.

———. "The Problem of Conceptual Unity in Hsün Tzu, and Li Kuo's Solution." *Philosophy East and West* 39.2 (1989), pp. 115–134.

———. "The Quasi-Empirical Aspect of Hsün Tzu's Philosophy of Human Nature." *Philosophy East and West* 28.1 (1978), pp. 3–19.

———. "Review of *Xunzi: A Translation and Study of the Complete Works*, vol. 1, books 1–6, John Knoblock." *Philosophy East and West* 41.2 (1991), pp. 215–227.

———. "Some Aspects of Ethical Argumentation: A Reply to Daniel Dahlstrom and John Marshall." *Journal of Chinese Philosophy* 14.4 (1987), pp. 501–516.

Dubs, Homer H. *Hsüntze: Moulder of Ancient Confucianism*. London: Arthur Probsthain, 1927.

———. "Mencius and Sun-dz on Human Nature." *Philosophy East and West* 6.3 (1956), pp. 213–222.

———. " 'Nature' in the Teaching of Confucius." *Journal of the American Oriental Society* 50 (1930), pp. 233–237.

Duyvendak, J. J. L. "The Chronology of Hsüntzu." *T'oung-Pao* 26 (1929), pp. 73–95.

———. "Hsün-tzu on the Rectification of Names." *T'oung-Pao* 23 (1924), pp. 221–254.

———. "Notes on Dubs' Translation of *Hsün-tzu*." *T'oung-Pao* 29 (1932), pp. 1–42.

Fehl, Noah. *Li: Rites and Propriety in Literature and Life*. Hong Kong: Chinese University of Hong Kong Press, 1971.

Fraser, Chris. "Zhuangzi, Xunzi, and the Paradoxical Nature of Education." *Journal of Chinese Philosophy* 33.4 (2006), pp. 529–542.

Gier, Nicholas F. "Xunzi and the Confucian Answer to Titanism." *Journal of Chinese Philosophy* 22.2 (1995), pp. 129–151.

Goldin, Paul R. *Rituals of the Way: The Philosophy of Xunzi*. Chicago: Open Court, 1999.

———. "Xunzi in the Light of the Guodian Manuscripts." *Early China* 25 (2000), pp. 113–146.

Goodrich, Chauncey S. "A New Translation of the Hsün-Tzu." *Journal of the American Oriental Society* 110.3 (1990), pp. 487–492.

Hagen, Kurtis. "Artifice and Virtue in Xunzi." *Dao* 3.1 (2003), pp. 85–107.

———. "The Concepts of *Li* and *Lei* in the *Xunzi*: Constructive Patterning of Categories." *International Philosophical Quarterly* 41.2 (2001), pp. 183–197.

———. "A Critical Review of Ivanhoe on Xunzi." *Journal of Chinese Philosophy* 27.3 (2000), pp. 361–373.

———. *The Philosophy of Xunzi: A Reconstruction*. Chicago: Open Court, 2007.

———. "Sorai and Xunzi on the Construction of the Way." *Asian Philosophy* 15.2 (2005), pp. 117–141.

———. "Xunzi and the Nature of Confucian Ritual." *Journal of the American Academy of Religion* 71.2 (2003), pp. 371–403.

———. "Xunzi's Use of *Zhengming*: Naming as a Constructive Project." *Asian Philosophy* 12.1 (2002), pp. 35–51.

Hang, Thaddeus T. C. "Understanding Evil in the Philosophies of Mencius, Hsün Tzu, and Lao Tzu." In Sandra A. Wawrytko, ed., *The Problem of Evil: An Intercultural Exploration*. Amsterdam: Rodopi, 2000, pp. 1–9.

Harbsmeier, Christoph. "Xunzi and the Problem of Impersonal First Person Pronouns." *Early China* 22 (1997), 181–220.

Harold, James. "Is Xunzi's Virtue Ethics Susceptible to the Problem of Alienation?" *Dao* 10.1 (2011), pp. 71–84.

Hay, Eldon R. "Religion and the Death of God: Hsün Tzu and Rubenstein." *South East Asia Journal of Theology* 11.1 (1970), pp. 83–93.

Hsieh, Shan-yuan. "Hsün-tzu's Political Philosophy." *Journal of Chinese Philosophy* 6.1 (1979), pp. 69–90.

Hutton, Eric L. "Does Xunzi Have a Consistent Theory of Human Nature?" In T. C. Kline III and Philip J. Ivanhoe, eds., *Virtue, Nature, and Moral Agency in the "Xunzi."* Indianapolis, IN: Hackett, 2000, pp. 220–234.

———. "Moral Reasoning in Artistotle and Xunzi." *Journal of Chinese Philosophy* 29.3 (2002), pp. 355–384.

———. "On the Meaning of *Yi* for Xunzi." Unpublished MA thesis, Harvard University, 1996.

Ivanhoe, Philip J. "Human Nature and Moral Understanding in the *Xunzi*." In T. C. Kline III and Philip J. Ivanhoe, eds., *Virtue, Nature, and Moral Agency in the "Xunzi."* Indianapolis, IN: Hackett, 2000, pp. 237–250.

———. "Mengzi, Xunzi, and Modern Feminist Ethics." In Li Chenyang, ed., *The Sage and the Second Sex*. Chicago, IL: Open Court, 2000, pp. 57–74.

———. "Thinking and Learning in Early Confucianism." *Journal of Chinese Philosophy* 17.4 (1990), pp. 473–493.

Jiang, Tao. "Two Notions of Freedom in Classical Chinese Thought: The Concept of Hua in the *Zhuangzi* and the *Xunzi*." *Dao* 10.4 (2011), pp. 463–486.

Kensig, Steve. "Ritual Versus Law in *Hsün Tzu*." *Journal of Chinese Philosophy* 3.1 (1975), pp. 57–66.

Kjellberg, Paul. "Sextus Empiricus, Zhuangzi, and Xunzi on Why Be Skeptical?" In Paul Kjellberg and Philip J. Ivanhoe, eds., *Essays on Skepticism, Relativism, and Ethics in the "Zhuangzi."* Albany: State University of New York Press, 1996, pp. 1–25.

Kline, T. C., III. "Moral Cultivation through Ritual Participation: Xunzi's Philosophy of Ritual." In Kevin Shilbrack, ed., *Thinking through Ritual*. New York: Routledge, 2004, pp. 188–206.

———. "Moral Agency and Motivation in the *Xunzi*." In T. C. Kline III and Philip J. Ivanhoe, eds., *Virtue, Nature, and Moral Agency in the "Xunzi."* Indianapolis, IN: Hackett, 2000, pp. 155–175.

———. "The Therapy of Desire in Early Confucianism: Xunzi." *Dao* 5.2 (2006), pp. 235–246.

Kline, T. C., IIII, and Philip J. Ivanhoe, eds. *Virtue, Nature, and Moral Agency in the "Xunzi."* Indianapolis, IN: Hackett, 2000.

Knoblock, John. "The Chronology of Xunzi's Works." *Early China* 8 (1982–1983), pp. 28–52.

———. *Xunzi: A Translation and Study of the Complete Works*, 3 vols. Stanford, CA: Stanford University Press, 1988, 1990, 1994.

Kuller, Janet A. H. "Anti-Taoist Elements in Hsün Tzu's Thought and Their Social Relevance." *Asian Thought and Society* 3.7 (1978), pp. 53–67.

———. "The 'Fu' of the *Hsün Tzu* as an Anti-Taoist Polemic." *Monumenta Serica* 31 (1974–1975), pp. 205–218.

Kupperman, Joel J. "Xunzi: Morality as Psychological Constraint." In T. C. Kline III and Philip J. Ivanhoe, eds., *Virtue, Nature, and Moral Agency in the "Xunzi."* Indianapolis, IN: Hackett, 2000, pp. 89–102.

Lau, D. C. "Theories of Human Nature in *Mencius* and *Xunzi*." In T. C. Kline III and Philip J. Ivanhoe, eds., *Virtue, Nature, and Moral Agency in the "Xunzi."* Indianapolis, IN: Hackett, 2000, pp. 188–219.

Lee, Janghee. *Xunzi and Early Chinese Naturalism*. Albany: State University of New York Press, 2004.

Lewis, Thomas A. "Frames of Comparison: Anthropology and Inheriting Traditional Practices." *Journal of Religious Ethics* 33.2 (2005), pp. 225–253.

Li, Chenyang. "Xunzi on the Origin of Goodness: A New Interpretation." *Journal of Chinese Philosophy* 38s (2011), pp. 46–63.

Liang, Ch'i-hsiung. "A Descriptive Review of Hsün-Tzu's Thought." *Chinese Studies in Philosophy* 6 (1976), pp. 4–60.

Lin, Chung-I. "Xunzi as a Semantic Inferentialist: *Zhengmin, Bian-Shuo* and *Dao-Li*." *Dao* 10.3 (2011), pp. 311–340.

Lodén, Torbjörn. "Reason, Feeling, and Ethics in Mencius and Xunzi." *Journal of Chinese Philosophy* 36.4 (2009), pp. 602–617.

Machle, Edward J. "Hsün Tzu: A Revisionist View." *Iliff Review* 32.3 (1975), pp. 19–31.

———. "The Mind and the *Shen-ming* in the *Xunzi*." *Journal of Chinese Philosophy* 19.4 (1992), pp. 361–386.

———. *Nature and Heaven in the "Xunzi": A Study of the "Tian Lun."* Albany: State University of New York Press, 1993.

Malmquist, Göran. "Cherng shianq." *Bulletin of the Museum of Far Eastern Antiquities* 45 (1973), pp. 63–91.

———. "A Note on the Cherng shiang Ballad in the *Shyun Tzyy*." *Bulletin of the Oriental and African Society* 36 (1973), pp. 352–358.

Martin, Michael. "Ritual Action (*Li*) in Confucius and Hsün Tzu." *Australian Journal of Philosophy* 73.1 (1995), pp. 13–30.

Mei, Y. P. "Hsün Tzu on Terminology." *Philosophy East and West* 1.2 (1951), pp. 51–56.

———. "Hsün-tzu's Theory of Education." *Qinghua xuebao* 2 (1961), pp. 361–379.

———. "Hsün-tzu's Theory of Government." *Qinghua xuebao* 7 (1970), pp. 36–83.

Munro, Donald J. "A Villain in the *Xunzi*." In Philip J. Ivanhoe, ed., *Chinese Language, Thought, and Culture: Nivison and His Critics*. Chicago: Open Court, 1996, pp. 202–223.

Nivison, David S. "Critique of David B. Wong, 'Xunzi on Moral Motivation.' " In Philip J. Ivanhoe, ed., *Chinese Language, Thought, and Culture: Nivison and His Critics*. Chicago: Open Court, 1996, pp. 323–231.

———. "Response to James Behuniak." *Philosophy East and West* 50.1 (2000), pp. 110–115.

———. "Xunzi and Zhuangzi." In T. C. Kline III and Philip J. Ivanhoe, eds., *Virtue, Nature, and Moral Agency in the "Xunzi."* Indianapolis, IN: Hackett, 2000, pp. 176–187.

———. "Xunzi on Human Nature." In Bryan W. Van Norden, ed., *The Ways of Confucianism: Investigations in Chinese Philosophy*. Chicago: Open Court, 1996, pp. 123–141.

Parker, E. H. "Liu Hsiang and Tsien Tahien on Suntsz." *New China Review* 4.6 (1922), pp. 443–449.

———. "The Philosopher Suntsz." *New China Review* 4.1 (1922), pp. 1–19.

Peterson, Willard J. "Review of *Xunzi: A Translation and Study of the Complete Works*, vol. 1, by John Knoblock." *American Historical Review* 95.5 (1990), p. 1600.

Radcliffe-Brown, A. R."Religion and Society." In *Structure and Function in Primitive Society.* New York: The Free Press, 1965, pp. 153–177.

Robins, Dan. "The Development of Xunzi's Theory of Xing, Reconstructed on the Basis of a Textual Analysis of *Xunzi* 23, 'Xing'e' (Xing Is Bad)." *Early China* 26–27 (2001–2002), pp. 99–158.

———. "Review of *Rituals of the Way: The Philosophy of 'Xunzi'* by Paul R. Goldin." *Journal of Asian Studies* 60.4 (2001), pp. 1152–1155.

Rosemont, Henry, Jr. "State and Society in the *Xunzi*: A Philosophical Commentary." In T. C. Kline III and Philip J. Ivanhoe, eds., *Virtue, Nature, and Moral Agency in the "Xunzi."* Indianapolis, IN: Hackett, 2000, pp. 1–38.

Sato, Masayuki. *The Confucian Quest for Order: The Origin and Formation of Xun Zi's Political Thought.* Leiden: Brill, 2003.

———. "The Evolutionary Change of Pre-Qin Conceptual Terms and Their Incorporation into Xunzi's Thought." In J. Meyer and P. Engelfriet, eds., *Linked Faith.* Leiden: Brill, 2000, pp. 18–40.

Scarpari, Maurizio. "The Debate on Human Nature in Early China." *Philosophy East and West* 53.3 (2003), 323–339.

Schofer, Jonathan W. "Virtues in Xunzi's Thought." In T. C. Kline III and Philip J. Ivanhoe, eds., *Virtue, Nature, and Moral Agency in the "Xunzi."* Indianapolis, IN: Hackett, 2000, pp. 69–88.

Schwitzgebel, Eric. "Human Nature and Moral Education in Mencius, Xunzi, Hobbes, and Rousseau." *History of Philosophy Quarterly* 24.2 (2007), pp. 147–168.

Sciban, Lloyd. "Review of *Ethical Argumentation: A Study in Hsün Tzu's Moral Epsitemology*, by A. S. Cua." *Philosophy East and West* 40.2 (1990), pp. 266–268.

Shih, Joseph. "Secularization in Early Chinese Thought: A Note on Hsün Tzu." *Gregorianum* 50.2 (1969), pp. 391–404.

Shih, Vincent Y. C. "Hsüntzu's Positivism." *Qinghua xuebao* 4 (1963), pp. 152–174.

Shun, Kwong-loi. "Mencius, Xunzi, and Dai Zhen: A Study of the *Mengzi ziyi shuzheng*." In Alan K. L. Chan, ed., *Mencius: Contexs and Interpretations.* Honolulu: University of Hawaii Press, 2002, pp. 216–241.

———. "Review of *Ethical Argumentation: A Study in Hsün Tzu's Moral Epistemology*, by A. S. Cua." *Philosophy East and West* 41.1 (1991), pp. 111–117.

Soles, David E. "The Nature and Grounds of Xunzi's Disagreement with Mencius." *Asian Philosophy* 9.2 (1999), pp. 123–133.

Spence, Jonathan D. "Remembrance of Ming's Past." *New York Review of Books* 41.12 (1994), pp. 24–29.

Stalnaker, Aaron. "Aspects of Xunzi's Engagement with Early Daoism." *Philosophy East and West* 53.1 (2003), pp. 87–129.

———. "Comparative Religious Ethics and the Problem of 'Human Nature.'" *Journal of Religious Ethics* 33.2 (2005), pp. 187–224.

———. *Overcoming Our Evil: Human Nature and Spiritual Exercises in Xunzi and Augustine*. Washington, DC: Georgetown University Press, 2006.

———. "Rational Justification in Xunzi: On His Use of the Term *Li* 理." *International Philosophical Quarterly* 44.1 (2004), pp. 53–68.

Stroud, Scott R. "Moral Cultivation in Kant and Xunzi." *Journal of Chinese Philosophy* 38.4 (2011), pp. 538–555.

Sungmoon, Kim. "From Desire to Civility: Is Xunzi a Hobbesian?" *Dao* 10.3 (2011), pp. 291–309.

Tan, Mingran. "A Reevaluation of Xunzi's Moral Theory from the Aspect of Mind." *Journal of Chinese Philosophy* 35.1 (2008), pp. 121–138.

T'ang, Hsiao-wen. "Why Is Hsün Tzu Called a Legalist?" *Chinese Studies in Philosophy* 8 (1976), pp. 21–35.

Tang, Paul C. L. "On the Special Logic Thesis in Chinese Philosophy." *Metaphilosophy* 28.4 (1997), pp. 371–384.

Tiwald, Justin. "Xunzi on Moral Expertise." *Dao* 11.3 (2012), pp. 275–293.

Van Norden, Bryan W. "Hansen on Hsün-tzu." *Journal of Chinese Philosophy* 20.3 (1993). pp. 365–382.

———. "Mengzi and Xunzi: Two Views of Human Agency." In T. C. Kline III and Philip J. Ivanhoe, eds., *Virtue, Nature, and Moral Agency in the "Xunzi."* Indianapolis, IN: Hackett, 2000, pp. 103–134.

———. "Review of *Nature and Heaven in the 'Xunzi': A Study of the Tian Lun*, by Edward Machle." *Journal of Asian Studies* 53.3 (1994), pp. 921–922.

Wang, Keping. "Mozi versus Xunzi on Music." *Journal of Chinese Philosophy* 36.4 (2009), pp. 653–665.

Watson, Burton. *Hsün Tzu: Basic Writings*. New York: Columbia University Press, 1963.

Wong, David B. "Dwelling in Humanity or Free and Easy Wandering." In Peter D. Hershock, Marietta Stepaniants, and Roger Ames, eds., *Technology and Cultural Values: On the Edge of the Third Millenium*. Honolulu: University of Hawaii Press, 2003, pp. 400–415.

———. "Xunzi on Moral Motivation." In T. C. Kline III and Philip J. Ivanhoe, eds., *Virtue, Nature, and Moral Agency in the "Xunzi."* Indianapolis, IN: Hackett, 2000, pp. 135–154.

Yearley, Lee H. "Facing Our Frailty: Comparative Religious Ethics and the Confucian Death Rituals." Gross Memorial Lectures, Valparaiso University, 1995.

———. "Hsün Tzu on the Mind: His Attempted Synthesis of Confucianism and Daoism." *Journal of Asian Studies* 39.3 (1980), pp. 465–480.

Yu, Anthony. "Cratylus and Xunzi on Names." In Steven Shankman and Stephen W. Durrant, eds., *Early China/Ancient Greece: Thinking Through Comparisons*. Albany: State University of New York Press, 2002, pp. 235–250.

Yu, Jiyuan. "Human Nature and Virtue in Mencius and Xunzi: An Aristotelian Interpretation." *Dao* 5.1 (2005), pp. 11–30.

Yu, Mingguang. "Xunzi's Philosophy and the School of Huang-Lao." *Contemporary Chinese Thought* 34.1 (2002), pp. 37–60.

Zhao, Yanxia. *Father and Son in Confucianism and Christianity: A Comparative Study of Xunzi and Paul.* Sussex: Sussex Academic Press, 2007.

GENERAL WORKS

Berkson, Mark. "Chapter Three: Death in the Xunzi." In *Death and the Self in Ancient Chinese Thought: A Comparative Perspective.* PhD dissertation, Stanford University, 1999, pp. 103–195.

———. "Conceptions of Self/No-Self and Modes of Connection: Comparative Soteriological Structures in Classical Chinese Thought." *Journal of Religious Ethics* 33.2 (2005), pp. 293–331.

Berthrong, John. "From Xunzi to Boston Confucianism." *Journal of Chinese Philosophy* 30.3–4 (2003), pp. 433–450.

Chan Wing-tsit. "Naturalistic Confucianism: Hsün Tzu." In *A Source Book in Chinese Philosophy.* Princeton, NJ: Princeton University Press, 1963, pp. 115–135.

Creel, Herrlee G. "Chapter Seven: The Authoritarianism of Hsün Tzu." In *Chinese Thought from Confucius to Mao Tse-tung.* Chicago: University of Chicago Press, 1953, pp. 115–134.

Eno, Robert. "Chapter Six: Ritual as a Natural Art: The Role of T'ien in the *Hsun Tzu.*" In *The Confucian Creation of Heaven: Philosophy and the Defense of Ritual Mastery.* Albany: State University of New York Press, 1990, pp. 131–170.

Fehl, Noah E. *Li: Rites and Propriety in Literature and Life—A Perspective for a Cultural History of Ancient China.* Hong Kong: Chinese University of Hong Kong, 1971.

Fung Yu-lan. "Chapter Twelve: Hsün Tzu and His School of Confucianism." In *A History of Chinese Philosophy: Volume I—The Period of the Philosophers,* trans. Derk Bodde. Princeton: Princeton University Press, 1952, pp. 279–311.

Geaney, Jane. *On the Epistemology of the Senses in Early Chinese Thought.* Honolulu: University of Hawaii Press, 2002.

———. "Xunzi: Eye/Action and Ear/Speech." In *Language and Sense Discrimination in Ancient China,* PhD dissertation, University of Chicago, 1996, pp. 103–143.

Graham, Angus C. "Hsün-tzu's Confucianism: Morality as Man's Invention to Control His Nature." In *Disputers of the Tao: Philosophical Argument in Ancient China.* Chicago: Open Court, 1989, pp. 235–266.

Hansen, Chad. "Xunzi: Pragmatic Confucianism." In *A Daoist Theory of Chinese Thought: A Philosophical Interpretation.* Oxford: Oxford University Press, 1992, pp. 307–334.

Hutton, Eric L., trans. "Chapter Six: *Xunzi.*" In Bryan W. Van Norden and Philip J. Ivanhoe, eds., *Readings in Classical Chinese Philosophy,* second ed. Indianapolis, IN: Hackett, 2006, pp. 255–309.

Ivanhoe, Philip J. "Chapter Three: *Xunzi.*" In *Confucian Moral Self Cultivation,* second ed. Indianapolis, IN: Hackett, 2000, pp. 29–42.

———. "Early Confucianism and Environmental Ethics." In Mary E. Tucker and John Berthrong, eds., *Confucianism and Ecology.* Cambridge, MA: Harvard University Press, 1998, pp. 59–76.

Lai, Karyn. "Confucian Moral Cultivation: Some Parallels with Musical Training." In Kim-chong Chong, Sor-hoon Tan, and C. L. Tan, eds., *The Moral Circle and the Self: Chinese and Western Approaches*. Chicago: Open Court, 2003, pp. 107–141.

Lewis, Mark E. "Custom and Human Nature in Early China." *Philosophy East and West* 53.3 (2003), pp. 308–322.

Makeham, John. "Chapter Three: Nominalist Theories of Naming in the Neo-Mohist Summa and Xun Zi." In *Name and Actuality in Early Chinese Thought*. Albany: State University of New York Press, 1994, pp. 51–64.

Mote, Frederick. "Early Confucianism: Hsün Tzu." In *Intellectual Foundations of China*, second ed. New York: McGraw-Hill, 1989, pp. 54–58.

Munro, Donald J. *The Concept of Man in Early China*. Stanford, CA: Stanford University Press, 1969.

Needham, Joseph. *Science and Civilization in China*, vol. 2. Cambridge: Cambridge University Press, 1954.

Neville, Robert "Chapter Seven: Ritual and Normative Culture." In *Normative Cultures*. Albany: State University of New York Press, 1995, pp. 163–195.

Nivison, David S. "The Classical Philosophical Writings." In Michael Loewe and Edward L. Shaughnessy, eds., *Cambridge History of Ancient China*. Cambridge University Press, 1999, pp. 745–812.

———. "Weakness of Will in Ancient Chinese Philosophy." In Bryan W. Van Norden, ed., *The Ways of Confucianism*. Chicago: Open Court, 1996, pp. 79–90.

Pocock, J. G. A. "Ritual, Language, Power: An Essay on the Apparent Political Meanings of Ancient Chinese Philosophy." In *Politics, Language and Time*. New York: Atheneum, 1973, pp. 47–79.

Puett, Michael. "Chapter 2: The Craft of Humanity: Debates Over Nature and Culture in Warring States China." In *The Ambivalence of Creation*. Stanford, CA: Stanford University Press, 2001, pp. 39–91.

———. "The Ethics of Responding Properly: The Notion of Qing in Early Chinese Thought." In Halvor Eifring, ed., *Love and Emotions in Traditional Chinese Literature*. Leiden: Brill, 2004, pp. 37–68.

Roetz, Heiner. "Xunzi's Rationalism." In *Confucian Ethics of the Axial Age: A Reconstruction under the Aspect of the Breakthrough Toward Postconventional Thinking*. Albany: State University of New York Press, 1993, pp. 213–226.

Schwartz, Benjamin I. "Hsün-tzu: The Defense of the Faith." In *The World of Thought in Ancient China*. Cambridge, MA: Harvard University Press, 1985, pp. 290–320.

Slingerland, Edward G. "Chapter Six: Wu-wei in the *Xunzi*." In *Effortless Action: Wu-wei as a Spiritual Ideal in Early China*. PhD dissertation, Stanford University, 1998, pp. 345–411.

———. "Straightening the Warped Wood: Wu-wei in the *Xunzi*." In *Effortless Action: Wu-wei as Conceptual Metaphor and Spiritual Ideal in Early China*. New York: Oxford University Press, 2003, pp. 217–264.

Tang, Yijie. "Emotion in Pre-Qin Ruist Moral Theory: An Explanation of '*Dao* Begins in *Qing*,'" trans. Brian Bruya and Hai-ming Wen. *Philosophy East and West* 53.2 (2003), pp. 271–281.

Taylor, Rodney L. "Confucianism: Scripture and the Sage." In *The Holy Book in Comparative Perspective*. Columbia: University of South Carolina Press, 1985, pp. 181–203.

———. "The Religious Character of the Confucian Tradition." *Philosophy East and West* 48.1 (1998), pp. 80–107.

Twohey, Michael. "Chapter Two: Xunzi and Ancient Chinese Authority." In *Authority and Welfare in China: Modern Debates in Historical Perspective*. New York: St. Martin's Press, 1999, pp. 13–28.

Yu, A. C. "Chapter II: Desire." In *Rereading the Stone: Desire and the Making of Fiction in "Dream of the Red Chamber."* Princeton, NJ: Princeton University Press, 1997, pp. 53–109.

Contributors

Mark Berkson is Professor and Chair of the Department of Religion at Hamline University. His publications include works on Confucian and Daoist thought, death and dying, and interfaith dialogue. His DVD/book project, *Cultural Literacy for Religion*, part of the Great Courses series, was released in 2012.

Philip J. Ivanhoe (PhD Stanford University) specializes in the history of East Asian philosophy and religion and its potential for contemporary ethics. He has written, edited, or coedited more than twenty books and published more than fifty articles as well as numerous dictionary and encyclopedia entries on Chinese and Western religious and ethical thought. Among his publications are: coedited with Yu Kam-por and Julia Tao, *Taking Confucian Ethics Seriously: Contemporary Theories and Applications* (State University of New York Press 2010), *The Essays and Letters of Zhang Xuecheng* (Stanford University Press 2009), coedited with Rebecca Walker, *Working Virtue: Virtue Ethics and Contemporary Moral Problems* (Oxford University Press 2007), *Confucian Moral Self Cultivation* (Hackett, revised second edition, 2006), and *The Daodejing of Laozi* (Hackett 2003).

T. C. Kline III is an independent scholar living in Maine. Much of his work examines Xunzi's philosophy, and he is the coeditor, with Philip J. Ivanhoe, of the companion to this volume, *Virtue, Nature, and Moral Agency in the "Xunzi"* (Hackett 2000).

Edward J. Machle is Professor Emeritus of Philosophy at the University of Colorado Boulder. He has published several important articles on Xunzi's philosophy, including a book-length study of the *Tianlun* 天論 chapter of the *Xunzi* entitled *Nature and Heaven in the "Xunzi": A Study of the Tian Lun* (State University of New York Press 1993).

ROBERT C. NEVILLE is Executive Director of the Danielsen Institute and Professor of Philosophy, Religion, and Theology at Boston University. His research covers topics in philosophy, religion, and theology. His most recent book on Confucian religious thought is *Boston Confucianism* (State University of New York Press 2000).

JAMES ROBSON is Associate Professor of East Asian Languages and Civilizations at Harvard. His research interests focus on Chinese religious thought, especially medieval Chinese Buddhism and Daoism. He is the author of *Power of Place: The Religious Landscape of the Southern Sacred Peak* (Nanyue 南嶽) *in Medieval China* (Harvard University Press 2009), which received the Stanislas Julien Prize for 2010 by the French Academy of Inscriptions and Belles-Lettres.

JUSTIN TIWALD is Associate Professor of Philosophy at San Francisco State University. He has published widely on issues at the intersections of ethics, political philosophy, and Chinese thought, including "Dai Zhen's Defense of Self-Interest" (*Journal of Chinese Philosophy*) and "Xunzi on Moral Expertise" (*Dao*).

LEE H. YEARLEY is the Evans-Wentz Professor of Religious Studies at Stanford University. Interested in both Christian and Chinese religious thought, he has published significant work in comparative religion, including *Mencius and Aquinas: Theories of Virtue and Conceptions of Courage* (State University of New York Press 1990).

Index